*Beachcomber's Guide to*
# Gulf Coast Marine Life

*Third Edition*

# Beachcomber's Guide to
# Gulf Coast Marine Life

## Third Edition

## Texas, Louisiana, Mississippi, Alabama, and Florida

Susan B. Rothschild, Ph.D.

A Roberts Rinehart Book
TAYLOR TRADE PUBLISHING
Lanham • New York • Dallas • Boulder • Toronto • Oxford

Published by Taylor Trade Publishing
A Roberts Rinehart Book
A wholly owned subsidiary of The Rowman & Littlefield Publishing Group, Inc.
4501 Forbes Boulevard, Suite 200
Lanham, Maryland 20706

Distributed by NATIONAL BOOK NETWORK

**Library of Congress Cataloging-in-Publication Data**

Rothschild, Susan B.
  Beachcomber's guide to Gulf coast marine life : Texas, Louisiana, Mississippi, Alabama, and Florida / Susan B. Rothschild.—3rd ed.
     p. cm.
  Includes bibliographical references (p. ).
  ISBN 1-58979-061-8 (alk. paper)
  1. Marine invertebrates—Mexico, Gulf of. 2. Seashore biology—Mexico, Gulf of. I. Title.
QL134.R68 2004
592.177'364—dc21                                                    00-029420

# Contents

# Preface to the Third Edition

It is a pleasure to welcome you to this new edition of *Beachcomber's Guide to Gulf Coast Marine Life*. This latest version incorporates an increased recognition of a "Gulf endemic fauna," as the result of accumulating biogeographical studies on the morphology and genetics of species of the Carolinean Province. You will find some old friends with new names due to taxonomic revisions.

Most additions occur in the sea turtle chapter. The last decade witnessed much research on sea turtles under the auspices of marine protection programs around the globe. Implementation of the Endangered Species Act of 1983 and its subsequent amendments have engendered many conservation and research programs in the United States. Thus, this edition confirms and refines previous speculations about many aspects of the life history patterns of sea turtles. More research and new methods, such as mitochondrial DNA analysis, have helped to solve more of nature's mysteries. With increased information on the global linkages between sea turtle populations and recognition of the importance of marine turtle protection, progress is being made in reducing the mortality of sea turtles due to man's activities. The diversity of these activities is part of the problem in reversing downward population trends. However, the increased awareness of how man impacts sea turtles, either directly through harvesting or indirectly via fishery "by-catches," coastal economic development, and marine pollution, has helped to focus conservation efforts on critical life stages.

As our understanding of the ocean and its dynamic processes grows, so grows our appreciation of the complexities and linkages between organisms (us too!) and their environment. Understanding the small-scale physics of the ocean and its effect on the tiniest sea creatures that constitute the food chain foundation has been a major research impetus in the last few years. Factoring small-scale processes into large-scale processes promises the ultimate payoff of improved science for conservation and management of our living marine resources.

While scientists are often concerned with understanding how well abstract theories and associated models match or forecast nature, it is the individual organism and its response to its environment that underlies population dynamics. So, when we wander out into the surf zone, or peruse a mudflat, we can, while pondering nature's complexity, thrill at holding a fragile worm in our hands or marvel at the all the bumps and ridges on a crab's shell. We hope the *Beachcomber's Guide* will not only answer many of your questions, from "What is it?" to "What's it doing?" but inspire you to look closer and watch more intently as you make acquaintance with the marvelous variety of marine life inhabiting our shores.

We would like to thank the following colleagues for their assistance with this edition: Dr. Nancy B. Thompson and Wayne Witzell of the Southeast Fisheries Center, National Marine Fisheries Service, NOAA, Miami, Florida, and Dr. Donna Shaver-Miller, U.S. Geological Service, U.S. Dept. of the Interior at the CERC Field Research Station, Padre Island National Seashore, Texas for information on sea turtles; Dr. Carl Thurman of the University of Northern Iowa, Cedar Falls, Iowa and University of Texas Medical School, Houston, Texas for information on Gulf coast fauna; Kathleen K. Clark of Lopez High School, Brownsville, Texas for comments; research librarians at the University of Massachusetts Dartmouth, the Marine Biological Laboratory Library, Wood's Hole, Massachusetts and the Sea Turtle Online Bibliography, Archie Carr Center for Sea Turtle Research, University of Florida, Gainesville, Florida for assistance in obtaining reference materials; Dr. Brian Rothschild of the University of Massachusetts Dartmouth and Daniel Sheridan, Esq. of Owings Mills, Maryland for advice, and Mr. Tim Calk, of Gulf Publishing Company for guidance.

*Susan Brunenmeister Rothschild, Ph.D.*

# Preface to the Second Edition

Since the first publication of this guide fourteen years ago, there has been a proliferation of scientific literature concerning the biology and ecology of marine organisms as well as the biological and physical processes in the marine environment. In this edition, we have been able to update information on old friends and write about some new ones. In our new chapter on sea turtles, we have departed from our approach of exploring specific habitats and instead introduce each species separately. But taking any other approach would have been difficult, as not only do these ancient life forms occupy a variety of habitats throughout their lives—in terrestrial, neritic, and pelagic environments—but much is still to be learned about the activities in each of them.

As we increase our knowledge of the biosphere, we realize how much more there remains to explore and understand. In this regard, we can note that the biological and physical oceanographic features of the Gulf of Mexico that result in hypoxia and mass mortalities of bottom fauna in some nearshore regions are presently a focus of research that leads to more questions about the stability of marine ecosystems. While some of these pursuits are out of the realm of our discussion, they relate, however, to processes whose integration results in our finding a *Littorina* snail on a stalk of cordgrass or a shrimp on our dinner plate.

In relation to the preparation of this edition, we would like to thank Dr. Nancy B. Thompson and Mr. Wayne Witzell of the Southeast Fisheries Center, National Marine Fisheries Service for information on sea turtles; Ms. Cathy Heil, librarian at the University of Maryland, Chesapeake Biological Laboratory, for her assistance in obtaining materials; and Dr. Brian Rothschild of the University of Maryland, Chesapeake Biological Laboratory, for advice.

S.B.
N.F.

# Preface

This guide was designed as an aid to the student, fisherman, or beachcomber who wishes to become acquainted with the spectacular array of invertebrate animals living along the Gulf shore. The organisms described in this introductory guide are those which we believe are commonly encountered by the casual observer. The list of Gulf Coast invertebrates is by no means complete, and therefore, this guide should not be used as a taxonomic reference by the serious student of marine invertebrates. However, systematic sources for many taxa are included in the bibliography.

We wish to acknowledge the help of the numerous students of invertebrate zoology and marine biology at the University of Houston who assisted in making the collections on which this guide is based. We are especially indebted to B. R. Collins, proprietor of the West Bay Bait Camp, and to Archie Curl, a Texas City shrimp fisherman, for the generous use of their facilities for the collection of specimens. We thank Carl L. Thurman, J. B. Wills, and Ruth Ann Bagnall for their help in identifying fiddler crabs, polychaetes, and zooplankters, respectively. We are also indebted to many friends, especially Drs. Sewell H. Hopkins, Harold W. Harry, and Frank Fisher, for their numerous suggestions during the preparation of the manuscript. Conversations with Charles Allen, James Baker, Marion Johnson, Maurice Jones, Mary Kutac, Gary Penn, and Tom Scanland contributed greatly to the revision of this guide. We greatly appreciate the use of facilities of the University of Houston Coastal Center during our study of this fauna. We are also indebted to Anne Fotheringham for her typing skills and many helpful hints.

We would also like to thank Miss Patsy Menefee for her erxcellent drawings. All of the illustrations were drawn by Miss Menefee except the following, which were drawn by the authors: Fotheringham—1.1, 1.2, 2.1, 2.2, 2.13, 2.20–2.26, 3.1, 3.4, 3.6, 3.10, 3.13, 3.14, 3.16, 3.17, 3.32, 3.37–3.40, 4.1–4.6, 4.9, 4.13, 4.14, 5.1–5.29, 5.34–5.50, 6.4, 6.10, 6.13, 7.3, 7.13, 7.20–7.26, 7.31, 7.34, 8.1–8.29, 8.31–8.48, 9.3, 9.6, 9.7, 10.2, 10.3, 10.5, 10.7, 11.1–11.13; and Brunenmeister—2.4, 2.10, 2.16, 2.19, 3.20–3.23, 3.36, 3.42, 3.43, 4.12, 4.15, 5.30–5.32, 5.51, 6.6. 6.8, 6.11, 6.12, 7.5, 7.6, 7.8, 7.10–7.12, 7.19, 7.35, 9.2, 9.4, 9.5, 10.1, 12.1–12.9.

*Susan Brunenmeister*
*Nick Fotheringham*

# Introduction

Exploring the beach brings endless fascination and intrigue. Each breaking wave sweeps away the old beach face and unveils an array of curiosities. Forces staggering in variety and intensity abuse animal life along the beach, yet life clings to the shore and adapts. Crushing waves and the scouring currents they generate, the continuously changing tides, the baking sun, shorebirds probing with long bills and little fish darting into the shallows between waves all take their toll. The survivors have evolved with a special blend of characteristics that make survival in such an inhospitable environment possible. What reward could have stimulated such an effort?

The sea is the birthplace of life; the ancestors of many millions of inhabitants of forests and lakes emerged from the sea eons ago. The land promised new frontiers and a haven from old enemies for creatures from the sea. But the sea is a temptress, luring back the children of its emigrants with morsels of food cast upon the shore and the promise of more just beneath her surface. However, the seashore is a boundary that is often assailed but seldom bridged. Many have risen to her bait, but few have found its source and lived. Thus, the beach is a zone of conflict, an arena for developing peculiar lifestyles by species from both the sea and the land.

The most striking results of these experiments in living are found among the invertebrates. They exhibit many of nature's most exotic lifestyles. The invertebrates of the sea include species that can jump fifty times their own length, carry many times their own weight, bore into solid rock, change sex at will, change color to match their background, lay as many as half a billion eggs at one time, or regrow a head that has been cut off. These unusual abilities are adaptations to an unusual environment.

No special knowledge is required to discover the numerous intriguing secrets of these animals. Many engrossing hours may be spent at the seashore discovering how a mole crab burrows, how a ghost crab signals with its claws, how a sea anemone moves a bit of food placed on a tentacle to its mouth, how a barnacle captures food with its feet, how male fiddler crabs fight for possession of a burrow, or how an oyster drill drills an oyster. This book is a guide to the lifestyles of more than 300 of the most common invertebrates that the visitor to the shores of northwestern Gulf of Mexico is likely to encounter. It includes points of interest and ways to observe that will make a visit to the beach an enriching experience.

Unfortunately, many of the creatures cast at the feet of beachcombers have been torn from their usual habitats and lifestyles and are often lifeless, broken, or faded. Through the chapters on offshore habitats, the reader is transported to the environments in which these animals display morphological and behavioral adaptations seldom evident in beachwashed specimens.

Readers who are not familiar with the system of biological classification may wish to read the brief guide in Appendix A on page 144.

# CHAPTER ONE

# General Shore and Faunal Features

## *The Habitats*

The predominant coastal form along the northwestern coast of the Gulf of Mexico consists of a series of barrier islands enclosing several shallow bays (Figure 1.1). These islands and bays encompass a mosaic of marine and estuarine habitats that differ in substrate, exposure to surf, food resources, and environmental variability. Habitats on the outer side of the barrier islands receive more abuse from waves but undergo less abrupt changes in salinity and temperature than do habitats on the bay side of the islands. Sandy beaches and rock jetties are the major habitat types on the outer coast; mudflats, salt marshes, pilings, and oyster reefs are the major habitat types in the bays (Figure 1.2). The water itself forms an additional habitat for swimming and floating organisms.

I

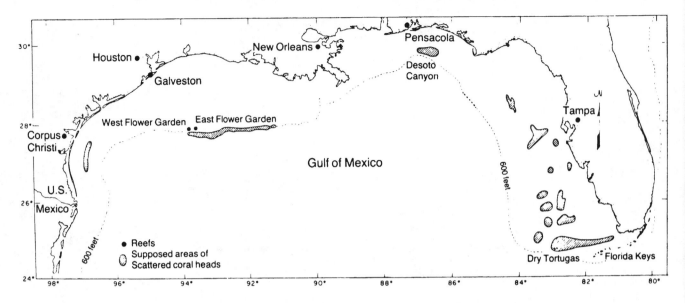

**FIGURE 1.1.** Northern Gulf Coast.

The jetties at Port Arthur, Galveston, Freeport, Port Aransas, and Port Isabel and along the Galveston seawall were designed to modify the pattern of nearshore circulation along the coast. They interrupt the flow of sand along the shore, thus reducing the erosion of adjacent beaches and the deposition of sand in navigation channels. Consequently, these structures and the organisms living on them are subjected to breaking waves laden with sand, strong currents, and fluctuating sand levels. At the same time, these waves bring moisture to organisms living high on the jetties, and the currents bring plankton, the microscopic life consumed by most of the jetty inhabitants.

Organisms living on the sandy beaches along the Gulf side of the barrier islands must also contend with surf, currents, and shifting sand. Most sandy-beach animals escape the physical hazards of their environment by burrowing. Thus, almost the entire community lives underground—and out of sight. Some species minimize the changes in their environment by migrating up and down the beach with the changing tide. Others avoid the surf by living high on the beach and returning to the sea only to wet their gills or to forage for bits of food left by the ebbing tide. Still others have very large gills to supply oxygen for the extra exertion demanded by a life in the surf zone or tufts of hairlike setae to protect sensitive structures from the constantly moving sand.

The barrier islands protect habitats in the bays from the severest effects of waves and currents. As a result of the slowed water movement, fine particles passing down the rivers and bayous into the bays settle to the bottom, producing a muddier substrate than is found on the outer shore. Moreover, the bays are shallow. They heat and cool faster and undergo more abrupt changes in salinity and oxygen content than the open Gulf.

The relatively stable and extensive soft bottom of the bays provides an ideal environment for numerous burrowing animals. Their major obstacle is the hydrogen-sulfide layer, a toxic layer of generally black mud characterized by an odor like that of rotting eggs, which forms at shallower depths in the bays than in the more turbulent outer-coast habitats. Due to the shallowness of the bays, broad mudflats are exposed during low tides, leaving nonburrowing species at the mercy of predators and the drying sun. Salt-tolerant plants known as halophytes may become established on the edges of these flats. These plants further impede the circulation near them, which causes additional sediment to be deposited during high tides. In this manner, salt marshes develop around the bay, and small islands may become established within the bay.

Two other submerged habitat types are commonly found within the bays—grass flats and oyster reefs. The grass flats on the northwestern Gulf Coast consist primarily of shoal grass, *Halodule wrightii*, and turtle grass, *Thalassia testudinum*, which, like the salt marsh, helps to stabilize the soft bottom. These grasses build low mounds by trapping sediment among their roots. Because they require light for photosynthesis, grass flats are only found in shallow water.

Oyster reefs, on the other hand, are composed of animals that do not depend directly on sunlight for their growth and survival. Oysters are therefore nearly independent of water depth but depend heavily on food-carrying currents. They secrete calcareous shells that are cemented to those of adjacent oysters, producing a massive habitat suitable to numerous other species.

The northern Gulf Coast has a highly variable climate. Hurricanes, northers, freshets, and freezes are sporadic events that may have tremendous effects on shore species. Animals dwelling near the waterline risk exposure to large and often abrupt changes in temperature, salinity, and water level caused by these events. Hurricanes and severe thunderstorms dump enormous quantities of freshwater water on the coastal zone, most of which runs off into the bays and then through the passes into the Gulf. Because it is lighter than seawater, much of this freshwater flows along the surface without mixing very deeply into the bays. However, the salinity along the shoreline will be reduced for several days and the water level will be higher than normal. Hurricanes may also alter coastal morphology and, consequently, the patterns of nearshore water circulation.

Northers blow the surface water away from the coast and sharply reduce the air temperature, chilling animals exposed by the receding water level. Some species escape these stresses by burrowing into the sediment or migrating into deeper water; others are physiologically versatile and are able to adjust to short-term alterations of their environment. Compound events, such as a freeze and a norther occurring simultaneously, stress nearshore animals more than either single event.

On the average, the northern coast of the Gulf of Mexico is a warm, humid, subtropical region. Mean air temperatures on the Galveston beach range from 12.2°C (54°F) during the coldest month (January) to 28.5°C (83°F) during the warmest month (August). Likewise, mean water temperatures range from 11.8°C (53°F) in January to 30°C (86°F) in August. The mean salinity at Galveston is 29.1 parts per thousand, but recorded salinities range as low as 3.2 parts per thousand and as high as 39.2 parts per thousand. This variability in the surface salinity results from the uneven distribution of the Gulf Coast's annual rainfall.

Organisms living between the tidemarks may be exposed to different temperature regimes depending upon whether or not the tide is covering them. If they are exposed to the air, they may experience temperatures as low as -13°C (8°F) or as high as 38°C (101°F). However, if they are underwater, the temperature will probably be within the recorded range of 4°C (39°F) to 33°C (91°F).

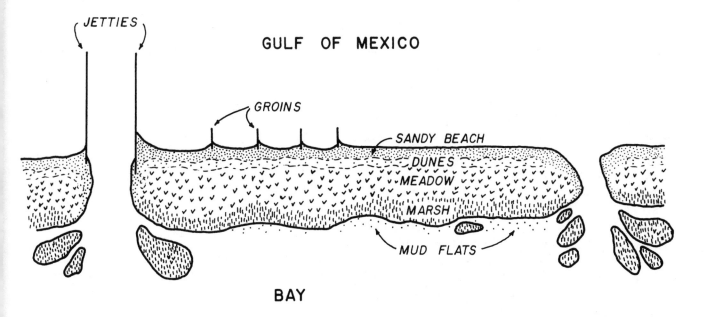

**FIGURE 1.2.** Locations of major coastal habitats on a barrier island.

## The Fauna

The fauna of the northern Gulf of Mexico has four elements: Carolinian, endemic, Caribbean, and cosmopolitan (species found around the world). It has great affinity with the fauna of the lower Atlantic Coast. Hence, zoogeographically this region is considered a disjunct segment of the Carolinian Province, which extends from Cape Hatteras, North Carolina, to southern Florida and across the northern Gulf of Mexico. These two regions were connected before the Florida peninsula was formed, permitting the migration of Atlantic species into the northern Gulf. Some species may have entered the Gulf later as the water temperatures of southern Florida were lowered to a level tolerable to northern species during the glacial ages. Today, the Florida peninsula and the Florida Current, which flows out of the Gulf, discourage such migrations. Many of our best-known species, such as the blue crab and the common oyster, are found on both coasts. More than 60 percent of the mollusks on the south Atlantic coast of the United States. and the northern coast of the Gulf of Mexico are the same.

Faunas of the eastern and western portions of the northern Gulf of Mexico are separated at a major faunal transition near Desoto Canyon (Figure 1.1). This faunal change is apparently related to a change in substrate, from calcareous in the east to terrigenous in the west. Predominant sediments along the coasts of Alabama and northwestern Florida arise from fossil and recent coralline deposits and hence are marine in origin. Sediments to the west are predominately silts and siliceous sands arising from continental erosion and are transported to the Gulf by numerous rivers, the largest being the Mississippi River. These sediments differ in grain size, density, pore space, and organic content and thus attract different species, particularly among those taxa that construct burrows or ingest sediment.

Another factor that contributes to this faunal difference is the Loop Current, which transports warm Caribbean water and entrained larvae of Caribbean species northward along the Florida coast. Thus, the eastern Gulf not only has a sediment type similar to that of the Caribbean, but also has access to a wide variety of tropical larvae. High turbidity of western Gulf waters discourages colonization by several taxa common in the eastern Gulf, such as sponges, reef-building corals, and algae.

Some of the Carolinian species have different lifestyles at the extremes of their geographical ranges. The common purple sea urchin spawns in summer in the northern portion of its range and in late winter in Texas. And the hermit crab, *Pagurus longicarpus*, migrates from shallow water into the deeper parts of the bays during the winter on the East Coast but migrates from deep water to the shallows during the winter in Texas. Several of these species also reach a larger size in the northern portion of their ranges than they do in the Gulf of Mexico.

Some of the species found in the Gulf have diverged evolutionarily, forming a fauna considered endemic or special to the Gulf. Zoogeographers estimate that 10 to 13 percent of Gulf species are endemic, and as investigations continue with new genetic techniques and greater scrutiny, more species in this category may be recognized.

The Caribbean or tropical element of the fauna of the northwestern Gulf Coast is generally a temporary one. It becomes established every few years when the local climate is sufficiently mild and largely disappears during severe winters. Most of these tropical species, such as the gorgonians, are most common south of 28° north latitude (Corpus Christi, Texas, and St. Petersburg, Florida). These species generally arrive as planktonic larvae carried north along the coasts of Mexico and Florida or across the Gulf from Yucatán.

Cosmopolitan species are often distributed by ships that visit Gulf Coast ports. Barnacles, hydroids, serpulid worms, and other sessile species are common fouling organisms found on the hulls of ships. Crabs and isopods that can tolerate exposure to air often find crevices on ships, especially wooden ships, that are suitable niches for a transoceanic voyage. Mud crabs, flatworms, and amphipods are often transported from one part of the world to another in shipments of seed oysters. Other species, such as the Portuguese man-of-war and the by-the-wind sailor, are carried across the ocean via currents and wind.

## Lifestyles

The animals that inhabit the northern Gulf Coast have diverse means of making a living. Perhaps the most common method of obtaining food is filter-feeding, i.e., by straining microscopic plankton from the water. Most filter-feeders set up a current of water by beating thousands of tiny cilia. This current is driven through small pores lined with bristles and coated with mucus. The plankton becomes entangled in the mucus, which is periodically sloughed off to the mouth, where the food is sorted and ingested. Filter-feeding is commonly employed by clams, oysters, mussels, slipper limpets, sponges, and some worms. Variations are exhibited by barnacles, whose long, curved legs strain plankton from passing water, and by sea anemones and hydrozoans, whose tentacles are armed with cells designed to immobilize and grasp plankters that brush against them.

Another common feeding mode is deposit-feeding. Many crabs obtain food by sifting through the sediment for minute food particles that are removed by specially adapted mouthparts. Some worms are even more direct—the sediment is simply swallowed and the sorting is done chemically in the gut. Scavenging is a related mode of feeding employed by larger crabs and some other crustaceans, such as isopods and amphipods. Scavengers are opportunists, exploiting the remains of animals that sporadically become available for larger bits of food. Many scavengers are also deposit-feeders or predators that are not adverse to picking up a bit of easy food.

Several animals on the jetties and in the salt marshes graze upon the algae that grows on the rocks and grass stalks. Limpets and littorine snails employ a radula, a thin, flexible band covered with numerous rows of teeth, which is rasped back and forth over the rock or plant surface to remove the microscopic algal film. Sea urchins and crabs eat larger algae, which can be grasped and torn from the rock.

Carnivorous snails exhibit various feeding modes. Some species bore a hole through the shell of their prey with the radula, frequently aided by chemical secretions. Others pry open or chip away the prey's shell with the lip of their own shell. Shell-chipping is a technique also employed by predaceous crabs when feeding on bivalves, snails, and hermit crabs. Other crabs and mantis shrimp are ambush predators, lying buried in the sand until a smaller animal wanders too near.

## Invertebrate Taxa

The sponge fauna of the northwestern Gulf of Mexico is not diverse, probably due to a combination of the cold winters and reduced salinities.

### PHYLUM PORIFERA
sponges

Sponges are much more prevalent in the eastern Gulf, especially where coral reefs occur. Sponges common to the northwestern Gulf Coast are boring sponges, which may be found in snails, clam and oyster shells, or encrusting sponges inhabiting artificial reefs.

### PHYLUM CNIDARIA
jellyfish, anemones, coral

The cnidarians are a very common and diverse group that includes the hydroids, jellyfish, sea anemones, sea pansies, gorgonians, and stony corals. Cnidarians are unique in possessing nematocysts, with which they immobilize their prey. Hydroids may be found on almost any firm substrate—rocks, pilings, shells, boats, buoys, crabs, and seaweeds. Although hydroids are very common, they are usually overlooked by the casual observer because they are small and look like plants. Jellyfish, or medusae, are generally much larger than hydroids, but they are difficult for the land-based naturalist to see unless they wash up on the beach or are large enough to be spotted from a jetty or pier. Sea anemones are common on the jetties, where they are often disguised by a covering of shell fragments, and on oyster reefs and hermit-crab shells. Sea pansies are found offshore on sandy bottoms. Although they occasionally wash ashore, they are most often observed in trawl samples. Gorgonians (sea whips and sea fans) may be found on the jetties below the waterline or attached to rocks or large shells offshore. Stony corals generally prefer warmer water than is found on this coast during the winter. Well-developed coral reefs may be found offshore at the Flower Gardens Bank, but only one species lives nearshore, on rocks or other solid objects.

## PHYLUM CTENOPHORA
comb-jellies

The ctenophores are a small group of medusalike animals, commonly called comb-jellies, which often become very abundant in the bays. The eerie light of their bioluminescence is a common sight to flounder fishermen. Ctenophores can be recognized by their eight rows of cilia. The beating of these tiny cilia propels the ctenophore through the water and brings it into contact with its planktonic food. In contrast to the cnidarians, most ctenophores lack nematocysts but have tentacles with adhesive structures that trap plankters. Two species are found along the northwestern Gulf Coast; one predominates in summer and the other in winter.

## PHYLUM PLATYHELMINTHES
flatworms

The flatworms are small, secretive animals and thus are easily overlooked. They have flattened, oval bodies and numerous eyes, often distributed in a band around the margin of the body. Species peculiar to this area can be found on oyster reefs, in shells occupied by hermit crabs, on *Sargassum*, or crawling over muddy sediments.

## PHYLUM RHYNCHOCOELA
proboscis worms

The nemerteans or proboscis worms are long, slender, fragile worms. The length of the proboscis in some species exceeds the length of the rest of the body. Everted by muscular contractions, it wraps around the prey and is then retracted, bringing the food to the mouth. The prey is usually swallowed whole, but if it is too large, its tissues are sucked out. Many nemerteans are very colorful, and some are patterned with bright stripes and bands. They may be found by straining mud or sand-mud through a sieve.

## PHYLUM ANNELIDA
round worms

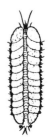

The most common marine annelid worms are the polychaetes. The bodies of these worms are conspicuously divided into numerous segments, each of which is equipped with a pair of lateral appendages. These appendages, called parapodia, are modified according to the worm's lifestyle. In tube-dwelling species, the parapodia are greatly reduced; in burrowing species, they are large, efficient locomotory devices. The sedentary species may be found attached to almost any solid object in the water, but they are most common on calcareous substrates such as shells. They may also be found in tubes or burrows in the mud. The errant species can be found by sifting through sediments and inspecting oyster shells, or by carefully examining other animals, such as sea stars, sea pansies, hermit crabs, and sea urchins for commensal species.

## PHYLUM MOLLUSCA
oysters, snails, clams, octopus

The mollusks are a very large and diverse group that includes familiar forms such as snails, clams, oysters, chitons, squids, and octopuses. Snails and bivalves are found in all nearshore environments and, being the object of many a collector's affection, are among the best-known marine invertebrates. Chitons live on hard substrates such as oyster shells. Squids and octopuses are best known to shrimp fishermen, in whose trawls they are frequently caught.

**PHYLUM ARTHROPODA**
crabs, shrimp

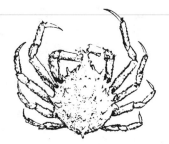

**PHYLUM BRYOZOA**
moss animals

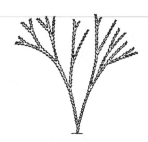

This is the largest animal phylum, primarily because it includes the insects. There are very few marine insects, however, and most of the marine arthropods belong to the class Crustacea. The crustaceans include the barnacles, copepods, amphipods, isopods, crabs, shrimp, and lobsters. Barnacles are among the more ubiquitous invertebrates in the sea; they are found on jetties, pilings, boat hulls, shells, crabs, turtles, whales, driftwood, and *Sargassum*. Copepods are one of the most important invertebrate taxa in the sea, forming a major food link between the microscopic plant life called phytoplankton and young fish. Isopods and amphipods may be found in damp crevices, among the seaweeds on the jetties, in edible beach drift, and in salt marshes. Various crabs may be found swimming in the bays, hiding among the boulders on the jetties, burrowing in the surf zone, or living in old tin cans. Likewise, various species of shrimp live on the muddy bay bottom, crawl about on the jetty boulders, cling to submerged grasses, or burrow into mudflats.

**PHYLUM ECHINODERMATA**
sea stars, urchins

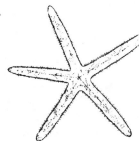

The echinoderms are generally large, benthic invertebrates such as the sea stars, brittle stars, sea urchins, sand dollars, and sea cucumbers. Sea stars and brittle stars can be found on sandy or sandy-mud bottoms from the surf zone to deep water. Brittle stars are also found on oyster reefs. Commonly found on jetties, sea urchins may also live on sandy bottoms. Beds of sand dollars may be found in sandy sediments just beyond the surf zone or in the passes. Sea cucumbers are usually found on grass flats.

The bryozoans are small, colonial animals whose colonies have two growth forms. One form closely resembles a hydroid colony, and the other form appears as a thin encrustation covering the surface of a shell or a rock. The latter form is more easily recognized and is common on shells inhabited by hermit crabs. The individuals within a colony may be modified for feeding, reproduction, or defense. Each feeding individual is equipped with a crown of tentacles that sweeps food out of the passing water toward the mouth.

**PHYLUM CHAETOGNATHA**
arrow worms

The arrow worms are long, slender, planktonic animals. They are equipped with lateral fins that aid in gliding through the water and with several pairs of long spines on the head that aid in food capture. They generally prefer saline water to brackish water but may occasionally be found in the bays when the salinity is high. They are voracious predators on plankters.

**PHYLUM CHORDATA**
sea squirts

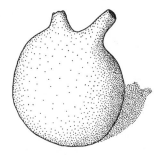

A few of the chordates lack vertebrae and hence are invertebrates. Among these are the sea squirts and the larvaceans. Sea squirts are round, gelatinous animals with two short siphons projecting from the body. Water laden with planktonic food is drawn into one of these tubes, the food is digested, and the water is forced out the other tube. They are sessile animals that can be found on oyster reefs, pilings, and old shells. Larvaceans are peculiar planktonic animals that resemble small tadpoles in which the tail is attached at right angles to the head. They live in disposable gelatinous "houses" equipped with filters for straining food from the water.

# CHAPTER TWO

# Jetties and Groins

Rocky intertidal habitats along the northwestern Gulf Coast are limited to man-made jetties designed to impede the movement of sand along the shore. Organisms living on these structures may be exposed to severe physical stresses from waves and currents. The more fragile animals must seek refuge in the crevices or on the leeward side of the boulders. Most of the animals on the jetties either filter plankton from the water, graze on algae or diatoms that grow on the rocks, or search for scraps of food left by the ebbing tide, gulls, or fishermen.

In spite of the paucity of rocky-shore habitats on the Gulf Coast, those that do exist share common features with most other rocky shores around the world. These features include zones of ecologically similar organisms that adapt to similar regimes imposed by the tides and surface waves of breaking waves.

On the tops of the jetties there may be a splash zone, wetted only by the spray of breaking waves. Below this lies a zone that is submerged during nearly all high tides and exposed during nearly all low tides—the littoral zone. Below that, uncovered by the lowest tides, is the sublittoral zone. Some marine biologists also recognize supralittoral and infralittoral fringes, which are wetted only by extreme high tides or high waves and exposed only by extreme low tides, respectively.

The most common animals found in rocky-shore habitats are the acorn barnacles, *Chthamalus frag-ilis* and *Balanus improvisus*; the zebra periwinkle, *Nodilittorina lineolata*; the false limpet, *Siphonaria pectinata*; the rock louse, *Ligia exotica*; the hermit crab, *Clibanarius vittatus*; the stone crab, *Menippe adina*; the porcelain crab, *Petrolisthes armatus*; the drill, *Stramonita haemastoma*; and the warty sea anemone, *Bunodosoma cavernata*.

## The Ubiquitous Barnacles

The fragile barnacle, *Chthamalus*, is the most common acorn barnacle at the higher levels on the jetties. It is generally small (about 5 mm), but its size and shape vary greatly depending upon its food supply and upon how crowded it is. Crowded barnacles are more elongate and thus are more easily broken off the rocks by waves than are the squatter, uncrowded barnacles.

Three other acorn barnacles—*Balanus improvisus*, *Balanus eburneus* (the ivory barnacle), and *Balanus amphitrite* (the striped barnacle)—are often found on jetties, pilings, driftwood, and shells. The acorn barnacles are distinguished by their shell structure, which is composed of a base, a wall consisting of six interlocking plates, and an operculum consisting of four valves. The bases and walls of the shells of the northwestern Gulf Coast species of *Balanus* are calcareous and porous. The base of *Chthamalus'* shell is membranous, and its wall is calcareous but solid. Moreover, the plates of the walls of these genera overlap differently (Figure 2. 1).

*Balanus eburneus* is the largest acorn barnacle in this area. It can be distinguished from *Balanus improvisus* and *Balanus amphitrite* by the longitudinal grooves on the larger pair of opercular valves (called scuta) and the broad zone of overlap (the radius) between the plates (Figure 2.2). *Balanus amphitrite* also has broad radii but lacks the longitudinally grooved scuta and is marked by thin gray

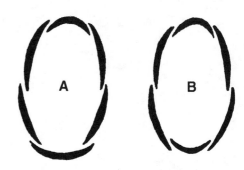

**FIGURE 2.1.** Configuration of shell wall plates for the acorn barnacles, *Balanus* (A) and *Chthamalus* (B).

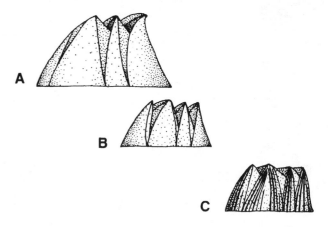

**FIGURE 2.2.** Lateral view of the acorn barnacles, *Balanus eburneus* (A), *Balanus improvisus* (B), and *Balanus amphitrite amphitrite* (C). (x5)

or purple stripes (except in old, bleached shells). *Balanus improvisus* has narrow radii and no longitudinal grooves on the scuta.

Barnacles are filter-feeders, screening plankton from the water with their featherlike legs. These legs are withdrawn behind the tightly closing opercular valves when the tide recedes. This keeps the barnacle moist for several hours. However, if the barnacle is not wetted by the returning tide or by the spray from a wave for a longer time, it may perish. This places an upper limit on the portion of the jetty that is inhabitable by *Chthamalus*. A lower limit may be created through crowding by other barnacle species or through predation by the snail *Stramonita haemastoma*. *Stramonita* is less tolerant of drying than is *Chthamalus*; thus, the higher levels on the jetty provide *Chthamalus* with a refuge from this predator.

The dense aggregations of barnacles are caused in part by the affinity that barnacle larvae have for rock that is or has been occupied by other barnacles of the same species. A chemical substance in the shells of older barnacles attracts the young to settle nearby. This is critical to barnacles, because individuals must cross-fertilize even though they are sessile, have internal fertilization, and are hermaphroditic (each individual produces both eggs and sperm). Only the eggs of barnacles settled close to each other can be fertilized. The fertilized egg hatches into a planktonic nauplius larva, which undergoes six molts and then develops into a second larva called a cypris. The planktonic stage of a barnacle's life usually lasts less than two weeks, but it may be prolonged if the cypris larva has difficulty locating a suitable habitat. The cypris larva uses a cement produced by special glands on its antennae to attach itself to a rock. Actually, a barnacle is an animal that spends its life standing on its head and capturing food with its feet.

The zebra periwinkle, *Nodilittorina lineolata* (Figure 2.3), can usually be found among the barnacles. This black-and-white snail is so tiny that it is often found inside the shells of dead barnacles. *Nodilittorina* scrapes algae and diatoms from the rock, often removing particles of rock in the process. Thus, it is a "bioeroder" and is partially responsible for numerous depressions in soft rocks such as sandstones. It is often found aggregated in crevices, of its own making or not, which help to protect it from pounding waves and drying wind.

**FIGURE 2.3.** The zebra periwinkle, *Nodilittorina lineolata*. (x5)

Another common grazer on the jetty is the false limpet, *Siphonaria pectinata* (Figure 2.4). Like barnacles, limpets have a conical shape that helps them to resist the force of waves breaking over them. Like *Nodilittorina*, *Siphonaria* grazes on microscopic algae and diatoms, and it often erodes a shallow depression into which its shell fits snugly. It is often camouflaged by filamentous algae that grow on its shell. This bioeroder is quite destructive to soft beach rocks in southeastern

**FIGURE 2.4.** The false limpet, *Siphonaria pectinata*. (x2)

Florida. Unlike most other marine snails, *Siphonaria* is a pulmonate gastropod, i.e., gases are exchanged across the lining of its mantle cavity rather than through a gill. Hence, it is called a "false" limpet. These snails are hermaphroditic, meaning that two individuals may fertilize each other's eggs. The eggs are laid in yellow or yellow-green ribbons 3–4 cm long. These gelatinous egg ribbons are often laid in a semicircle.

## Fleet-Footed Scavengers

Scurrying for shelter among the boulders, the isopod or rock louse, *Ligia exotica* (Figure 2.5), resembles a cockroach retreating from your approach. These fleet-footed scavengers, called sea slaters in England, migrate with the changing tide and thus are able to avoid many of the hazards of life in the intertidal zone. *Ligia* is most active near dusk or on overcast days; on warm, sunny days it stays in the cooler crevices between the boulders. *Ligia* stays near the

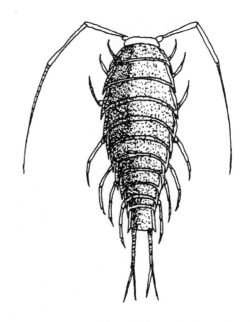

**FIGURE 2.5.** The rock louse, *Ligia exotica*. (x2)

water and shuns the warming rays of the sun because its platelike gills dry out easily. When it finds itself exposed to the sun's heat, water from its permeable cuticle evaporates and cools the isopod, but it must withstand considerable concentration of its blood resulting from the water loss. *Ligia* can often be observed wetting its gills at the water's edge. Because its gills are located under its abdomen, it needs to submerge only the posterior portion of its body. It replaces lost internal water by drinking, either through its mouth or, more commonly, through its anus. Anal drinking is aided by dilation of the rectum and antiperistalsis—i.e., reversing the flow through the alimentary canal.

*Ligia* can change its color by concentrating or dispersing a dark pigment called melanin in special cells called chromatophores under its cuticle. When the melanin is concentrated, it appears as black dots that are so tiny as to be nearly invisible; thus, the isopod as a whole seems pale. When the melanin is dispersed, the isopod seems dark gray. *Ligia* is usually found in its dark phase during the day and in its pale phase at night, except when influenced by a full moon or other bright light.

Unlike most other jetty invertebrates, *Ligia* does not have a planktonic larval stage. The young develop in a brood pouch between their mother's legs until they are old enough to fend for themselves on the jetty. As many as 120 young may be carried by a single female. Although this number seems trivial compared to the many thousands or millions of eggs produced by a blue crab or an oyster, *Ligia*'s young stand a better chance of survival because of their parental care.

A smaller isopod, *Sphaeroma quadridentatum* (Figure 2.6), can usually be found by searching carefully among the algae growing on the jetty or among the clusters of barnacles and littorines. Like its terrestrial relatives, the pill bugs, *Sphaeroma* will roll into a ball if threatened. It can often be found in this spherical form inside old barnacle shells. Unlike other American representatives of

**FIGURE 2.6.** The smooth-backed sphaeroma, *Sphaeroma quadridentatus.* (x4)

this genus, *Sphaeroma quadridentatum* lacks tubercles on its abdomen. Most members of this genus bore into wooden structures, and one species, *Sphaeroma terebrans*, is very destructive to the prop roots of red mangroves in southwestern Florida.

## Oyster Drills and Hermit Crabs

The drill or rock shell, *Stramonita haemastoma*, is a predator of barnacles and young oysters (spat) on the jetties. *Stramonita* is best known as an oyster predator found on oyster beds, but it is equally destructive to noncommercial species on rocky shores. Two varieties of this snail are found in Texas; some malacologists consider these to be subspecies. They are *Stramonita haemastoma floridana* and *Stramonita haemastoma canaliculata* (Figure 2.7). The latter is recognized most easily by the double row of large knobs on its shell and the numerous grooves on the inside of the lip. However, intermediate forms are common and there is serious doubt that these two forms deserve subspecific rank.

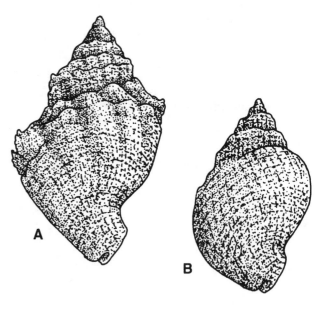

**FIGURE 2.7.** The rock shells, *Stramonita haemastoma canaliculata* (A) and *Stramonita haemastroma floridana* (B). (x1)

The shells of *Stramonita* are used by the striped hermit crab, *Clibanarius vittatus*, which is commonly found at or near the waterline along jetties. *Clibanarius* (Figure 2.8) can also be found occupying the shells of several species of snails that live on

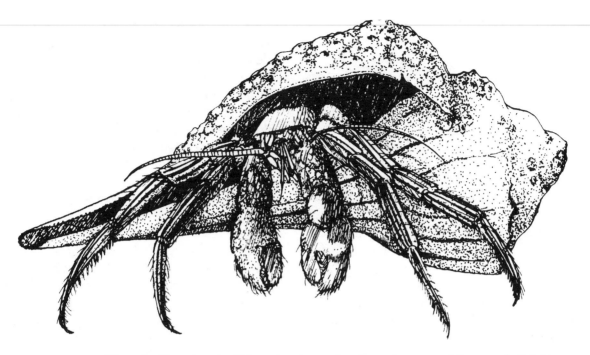

**FIGURE 2.8.** The striped hermit crab, *Clibanarius vittatus*, in a barnacle-encrusted *Busycon* shell. (x1)

sandy substrates offshore, typically, the moon snail, *Neverita duplicata*, and the whelks, *Busycon pulleyi* and *Busycotypus spiratum*. Young *Stramonita* (about 1 cm long) are usually found riding on the shells of adults or on shells inhabited by hermit crabs. *Clibanarius* is a scavenger, feeding on a wide variety of items such as algae, the remains of organisms that wash up on the rocks, and fishing bait. It disappears from the shallows around the jetty for two or three months during the winter. During this period, it can usually be found in the channels adjacent to the jetties. There it aggregates and often buries itself in the sediment.

*Clibanarius* is occasionally burdened by the parasitic isopod, *Bopyrissa wolffi* (Figure 2.9), which resides in its host's gill chamber. It occurs primarily in young hermit crabs and is easily detected by a pronounced swelling of the crab's carapace over the isopod. Male *Bopyrissa* are much smaller than the females and are thus more easily overlooked.

The shells of both snails and hermit crabs on the jetties are sometimes used as a substrate by the half-folded dove snail, *Anachis semiplicata* (Figure 2.10). *Anachis* may also be found on shells on the mudflats or on blades of shoal grass *(Halodule)* or turtle grass *(Thalassia)*. It attaches itself to the grass blade by a thin mucous thread. This tiny carnivore is most conspicuous when it forms clusters of ten or more individuals, possibly for breeding.

**FIGURE 2.9.** A female parasitic isopod, *Bopyrissa wolffi*. (x15)

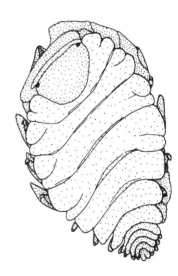

**FIGURE 2.10.** The half-folded dove shell, *Anachis semiplicata*. (x3)

The cancellate cantharus, *Cantharus cancellarius* (Figure 2.11), is another small snail that is often found on the jetties or on the sand flats adjacent to the jetties. It resembles *Stramonita* but has a more

**FIGURE 2.11.** The cancellate cantharus, *Cantharus cancellarius.* (x1.5)

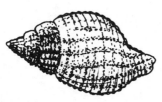

textured shell and rarely exceeds 3 cm in length. Its yellowish-brown shell usually supports an algal flora when the snail is alive. The tinted cantharus, *Pollia tincta*, may be found on the jetties from Port Aransas south. It is usually darker (blue-gray or chocolate brown) than the cancellate cantharus.

## Flowers in the Crevices

During low tides, the anemone *Bunodosoma cavernata* (Figure 2.12) is often exposed. Anemones are difficult to recognize out of water, because they shrink against the rock and fold in their tentacles. A more rewarding view may be found by seeking an anemone that is just below the waterline. Sea anemones are not plants, as they appear, but are sessile animals. A *Bunodosoma* on a jetty is usually light brown with vertical rows of pale blue dots on the stalk. Its tentacles have a blue stripe on the side nearest the mouth and are usually reddish on the opposite side. However, individuals from other habitats are often much duller in color than the jetty form.

Like most other anemones, *Bunodosoma* is capable of crawling. However, its temporary attachment to the rock is firm, and this anemone is often imbedded in a hole or crevice so that removing it in one piece is not a simple task. Some anemones, particularly those in contact with waterborne sand and debris, capture small fragments until they seem to have formed a shell crust. This "crust" protects them from a variety of hazards—desiccation, sunburn, abrasion from the sand, or attack by predators. Another jetty anemone, *Bunodactis texaensis*, is very similar in appearance to *Bunodosoma* and can only reliably be distinguished from it by a microscopic examination of the nematocysts. *Bunodactis* is usually light gray with dark gray streaks on the tentacles.

**FIGURE 2.13.** *Aiptasiomorpha texaensis.*(x4)

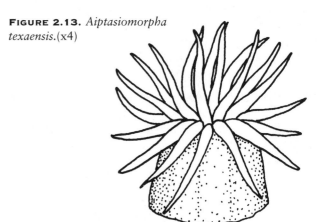

A small, pinkish anemone, *Aiptasiomorpha texaensis* (Figure 2.13), can be found near the far ends of jetties on rocks that are exposed only during extreme low tides. It is only about 5 mm in diameter and is usually found in clusters. *Aiptasiomorpha* reproduces asexually by budding off tiny juveniles, which can occasionally be seen attached to their parent's stalk. When completely formed, these young anenomes crawl off onto the substrate and colonize the area around the parent, forming a cluster, or clone, of genetically identical individuals. *Aiptasiomorpha* is tolerant of low salinities and is often found on oyster reefs as well as on jetties.

**FIGURE 2.12.** The warty sea anemone, *Bunodosome cavernata.* (x1)

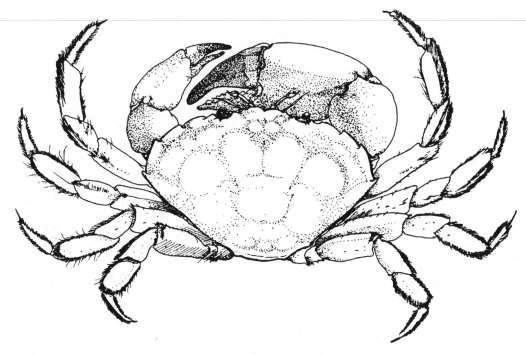

**FIGURE 2.14.** The stone crab, *Menippe adina.* (x0.7)

An anemone's nematocysts are long, barbed filaments that remain coiled inside cells on the tentacles until disturbed by contact with a potential food item, such as a fish or a finger. They then eject very rapidly toward the food, and if it is small enough to be held by the nematocysts, the prey is passed by the tentacles to the mouth. Some nematocysts carry a toxin to weaken the prey. These nematocysts are not dangerous to humans, but they do provide a sticky sensation when the tentacles are touched. The anemone does not have an anus, so any undigestible portions of its prey must be ejected through the mouth.

## Crabs and Shrimp on the Jetty

A close look into the pools between the boulders at low tide may reveal one or more stone crabs, *Menippe adina* (Figure 2.14). *Menippe* is generally a scavenger on the jetties, depending upon the water currents and the fishermen who keep it supplied with free food. In the absence of such easy food, it is quite capable of breaking open oyster spat or chipping away the shells of hermit crabs with its powerful claws. Fingers are no match for these claws either, so these crabs should be handled very carefully. *Menippe adina* is a western Gulf species, recently separated from *Menippe merce-*

*naria*, which occurs in Florida. In northwestern Florida, in Apalachee Bay, hybrid forms occur. *Menippe adina* is more evenly colored on its carapace and legs than *M. mercenaria*, which has poorly defined yellow spots on its carapace and distinct bands on the carpi and propodi of its legs.

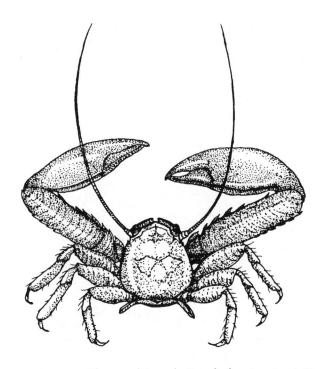

**FIGURE 2.15.** The porcelain crab, *Petrolisthes armatus.* (x2)

The porcelain crab, *Petrolisthes armatus* (Figure 2.15), may be found clinging to the bottoms of rocks in these pools. This small crab (3–4 cm) is aptly named, because it is extremely fragile. Its flattened claws are readily autotomized, or cast off, even with a minimum of human handling. *Petrolisthes* is a filter-feeder. It clings to the rock surface and alternatively waves its maxillipeds through the water above its head. These maxillipeds have a fringe of long setae that strain planktonic food from the water. Other mouthparts intermittently remove this food from the setae and transfer it to the mouth. *Petrolisthes* occasionally supplements its planktonic diet by scraping algae off rocks and shells or by scavenging dead animals that it is fortunate enough to come upon.

The persistent jetty explorer will be rewarded with a glimpse of the beautiful little peppermint shrimp, *Lysmata wurdemanni* (Figure 2.16). As its name suggests, this shrimp is translucent with delicate red stripes. The peppermint shrimp is most abundant near the tips of the southern jetties, where it resides deep in the crevices. *Lysmata* is closely related to the "cleaning shrimp," which remove parasites and infected tissue from the bodies of fish. Cleaning shrimp often set up stations to which the fish come to be treated. Although this behavior has not been reported in the peppermint shrimp, *Lysmata* will pick at sores and hairs if permitted to crawl about on one's hand. This annoying behavior is related to its probable habit of scavenging among the subtidal organisms encrusting the jetty.

## Migration of the Sea Hare

Another sight familiar to visitors to the South Texas jetties in late spring and early summer is the migration of the sea hare, *Aplysia brasiliana* (Figure 2.17), as it passes through the channel on its way to breed in the grass flats of the bays. Such a migration also occurs during the late winter and early spring on the west coast of Florida, where these adult mollusks congregate to breed in shallow bays. *Aplysia* is a benthic herbivore that grazes on algae growing on the rocks. It is a surprisingly strong swimmer with the aid of its pair of large "wings." These wings, which fold over the sea hare's back, are actually extensions of the snail's foot. Sea hares vary their swimming speed according to the water current. They swim with greatest thrust when going against a current and can make headway against currents weaker than 0.75 km/hour. Thus, they travel the greatest distances riding the tides. Although *Aplysia* appears shell-less, it has a very thin internal shell that lies over the hump of organs on the posterior of the animal. It is hermaphroditic, and each individual may lay up to half a billion eggs in a tangled mass of yellow strings. *Aplysia* dies soon after it lays its eggs; it has a life span of only one year. If molested, the sea hare releases a purple ink into the water.

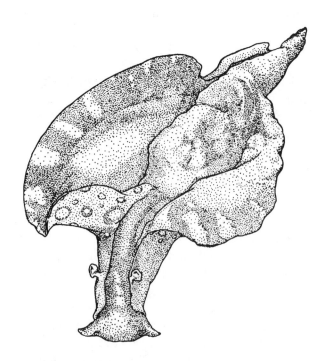

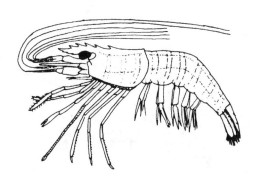

**FIGURE 2.16.** The peppermint shrimp, *Lysmata wurdemanni.* (x2)

**FIGURE 2.17.** The sea hare, *Aplysia brasiliana,* shown swimming. (x0.6)

## Spiny Delicacies

The South Texas jetties are also the home of the sea urchin *Arbacia punctulata* (Figure 2.18). This purple urchin is also a herbivore that enjoys large, leafy seaweeds. Its long spines protect it from many potential predators, but it is still vulnerable to the crushing force of waves breaking against the jetties and to the strong jaws of some aggressive fishes. Hence, it prefers to stay in crevices and on the leeward side of jetties. The sea urchin's gonads are eaten as a delicacy in many parts of the world. The shell of a sea urchin is called a "test," and the bumps on the test represent the points where the spines were attached. The test is composed of fused calcareous plates, fitted together in a sturdy zigzag pattern. Fast-growing *Arbacia* tend to have longer spines than slower-growing individuals. Spine length varies geographically, too. Populations in the Gulf of Mexico have longer spines than those in the northeastern Atlantic, although this difference is genetically determined. Hybrids produced by crossing parents from each locale have spines of intermediate length.

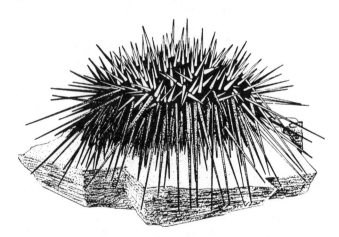

**FIGURE 2.18.** The sea urchin, *Arbacia punctulata*. (x0.5)

The rows of tiny holes in an *Arbacia* test are openings for the tube feet. Tube feet have a hollow core filled with seawater and a sucker at the tip. The sea urchin extends its feet by forcing seawater into them until the sucker touches and attaches to the substrate. By contracting muscles in the tube feet, the urchin shortens its feet and pulls itself toward the point where the sucker is attached. By coordinating the movements of its tube feet, and with some help from its spines, the urchin is able to move quite easily across either horizontal or vertical surfaces. The spines on the top and bottom of the urchin are shorter than those around its equator, making it easier for the tube feet to contact the substrate.

The two larger openings in the test are for the mouth and anus. The anus is located on the top side of the urchin, and the mouth is located on the side nearest the substrate. The mouth contains an unusual chewing apparatus called the "Aristotle's lantern." It consists of the housing and musculature for five long teeth, which meet at th'r tips to form a five-sided bite.

*Arbacia* is easily confused with another jetty urchin, *Echinometra lucunter*. Both species are approximately the same size and color and are nearly equally abundant on South Texas jetties. However, they can be distinguished by close inspection of the plates surrounding the anal opening on the upper surface. In *Arbacia*, these plates are four in number (sometimes three or five) and are sculptured with fine grooves in a reticulate pattern. In *Echinometra*, there are numerous plates of various sizes with assorted bumps similar to those on which the spines pivot. Moreover, the spines around *Echinometra*'s mouth have sharp tips, as opposed to the flattened tips of the oral spines of *Arbacia*.

## Beach Fleas and Skeleton Shrimp

The rocks on the sides of the jetties sometimes seem to be coated with a layer of slippery mud. On close inspection, this mud is often found to contain thousands of tiny holes. These holes mark the burrows of the tube-building amphipod, *Corophium louisianum* (Figure 2.19). *Corophium* produces a

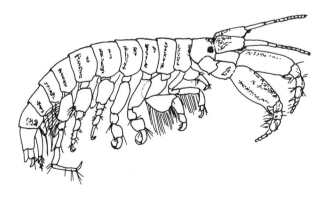

**FIGURE 2.19.** The tube-building amphipod, *Corophium louisianum*. (x15)

sticky substance that it uses to reinforce the walls of its tube. It is a detritus-feeder and will often make short forays from its burrow during high tide to search for food.

Another amphipod commonly found on the jetties is the beach flea, *Orchestia grillus* (Figure 2.20). *Orchestia* is larger than *Corophium* but is still only about 5 mm long. It is most abundant when green, filamentous algae are especially lush on the jetty. Its green color helps to camouflage it in this setting. If it is discovered, its powerful hind legs and curled abdomen act like a spring to propel it on a leap of up to 50 times its own length. *Orchestia*'s legs are poor for supporting it, so it is usually seen lying or crawling on its side.

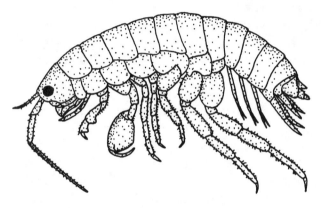

**FIGURE 2.20.** The beach flea, *Orchestia grillus*. (x7)

One of the most bizarre amphipods on the jetty is the so-called "skeleton shrimp," *Caprella equilibra* (Figure 2.21). Its long, slender body helps disguise it among the algal strands and hydroids to which it clings. *Caprella* is an ambush predator, lying in wait for an unsuspecting copepod, which it grabs with the claws on its second pair of legs.

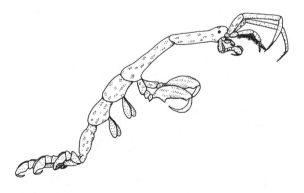

**FIGURE 2.21.** The skeleton shrimp, *Caprella equilibra*. (x8)

The smaller claws on its first legs then tear loose pieces of the prey and pass them to the mouth. *Caprella* is very sensitive to small water currents created by passing plankters. It may supplement its diet by scraping the diatom-rich slime from the surface of the hydroid or grass to which it clings. *Caprella* has also been found on bryozoans, sea squirts, soft corals, and the egg mass of the blue crab.

## Jetty Animals That Resemble Plants

On the undersides of boulders and deep in the crevices, where direct sunlight seldom reaches, one frequently finds what appears to be brown or gray algae. On close inspection this "algae" is usually identifiable as one or more hydroid colonies. These hydroids also appear as a coarse fuzz on pieces of driftwood or *Sargassum* that wash up on the jetties. A hydroid colony typically consists of a flexible stem, which may be branched; several individuals called zooids attached to the stem; and a base by which the stem is attached to the substrate. The zooids are polymorphic; i.e., several forms exist. The two most common forms are gastrozooids, which are feeding individuals, and gonozooids, which are reproductive individuals. The gastrozooids have a crown of nematocyst-bearing tentacles for food capture and resemble miniature anemones. The gonozooids typically consist of a stalk upon which several medusae are formed. In some species, the medusae are released to become part of the plankton. The medusae produce gametes that are released into the sea. The fertilized egg develops into a larva called planula, which eventually settles to the bottom to become another hydroid colony.

A third type of zooid found in some species is the dactylozooid, which is a protective zooid usually resembling a long tentacle armed with nematocysts. Except for openings for the tentacles, the entire colony is surrounded by a chitinous covering called a perisarc.

Among the more common Texas jetty hydroids are *Bougainvillia inaequalis* (Figure 2.22) and *Obelia dichotoma* (Figure 2.23). *Bougainvillia* forms a large, heavy colony (to 10 cm high) with a very wrinkled perisarc. *Obelia* is smaller (usually 1 to 1.5 cm high) and more delicate. Its perisarc is marked at nearly regular intervals by series of grooves, giving it an accordionlike appearance.

The gorgonian *Leptogorgia virgulata* (Figure 2.24) grows on the South Texas jetties. *Leptogorgia* is

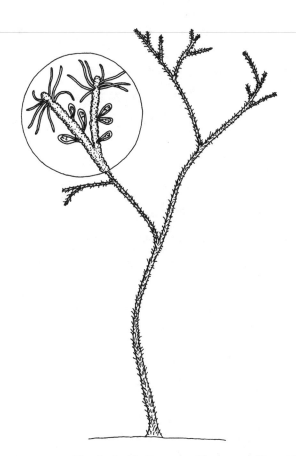

**FIGURE 2.22.** The hydroid, *Bougainvillia inaequallis,* with magnification of feeding and reproductive zooids. (x15)

most accessible to divers because it is never found above the water level, even during low tides. Though it resembles a stringy seaweed, the gorgonian is a soft coral and its limbs are lined with minute polyps. It exists in two color phases—yellow and reddish purple. *Leptogorgia* hosts a small parasitic snail, *Simnialena uniplicata.* The shell of *Simnialena* is long and slender, so it has a low profile as it crawls along the gorgonian's branches. It also has two color phases that match those of its host.

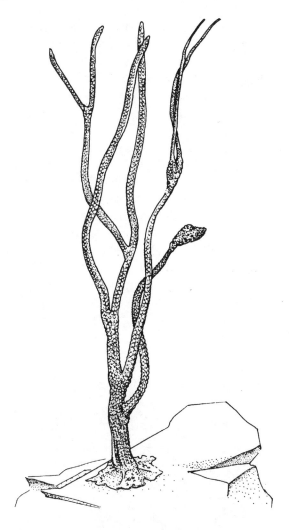

**FIGURE 2.24.** The gorgonian, *Leptogorgia virgulata,* with galls formed over damaged area. (x0.4)

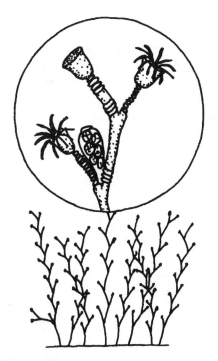

**FIGURE 2.23.** The hydroid, *Obelia dichotoma,* with magnification of feeding and reproductive zooids. (x7)

*Leptogorgia* typically grows as a fan-shaped colony oriented perpendicular to the prevailing tidal currents, enabling it to maximize its catch of drifting food. The colony is supported by a horny axial rod, which is sufficiently flexible to permit the colony to bend in response to wave surge or strong currents, as a sapling bows to the wind. Additional support for the polyps and resistance to abrasion is obtained from a loose skeleton of calcareous spicules. These ornate spicules (Figure 8.5) can be easily observed under a microscope after dissolving the tissue in a solution of sodium hypoclorite (Clorox).

The stony corals that construct massive reefs in tropical seas are intolerant of the cold winters along the northern Gulf Coast. Such reefs may be found on salt domes on the continental shelf but are not found in shallow water nearshore. Only one stony coral, *Astrangia poculata* (Figure 2.25), lives in shallow water along the northwestern Gulf Coast. It is a colonial coral consisting of a few to several dozen polyps, each about 5–6 mm in diameter and connected to a common base. Pieces of coral skeleton are often found among shells cast up on the beach, and living colonies can be found on rocks and debris dredged from the bottom near the jetties. Colonies probably live on the jetties below the low-tide level. The polyps are anemonelike and are white or pale pink in color. Unlike anemones, they grow in tight clusters and are supported by an intricate calcareous skeleton. As an *Astrangia* colony grows, new polyps are added by fission, i.e., the division of an old polyp into two new polyps, or by budding, i.e., the formation of a new (smaller) polyp as a bud off of an old polyp.

The fanworm *Hypsicomus elegans* (Figure 2.26)

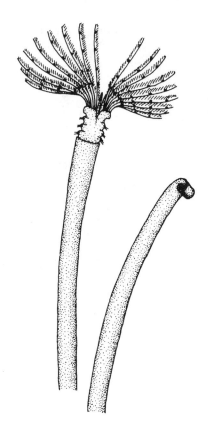

**FIGURE 2.26.** The fan worm, *Hypsicomus elegans*, expanded (left) and withdrawn (right). (x7)

may also be found on shells or rocks dredged from the bottom adjacent to the jetties. Although its color is variable, it usually has a deep purple body and frequently has purple-and-white-banded radioles. *Hypsicomus* constructs a tube from mucus and sand grains, which usually extends into a shell or calcareous rock. When disturbed, the fanworm withdraws into its tube and the tip of the tube often rolls up, sealing the aperture.

The jetties along the South Texas coast are the haunt of the Antillean nerite, *Nerita fulgurans* (Figure 2.27). This oddly shaped snail has a flattened spire and a very large aperture, which rapidly constricts to a relatively narrow slit inside the lip. *Nerita* is a grazer found near the high-tide level on jetty rocks and pilings. It has a tightly fitting operculum that enables it to withstand long periods out of the water.

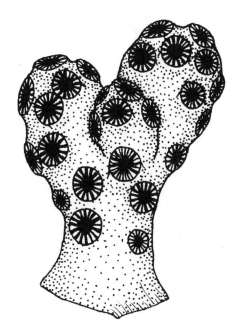

**FIGURE 2.25.** The stony coral, *Astrangia poculata*. (x3)

**FIGURE 2.27.** The Antillean nerite, *Nerita fulgurans*. (x2)

# CHAPTER THREE

# Sandy Beaches

Pounding surf, abrasive sand, and alternate periods of wetness and dryness of the sand beach present a harsh environment to organisms. Organisms in other environments must also deal with some of these factors, but on a sandy beach there is no solid substrate. There is nothing to hold on to in order to prevent one from being jostled about by wave action or washed in and out by the tide. The only refuge is within the sand. Consequently, most animals, except those that can swim well or crawl rapidly, burrow in the sand. Because many intertidal animals are concealed by their burrowing habit, a good clue to the abundance of the fauna in a particular area is the presence of feeding shorebirds such as sandpipers, sanderlings, and godwits.

Beach sand is composed of grains of various sizes and shapes. Although sand may be coarser or finer in different areas of the beach due to wave action, the space between the grains (pore space) is constant, averaging about 20 percent of the total volume.

The pore space, which is determined by the degree of particle packing, affects the water level within the sand. This level is highest in fine sand. The capillary action allows for the maintenance of water in the sand above sea level. Sand above the water level is damp due to the adhesion of water to the sand particles and the presence of water vapor in the interstitial spaces. Thus, a burrowing intertidal animal is in little danger of drying out at low tide. The presence of a water table in the sand is also important to animals living further back from the surf. By burrowing, they, too, can reach damp sand to protect themselves from desiccation.

In addition to protecting organisms against desiccation, a sand beach provides protection against temperature and salinity changes. Even a few millimeters of sand will protect against the hazards of insolation, i.e., exposure to the sun's rays. An animal that can burrow a few centimeters into the sand can survive intolerable surface temperatures. Salinity is relatively constant a few centimeters beneath the surface, enabling an organism to survive a period of freshwater runoff after a rain or, alternately, a drought.

A phenomenon called thixotropy is another physical aspect of sand that is important to burrowing animals. Thixotropy, strictly defined, is the ability of a gel to become liquid when stirred. Seemingly solid wet sand in the surf zone will "liquefy" if agitated slightly. The burrowing movements of an animal are sufficient agitation to loosen the sand and allow an animal to dig in quickly.

On the other hand, sand is moved about by wave action, putting animals that do not burrow deeply in constant danger of being washed out. The few animals that make permanent burrows in the surf zone must strengthen them by actually building tubes or strengthening the sand around the burrow with mucus. Animals that do not make permanent burrows but that move constantly through the sand are generally streamlined and smooth-surfaced. Such form permits faster and easier burrowing.

## Life on the Upper Beach

Having considered some of the factors that affect the inhabitants of sandy beaches, let's look at the animals and their adaptations concerning these factors. Like the jetties, the beach can be partitioned into supralittoral, littoral or intertidal, and sublittoral zones (Figure 3.1). The supralittoral zone begins at the base of the dunes and extends to the high tide line. One of the most conspicuous signs of animal life along the dunes is the rather large burrow of the ghost crab, *Ocypode quadrata* (Figure 3.2). This crab is active early in the morning, at dusk, and at night but usually remains in its burrow during the heat of the day. The depth of the burrow depends upon the water level within the sand, so it is wise to think twice before attempting to dig up a crab living

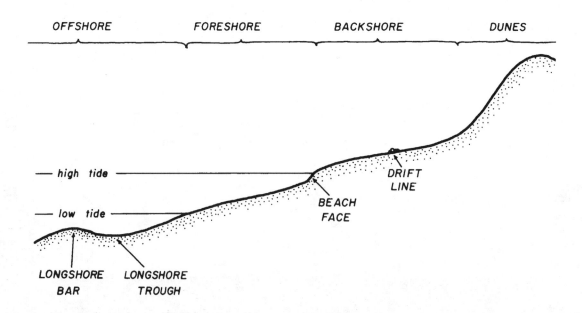

**FIGURE 3.1.** Profile of a sandy beach.

**FIGURE 3.2.** The ghost crab, *Ocypode quadrata.* (x0.7)

at the base of the dunes. Its burrow may be as deep as 1.3 m (4 ft) and may have a second entrance. Smaller crabs tend to live a little closer to the water, and consequently their burrows are shallower.

*Ocypode* is active from March through mid-December. During the colder months of the year, it plugs its burrow entrance with packed sand and remains dormant. Females that were spawned early in the previous summer mature and ovulate once in April and again in August. In the following year, they may or may not ovulate and usually do not survive a third winter. Mating probably occurs throughout the year, and unlike the blue crab *Callinectes, Ocypode* mates even when the female's integument is hard. Therefore, females can mate anytime after puberty. The female carries the eggs beneath her body and releases the developed larvae in the surf.

The ghost crab is a predator whose diet consists largely of mole crabs and bean clams, but it is also an opportunist. *Ocypode* will consume dead fish and the remains of animals found in beach debris, including stranded Portuguese men-of-war, *Physalia physalis,* which may be dragged to the burrow entrance. *Ocypode* is also capable of deposit feeding, like *Uca,* the fiddler crab. Both chelae are used to scoop sand to the mouth, where food particles are separated. Although they lack the specialized spoon-tip setae on their mouthparts that *Uca* uses to scrape food off sand grains, as feeders they are nearly as efficient. *Ocypode* is common in the surf at night because it must peri-

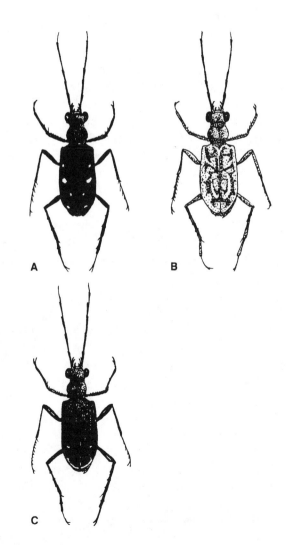

**FIGURE 3.3.** The tiger beetles, *Cicindela ocellata* (A), *Cicindela hamata* (B), and *Cicindela severa* (C). (x1.5)

odically exchange the seawater carried in its gill chamber. Its special adaptations to the supralittoral zone include thick setae around the openings to its gill chambers, which are used to take up capillary water from the sand. When dehydrated, *Ocypode* sits down, oscillating from side to side to work the tufts into the sand. The water is actually sucked into the gills by a vacuum that is produced in the gill chamber. How the vacuum is produced, though, is not known. Desiccation is also reduced by *Ocypode*'s relatively impermeable integument. It also has long antennae that can be flicked over its eyes to clear them of sand. These crabs interact socially with one another, communicating their intentions by the position of their chelae and by their body posture.

The tiger beetles, genus *Cicindela* (Figure 3.3), are another common, though often overlooked, resident of the upper shore and dunes. These small, fast-moving predators are characteristic of open, saline habitats such as beaches, mudflats, and the edges of salt marshes. More than 30 species are known from the northwestern Gulf Coast. They range in color from white to dark brown. They can be most easily recognized in the field by their behavior; when approached, they first run rapidly along the ground and then fly for a short distance if you get too close.

## Life on the Littoral Beach

The intertidal zone is inhabited by some interesting animals, to which most of the discussion of physical factors applies. One of the most common animals here is the coquina or bean clam, *Donax variabilis roemeri* (Figure 3.4), which comes in a variety of colors. Another species, *Donax texasiana*, is also fairly common and is usually uniform in color, in contrast to the rayed coloration of *Donax roemeri*. During the spring, these species are found together at the water's edge. In the summer, only *Donax roemeri* occurs in the intertidal zone, because *Donax texasiana* moves into the shallow sublittoral zone. During the winter, both occur in the sublittoral. *Donax roemeri* is distinguished from *Donax texasiana* by the overlap of the latter's valves in addition to the uniformity of the ventral teeth along its valve margins.

*Donax* is known to move up and down the beach slope with high and low tide, respectively. This migration is cued by vibrations in the sand pro-

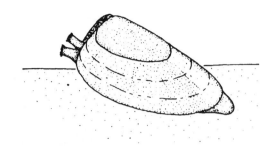

**FIGURE 3.4.** The bean clam, *Donax variabilis roemeri*, with siphons and foot extended. (x2)

duced by the pounding waves. Its adaptations for life in the surf zone include a large foot and a smooth, streamlined shell, which enables it to burrow quickly into the sand. This little clam has short siphons that require it to stay near the beach surface. This enables the filamentous alga, *Enteromorpha flexuosa*, to attach to the posterior ends of larger individuals. *Donax* is eaten by a variety of animals, including plovers and sanderlings, drum, various crabs, and the moon snail, *Neverita duplicata*. The gonads of large *Donax* are frequently parasitized by the larval stages of flukes, which either severely impair or prohibit reproduction. In uninfected individuals, reproduction apparently occurs in the spring and summer, and the recruitment of young is greatest in May and October. These young overwinter and then mature, reproduce, and die in the ensuing year. Their growth is greatest in the fall and winter and lowest in the summer, when energy is shunted into reproduction rather than into growth.

Another inhabitant of the surf zone, the mole crab *Emerita portoricensis* (Figure 3.5), is also gregarious. This small, cylindrical-shaped crab is covered dorsally by a very smooth carapace. It has short, stout legs and a long, bladelike telson that is held flexed beneath the body. The quick strokes of its legs and the shovellike action of the telson enable it to burrow quickly, posterior end first. It periodically cleans its antennules of adhering sand grains by flicking them across a special set of curved setae on the antennae. The *Emerita* that are commonly encountered are females. The males are much smaller than the females, and, when mature, they locate a female and inconspicuously cling to her body. The bright orange eggs are laid in late spring and are brooded beneath the female's abdomen until they hatch. The planktonic larvae are dispersed by ocean currents to other beaches,

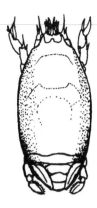

FIGURE 3.5. The mole crab, *Emerita portoricensis.* (x1.5)

## Snails That Leave Trails

Two snails are common in the intertidal zone. Both the lettered olive, *Oliva sayana* (Figure 3.7), and the moon snail, *Neverita duplicata*, are predacious. These snails glide along just beneath the surface of the sand at a depth determined by the lengths of their siphons. As they push the sand around their shells, they leave a furrow behind them which the knowledgeable collector can follow to locate the snail. Each has a large foot with the front portion (the propodium) modified for efficient burrowing. *Oliva* moves by extending the foot and then pulling the shell forward. This type of movement is termed "locomotor gallop" and is made only by a few gastropod species. Its golden-patterned mantle almost completely covers the shell when it is expanded. This probably reduces friction with the sand during movement and protects the shell from abrasion. The shell of this snail is highly polished and cylindrical in shape—further adaptations for the sandy beach environment.

and the less fortunate ones are carried far from shore, where they perish. The larvae undergo a series of molts, during which the structures required in adult life are acquired, and settle to the bottom to begin their lives in the surf zone. Another little crab, *Lepidopa websteri* (Figure 3.6), shares the surf zone with *Emerita*. This square-shaped crab also digs itself in backwards. Note its long, brushy antennules, which act as "straws" in bringing water from the surface.

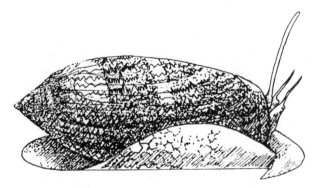

FIGURE 3.7. The lettered olive, *Oliva sayana*, with siphon, tentacles, and foot extended. (x1.5)

*Oliva* preys on *Donax* and other small, smooth-surfaced clams, which it presumably smothers with its foot. Its eggs are laid on the surface of the sand in transparent capsules containing from 20 to 50 eggs that develop into veliger larvae within a week. These veligers break out of the capsule and assume a planktonic existence until metamorphosing into the adult form.

The common Atlantic slipper shell, *Crepidula fornicata* (Figure 3.8), frequently washes ashore attached to an old *Oliva* shell or another suitable substrate, including another *Crepidula*. This slipper shell often lives in piles or chains as a result of its tendency to attach to the shells of each other.

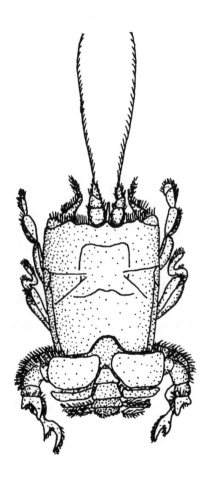

FIGURE 3.6. *Lepidopa websteri.* (x3)

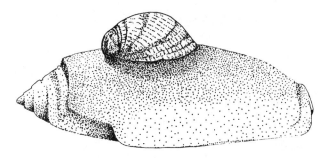

**FIGURE 3.8.** The common Atlantic slipper shell, *Crepidula fornicata*, attached to the shell of *Oliva sayana*. (x2)

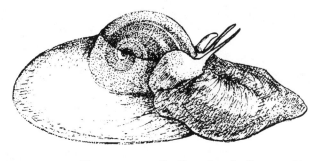

**FIGURE 3.9.** The moon snail, *Neverita duplicata*, with siphon, tentacles, and foot extended. (x0.7)

The largest and oldest members in a chain are females, while the smaller and most recent arrivals are males. A hormone secreted by the females causes the upper individuals to remain males. As the lower females die, the males change sex and replace them. *Crepidula* is a filter-feeding snail. A coarse mucous web secreted across the entrance to the mantle cavity prevents large particles from entering the inhalant stream of water that flows over the gills. These large particles are trapped in the mucus and sloughed off as pseudofeces. Smaller particles that enter the mantle cavity are filtered out by the gills and passed to the mouth in mucous strings. An increase in water turbidity decreases the rate of growth, because much energy is spent in preventing fouling of the mantle cavity. Under good conditions, *Crepidula* can increase up to 6 mm in length in three weeks. The inner shelf of *Crepidula* shells supports the internal organs and is overlaid by the circular foot. Attachment to the substrate is maintained by the foot's suction. Seventy to one hundred eggs are laid in each of several thin-walled capsules attached to the substrate. The young emerge from these capsules as veliger larvae.

*Neverita duplicata* (Figure 3.9) is a voracious predator of clams, its favorites being *Donax* and *Dosinia*, although it is a cannibal when other prey is not available. It holds the clam or snail within the folds of its foot and drills a hole through the shell with its radula. The radula is supported by a structure called an odontophore. As muscles pull the radula back and forth over the odontophore, the whole apparatus is rotated and a round hole is gradually rasped through the shell of the victim. When the hole is complete, *Neverita* inserts its tubular proboscis and eats the meat inside. If you examine beached shells, you will find many that have been bored by *Neverita*. Its work is identified by the countersunk hole left in the shell of its prey. Although the size of the rim of the hole is related to the size of the attacking *Neverita*, the size of the perforation can vary according to whether or not the prey was actually eaten. Very active prey often escapes, even after drilling proceeds long enough for a small opening to be made. Thus, if the diameter of the perforation is less than half that of the rim, the attacker probably went hungry for his efforts.

Another gastropod that can sometimes be found in the surf zone is the auger shell, *Hastula salleana* (Figure 3.10). This bluish-gray to brown shell is shaped like an awl. Little is known of the habits of this species. It has been supposed that these snails prey on marine worms, although they may be carnivorous scavengers. *Hastula* has a large foot that is used to plow through the sand. The foot can also be expanded to serve as a "sail," which carries the snail into deeper water with receding waves. This behavior is most pronounced during ebbing tides and keeps the auger from being stranded during low tide.

**FIGURE 3.10.** Salle's augur, *Hastula salleana*. (x2)

A common inhabitant of the shells of *Neverita*, *Oliva*, and *Hastula* after the snail's death is the hermit crab *Isocheles wurdemanni* (Figure 3.11). This hermit crab is distinguished from *Pagurus* and *Clibanarius* by its very setose ("hairy") antennae, its small, equal-sized claws, and its small eyes. *Isocheles* scavenges in shallow water for edible matter and, like

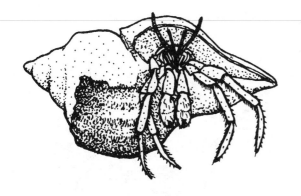

FIGURE 3.11. The hermit crab, *Isocheles wurdemanni*, in a bryozoan-encrusted shell. (x1)

other hermit crabs, is always on the lookout for a more suitable shell. Unlike *Pagurus*, *Isocheles* appears to be confined to the surf beach.

## Worms in the Surf Zone

The tube-building worm, *Diopatra cupraea* (Figure 3.12), is a common inhabitant of the sandy subtidal zone and is sometimes found intertidally. Its tubes, usually vacant, are often washed ashore during storms. The end of the tube extends three to four centimeters above the surface of the sand and is camouflaged and reinforced with small shells, fragments of shells, and bits of seaweed. The tube

extends a foot or more beneath the sand and thus is firmly anchored. This tube is constructed of mucus secreted by glands in the worm's parapodia. Upon contact with seawater, the mucus hardens to a parchmentlike material.

As the worm grows, it enlarges the tube by cutting a slit down the length of the tube, spreading the sides apart and adding a patch to the gap. The reinforced chimney may simply be cut away, discarded, and constructed anew. *Diopatra* is a scavenger that captures bits of food that are washed near its tube or small animals that are attracted to the tube. It does not usually leave its tube entirely; however, in calm water it may make a quick sortie after a tasty meal lying just out of reach. The worm itself is quite handsome. Its reddish-brown body is iridescent and on each side of the head are bright red gills. Attempts to dig this animal up are frequently unsuccessful, because it simply escapes through the bottom of the tube.

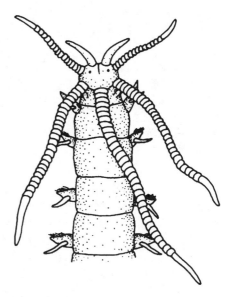

FIGURE 3.13. The anterior portion of the polychaete *Onuphis eremita oculata*. (x8)

*Onuphis eremita oculata* (Figure 3.13) is another tube-building polychaete living along the beach. It is a very long, slender worm that constructs a thin, membranous tube covered by a layer of fine sand grains. The worm is usually reddish in color due to the presence of large blood vessels near the surface. It can be captured by straining sand from the surf zone or from farther offshore through a sieve. Unfortunately, it is a very fragile worm and so is difficult to collect in one piece.

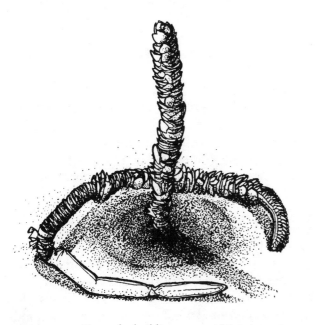

FIGURE 3.12. Two tube-building worms, *Diopatra cupraea*. The vertical tube is in its natural position; another worm is slightly extended from the exposed tube in which the unreinforced portion of the tube is also visible. (x1.5)

## Life Below the Littoral Zone

If one ventures into the subtidal zone and wades to about the second or third sandbar, one may find clusters of the sand dollar, *Mellita quinquiesperforata* (Figure 3.14). It prefers habitats where the salinity is usually greater than 23 parts per thousand; hence it is most common in the Gulf or in inlet-influenced areas in the bays. It also prefers a clean, sandy substrate because it has difficulty burrowing in other sediments.

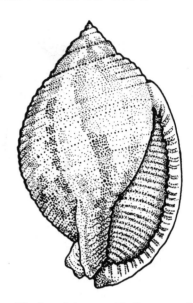

**FIGURE 3.15.** The Scotch bonnet, *Phalium granulatum.* (x1)

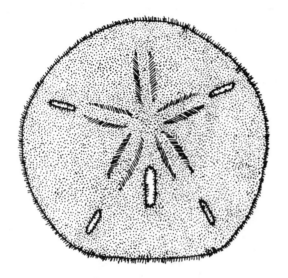

**FIGURE 3.14.** Dorsal view of a live, five-lunuled sand dollar, *Mellita quinquiesperforata.* (x1)

Sand dollars are closely related to sea urchins. Their skeletons are the waferlike tests so well known to beachcombers. While alive, their bodies are covered by numerous short spines that are used for locomotion as well as for protection. Both the mouth and the anus are located on the bottom (flat) surface. Potential food particles are removed from the sediment by hundreds of tiny podia and moved to the mouth with the aid of mucus and cilia. *Mellita quinquiesperforata* has five oval holes or lunules through its test. The function of these holes is not clearly understood.

*Mellita* is very gregarious, a habit that is advantageous during its breeding season in the late spring and summer. The gametes are shed into the seawater and depend upon the proximity of the adults and the synchrony with which the gametes are shed for fertilization to occur. The fertilized ova develop into planktonic larvae that spend four

to six weeks adrift. Young sand dollars ingest sand and store it in part of the gut as a "weight belt" to help hold them on the bottom.

The Scotch bonnet, *Phalium granulatum* (Figure 3.15), preys on *Mellita* and sea urchins. This orange-and-cream-colored snail bores holes approximately 2 mm in diameter through the test of *Mellita* and inserts its radula to rasp out the edible material. *Phalium* is fairly abundant offshore although unbroken shells are seldom washed ashore. *Phalium* lays its eggs in capsules that are cemented together into a tower.

## Starfish and Sea Pansies

Two sea stars, *Luidia clathrata* and *Luidia alternata* (Figure 3.16), are common along the beach and are occasionally caught in seines or with bait while crabbing. *Luidia clathrata* is uniformly cream- or flesh-colored, while *Luidia alternata* has dark brown bands alternating with a cream-colored background on the arms. These are relatively large sea stars, 20–25 cm in diameter, with fairly slender arms. They prey on other echinoderms, especially brittle stars, but they will also consume dead bait thrown overboard by fishermen. Their tube feet (or podia) lack the suckers used by many rocky-shore sea stars to open bivalves. Thus, they swallow their food whole and regurgitate the undigestible parts. This can be a hazard, because at least one *Luidia* is reported to have died after swallowing a whole sand dollar. Close inspection of the

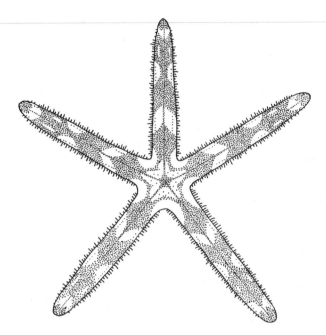

FIGURE 3.16. The banded sea star, *Luidia alternata.*(x0.3)

The reddish-purple sea pansy, *Renilla mulleri* (Figure 3.18), is one of the most fascinating sublittoral invertebrates. It consists of a flattened disk upon which numerous polyps are located and a stalk or peduncle that anchors it in the sediment. Like the related corals and gorgonians, *Renilla* is a colony of zooids. The longest polyps are feeding zooids, which capture small animals in their eight featherlike tentacles. The short, stubby polyps are responsible for maintaining a flow of water through the disk, which circulates respiratory gases and helps to keep the disk inflated.

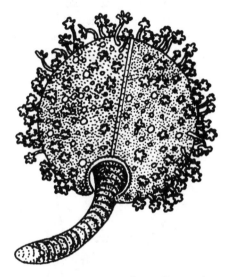

FIGURE 3.18. The sea pansy, *Renilla Mulleri*, with expanded polyps. (x1.75)

grooves on the underside of the sea star's arms may reveal one or more scaleworms, *Lepidonotus sublevis*. These short, fat worms are also commensal with hermit crabs and sea pansies.

A smaller sea star, *Astropecten duplicatus* (Figure 3.17), is more common than *Luidia* in deep water. This species is often caught in trawls on the shrimping grounds. It can be readily distinguished from *Luidia* by the rows of large plates along the sides of its arms. Like *Luidia*, *Astropecten* lacks suckers on its podia and must swallow its prey whole.

*Renilla* is well adapted for living in turbulent water. Its anchoring peduncle can be inflated and deflated independently of its disk, enabling it to inflate its buried peduncle while deflating its disk and minimizing its resistance to currents. Under more moderate conditions, it can increase its feeding surface up to 25 percent by inflating the disk. Small individuals can hold on in more turbulent water, i.e., closer to the surf, than large individuals, providing them greater protection from predators. *Renilla*'s enemies include the sea star *Astopecten*, from which it defends itself by expanding its polyps to bring its nematocysts into play or by raising one edge of its disk such that the current carries it to safer ground. *Renilla* is a suspension feeder whose diet consists largely of small crustaceans and unicellular algae.

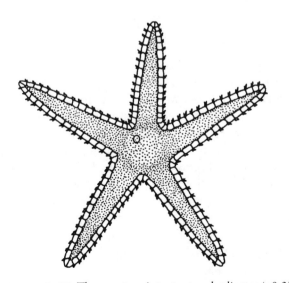

FIGURE 3.17. The sea star, *Astropecten duplicatus.*(x0.3)

## Yellow and Purple Whips

The sea whip, *Leptogorgia setacea* (Figure 3.19), is sometimes washed ashore in great tangled masses. This gorgonian attaches to shell fragments or other solid objects by a tuft of stolons, in contrast to the jetty species, *Leptogorgia virgulata*, which attaches by a basal plate. An uprooted *Leptogorgia setacea* may survive for several weeks if it is not washed into the surf zone and beached. Beach-washed specimens may be abraded down to the axial rod, which looks like a dark brown wire. During the sea whip's life, this rod is surrounded by an epithelium that secretes the skeleton to which the polyps are attached. This skeleton may be either yellow or reddish-purple, although the yellow form seems to be more common along the Texas coast. The polyps can be partially retracted during unfavorable conditions. *Leptogorgia setacea* hosts the snail, *Simnialena uniplicata* (Figure 3.19), which grazes on the gorgonian's polyps. Male *Simnialena* maintain territories; the female lays her eggs on the sea whip in clumps of capsules, each containing many eggs. *Simnialena* comes in yellow or purple, usually matching the color of its host. Its color is probably due to its diet rather than to a genetic trait.

## Life Beyond the Breakers

### Crabs

The calico crab, *Hepatus epheliticus* (Figure 3.20), lives offshore in shallow water. This brightly colored crab can be recognized by the red patches on its gray to pale yellow carapace and by its heavy claws. Berried females have been found in July; thus, this crab reproduces in summer. The sea anemone, *Calliactis tricolor*, is often found on *Hepatus'* back.

**FIGURE 3.20.** The calico crab, *Hepatus epheliticus.*(x1.0)

Another offshore crab, rarely found in the beach drift, is *Calappa sulcata* (Figure 3.21). This crab preys on hermit crabs and gastropods, such as the tulip shells *Fasciolaria* spp., by chipping the shell with its chela. The chela has a large tooth on its movable finger and two large teeth on its immovable finger that fit together such that when the lip of a shell is held between them, a chip is easily broken off. The shell is chipped successively until the animal inside is exposed, drawn out, and eaten. This modified claw is one of the most refined shell-opening mechanisms found in the crustaceans. *Calappa* can be recognized by its boxlike, ovate shape and its heavy claws.

The giant red hermit crab, *Petrochirus diogenes* (Figure 3.22), a common offshore species, is proba-

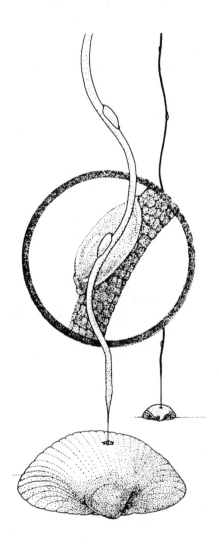

**FIGURE 3.19.** The sea whip, *Leptogorgia setacea,* attached to a large *Laevicardium* shell with magnification of the parasitic snail *Simnialena uniplicata.*(x0.7)

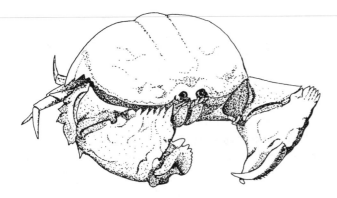

FIGURE 3.21. The crab, *Calappa sulcata*. (x0.5)

FIGURE 3.22. The giant red hermit crab, *Petrochirus diogenes*, emerging from the shell of a horse conch, *Pleuroploca gigantea*. (x0.7)

FIGURE 3.23. The porcellanid crab, *Porcellana sayana*, with fringes of setae on its claws. (x2.5)

bly a frequent prey of *Calappa*. It is found on mud, shell, and sandy bottoms in large shells, such as those of *Hexaplex*, *Busycon*, and *Fasciolaria*. *Petrochirus* is the largest hermit crab of the northwestern Gulf Coast and carries a number of commensals, the most notable of which is the porcellanid crab, *Porcellana sayana* (Figure 3.23). Like its host, *Porcellana* is reddish in color. It is a small crab with a fringe of long hairs on the outer edges of its claws.

## Snails

The giant eastern murex, *Hexaplex fulvescens* (Figure 3.24), is common just offshore and in the sand adjacent to the jetties. It can open oysters by pulling the valves apart with its large, muscular foot, which is capable of exerting a pull of 7–10 kilograms. It also opens mussels and clams by chipping the prey shell with its own shell until it makes an opening large enough for its proboscis to enter. After feeding, *Hexaplex* burrows into the sand and remains relatively stationary. During this time, new shell may be secreted. During the process of shell growth, the base of the spines around the lips is chemically dissolved. New shell is deposited, and a new ridge of spines is formed at the edge of the lip. The ridges of spines, or varices, around the shell represent former positions of the shell lip. Removal of the spines and formation of a new varix takes about ten days. *Hexaplex* lays its eggs in small capsules,

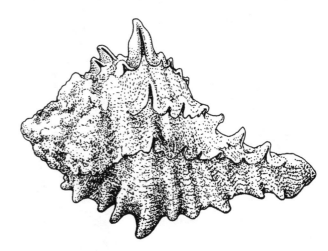

FIGURE 3.24. The giant eastern murex, *Hexaplex fulvescens*. (x0.7)

which are attached in protected areas under rocks.

The banded tulip, *Fasciolaria lilium lilium* (Figure 3.25), is also a sublittoral, predacious snail. Its smooth shell is mottled with reddish-brown on a cream background and banded with thin, brown, spiral bands. The animal itself is flame red. These snails prey on a variety of organisms. *Fasciolaria* does not drill but apparently pirates clams, such as *Chione* and *Mercenaria*, that have been drilled by other snails. It also chips the lips of small bivalves, including young oysters, but in this time-consum-

**FIGURE 3.25.** The banded tulip, *Fasciolarium lilium lilium.*(x1)

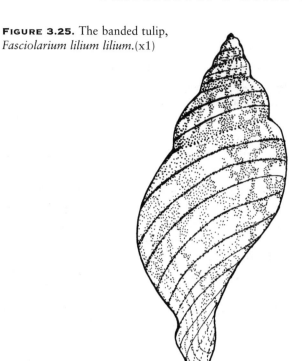

**FIGURE 3.26.** Tollin's wentletrap, *Epitonium tollini.*(x3)

**FIGURE 3.27.** The Atlantic distorsio, *Distorsio clathrata.* (x1.5)

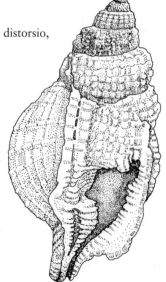

ing process it often damages its own shell, indicating that this mode of attack is rather inefficient. *Diopatra* and *Onuphis* worms are also included in its diet, but considering the lengths of the tubes of these worms, successful attack probably depends a great deal on surprise. *Fasciolaria* eats these polychaetes by extending its proboscis down the tube and rasping away the worm's flesh with its radula. Small gastropods, including its own species and young *Hexaplex,* are also consumed; however, only snails smaller than the attacking *Fasciolaria* are successfully attacked. Carrion is sometimes eaten in the absence of other food.

*Fasciolaria* deposits its eggs in flattened, cornucopialike capsules. Several dozen eggs are deposited in each capsule, but some are not fertilized and serve as "nurse" eggs that are eaten by the developing snails. Approximately a month after the eggs are deposited, the young emerge from the capsules as diminutive adults.

Tollin's wentletrap, *Epitonium tollini* (Figure 3.26), is a small, predacious gastropod that lives along the sandy beach and in inlet-influenced areas in the bays. "Wentletrap" is a Dutch word meaning "spiral staircase" and refers to the numerous high ridges or varices ("stairs") on the shell. These varices originate as thickenings of the shell growth. *Epitonium* discharges a purple fluid when disturbed.

The Atlantic distorsio, *Distorsio clathrata* (Figure 3.27), lives on sandy bottoms from just beyond the surf zone to a depth of about 60 m. The shell of *Distorsio* provides a good example of episodic growth, in which the axis of coiling changes each time, to which its name no doubt refers. This shell is often washed ashore on southern beaches during storms.

## Clams

A number of bivalves are common offshore. The giant cockle, *Laevicardium robustum* (Figure 3.28), is quite abundant. The large, muscular foot of this cockle is dark red; its shell is mottled with deep red, brown, and cream. It thrusts this foot against the sand to move itself in a series of rolls and leaps. Its siphons are rather short and are adorned with small, fleshy projections that prevent sand and large particles from entering the mantle cavity.

The ark clam family, Arcidae, has many representatives along the northwestern Gulf Coast. Perhaps the most common is the incongruous ark,

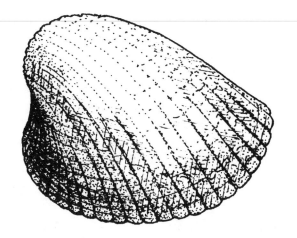

**FIGURE 3.28.** The giant cockle, *Laevicardium robustum.* (x0.7)

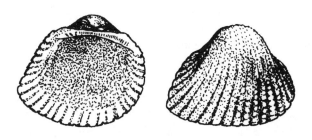

**FIGURE 3.29.** The incongruous ark, *Anadara brasiliana.* (x1)

**FIGURE 3.30.** The blood ark, *Anadara ovalis.* (x1)

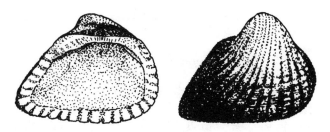

**FIGURE 3.31.** The ponderous ark, *Noetia ponderosa.* (x1)

*Anadara brasiliana* (Figure 3.29). This clam has unequal valves; the left valve overlaps the right valve when closed. The blood ark, *Anadara ovalis* (Figure 3.30), is also common. Unlike the former, it has a heavy, dark-brown periostracum (an organic covering that camouflages and protects the shell). The young of both of these species attach themselves to the substrate with a byssus, but they lose the byssus as they mature. The ponderous ark, *Noetia ponderosa* (Figure 3.31), has a heavier shell and is characterized by the lack of a byssus in the adult and the presence of a heavy periostracum.

The siphons of these filter-feeders are greatly reduced, and thus, they are shallow burrowers. The shallow-burrowing habit and shifting sand during storms account for the great numbers of these clams one sees on the beach after a storm. Members of this family can be immediately recognized by the hinge teeth on the valves. The tooth structure, called ctenodont, consists of a number of vertical grooves across the hinge line. These identical, comblike teeth constitute a primitive trait, as does the equal size of the anterior and posterior muscles (isomyarian) that close the shell.

The pen shells, *Atrina seminuda* and *Atrina serrata* (Figure 3.32), also live offshore in muddy-sand or sandy substrate. These olive-brown, wedge-shaped clams spin a heavy byssus that helps anchor them, pointed end down, in the substrate.

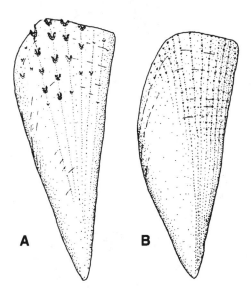

**A**　　**B**

**FIGURE 3.32.** The pen shells, *Atrina serrata* (A) and *Atrina seminuda* (B). (x0.5)

Once the clam is uprooted, its chances of reestablishing itself are small since the foot is quite reduced. This animal exhibits an anisomyarian muscle structure, in that the anterior adductor muscle is very small and the posterior adductor muscle is quite large. This is an adaptation related to its orientation in the substrate. These clams harbor commensal crabs of the genus *Pinnotheres* and pairs of commensal shrimp of the genus *Neopontonides*.

Another muddy-sand bottom dweller is the disk clam, *Dosinia discus* (Figure 3.33), a relative of the edible clam, *Mercenaria mercenaria*. *Dosinia* is laterally flattened and has a very smooth shell. It is an able burrower, and its long, fused siphons permit it to bury itself several inches beneath the surface. It is the frequent prey of the moon snail, *Neverita duplicata*, as evidenced by the many bored shells one finds on the beach.

The rose-petal tellin, *Tellina lineata*, and the alternate tellin, *Tellina alternata* (Figure 3.34), are two members of the family Tellinidae found along the Gulf Coast. Tellins, unlike the clams previously discussed, are not filter-feeders but deposit-feeders. They have very long, unfused siphons, enabling them to burrow deeply. The incurrent siphon acts as a vacuum cleaner, sweeping over the sediment for edible detritus and algae. The shell of *Tellina alternata* may be flushed interiorly with pink or yellow. The shell of *Tellina lineata* is smaller, less elongated and is flushed with pink. Of these two species, *Tellina alternata* is more common in beach wash along the northwestern Gulf Coast.

## The Edible Blue Crab and Its Kin

Perhaps the best-known crab along the Texas coast is the edible blue crab, *Callinectes sapidus* (Figure 3.35). Another species of this genus, *Callinectes ornatus*, also occurs here. It may be distinguished by the six frontal teeth on its carapace margin in contrast to the four frontal teeth of *Callinectes sapidus* (Figure 3.36). In addition, *Callinectes ornatus* is smaller, reaching a width of 93 mm in contrast to the maximum width of 230 mm in *Callinectes sapidus*. Hence, it is of little commercial value; however, *Callinectes ornatus* is the most abundant crab in the shallow offshore areas. Berried females have been found at all times of the year, although they are most abundant during the winter months. It is eaten by several species of fish, including the tarpon and the ling.

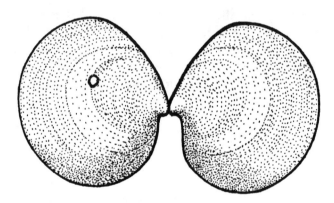

**FIGURE 3.33.** The disk clam, *Dosinia discus*, with a hole bored by *Neverita duplicata*. (x1)

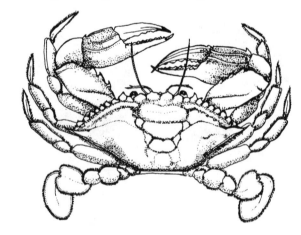

**FIGURE 3.35.** The blue crab, *Callinectes sapidus*. (x0.5)

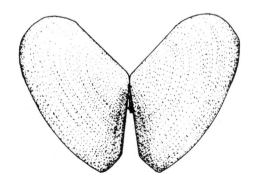

**FIGURE 3.34.** The alternate tellin, *Tellina alternata*. (x1.25)

Berried female *Callinectes sapidus* are found nearly year-round, the peak of the breeding season being in June and July. During the breeding season, one may often see a male carrying a female beneath his body, waiting for her to molt. Mating can occur only when the female molts and her shell is soft enough to permit

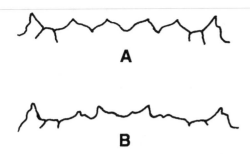

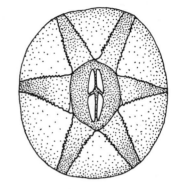

**FIGURE 3.36.** Frontal carapace margins of *Callinectes ornatus* (A) and *Callinectes sapidus* (B).

penetration of the male's penes through her genital pores. The transferred sperm are then used to fertilize the one to three million eggs produced by the female.

After mating, the female migrates into deeper water, where she attaches the fertilized eggs to her pleopods. The egg mass resembles a sponge, and the berried female is often called a "sponge" crab. The eggs hatch in about two weeks, releasing the young as zoeae (Figure 3.37). The zoeae eventually molt into megalops (Figure 3.38), which transform into diminutive adult forms; few of these millions of zoeae will escape predation and survive to adulthood. The crabs mature in one year, begin breeding, and live perhaps two more years.

**FIGURE 3.37.** A crab zoea larva. (x20)

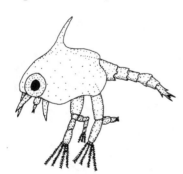

**FIGURE 3.39.** The acorn barnacles, *Chelonibia patula* (A) and *Chelonibia testudinaria* (B). (x4)

*Callinectes* is an omnivore; it eats fish, bottom invertebrates, vascular plants, and detritus. Old crabs, past their terminal molt, occasionally are found heavily encrusted with the barnacles *Balanus amphitrite amphitrite* and *Chelonibia patula*. *Chelonibia* (Figure 3.39) is a smooth-walled barnacle with a narrow operculum that seems too small for its aperture. When removed from the crab and turned upside-down, numerous long septa extend from the wall into the shell cavity of the barnacle. A larger relative, *Chelonibia testudinaria* (Figure 3.39), can be found on sea turtles. The shells of barnacles on the

**FIGURE 3.40.** The parasitic barnacle, *Octolasmis lowei*. (x10)

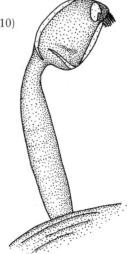

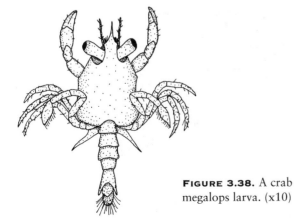

**FIGURE 3.38.** A crab megalops larva. (x10)

bottom of the turtle are usually well worn from frequent contacts with the sandy bottom. Blue crabs also host the parasitic barnacle *Octolasmis lowei* (Figure 3.40) in their gill chambers and may be infected with parasitic nemerteans and trematodes. *Octolasmis* resembles a miniature gooseneck barnacle with the calcareous valves reduced. It breeds in the summer, when its offspring develop through seven larval stages in the plankton before seeking a new host. This planktonic journey usually lasts about two weeks.

The speckled crab, *Arenaeus cribrarius* (Figure 3.41), is another representative of the swimming crab family found on this coast. *Arenaeus* is similar in shape to *Callinectes* but is immediately distinguished by its sandy color and the pebbled pattern on its carapace. These crabs are common in the surf zone and subtidally range from Massachusetts to Brazil. *Arenaeus* usually buries itself in the sand. The heavy coat of hairlike setae on the sides of its mouthparts keeps sand away from delicate structures. When buried, the chelipeds are held close to the body. It respires by drawing water in

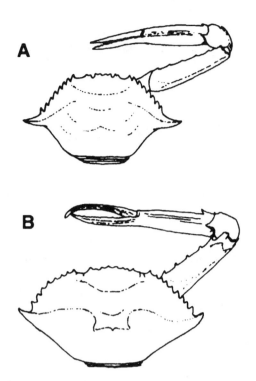

**FIGURE 3.42.** Carapace and cheliped of *Portunus gibbesii* (x0.75) (A) and *Portunus spinimanus* (x0.75) (B).

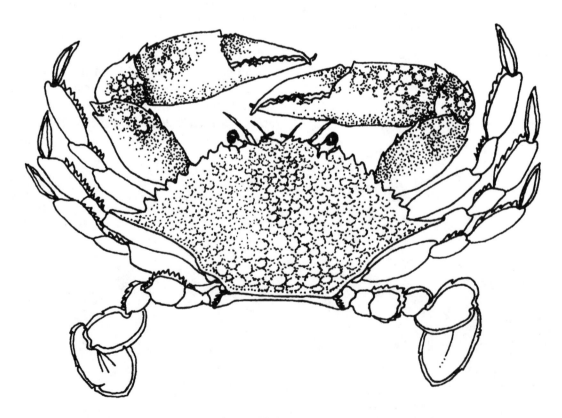

**FIGURE 3.41.** The speckled crab, *Arenaeus cribrarius*. (x1)

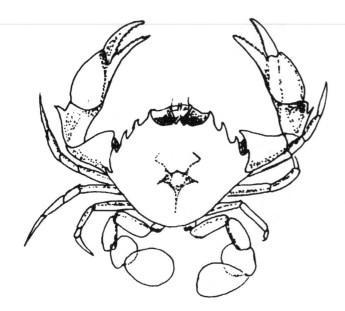

**FIGURE 3.43.** The lady crab, *Ovalipes quadulpensis.* (x1.0)

around the lateral and posterior margins of the carapace and pumping it through the gill chamber and out the anterior end through the space between its body and chelipeds. Its gills are large for a crab of its size, providing additional oxygen for the exertion required by life among the breaking waves.

Several other swimming crabs, members of the genus *Portunus,* are found along this coast, but none are especially common nearshore. The species that are usually found nearshore are *Portunus gibbesii* and *Portunus spinimanus* (Figure 3.42). The carapace of the latter species is less than

twice as wide as it is long; the carapace of the former species is at least twice as wide as it is long. *Portunus* closely resembles *Callinectes,* but males may be easily distinguished—male *Portunus* have triangular abdomens, while male *Callinectes* have "T-shaped" abdomens.

The lady crab, *Ovalipes guadulpensis* (Figure 3.43), also belongs to the family Portunidae. It is a very colorful crab, the carapace being yellow-gray to light lavender-gray with dull yellow spots. The spines on the carapace are purple. The last pair of walking legs, which are modified as paddles as in all portunid crabs, are lemon yellow. It lives primarily on sandy bottoms and is occasionally found swimming near the jetties.

The purse crab, *Persephona aguilonaris* (Figure 3.44), is slow moving and cryptic in its behavior. It buries itself in the sand by vertical movement of its legs until only its eyes and the front portion of its carapace remain exposed. Its common name derives from the size and shape of the female's abdomen, which extends over the entire undersurface of the crab. When *Persephona* is gravid, this abdomen covers the eggs attached to the pleopods. It is easily recognized by its circular carapace, which is cream colored with red blotches.

## Spider Crabs

Two species of spider crabs occur along the Gulf coast—*Libinia emarginata* and *Libinia dubia* (Figure 3.45), which can be distinguished by the num-

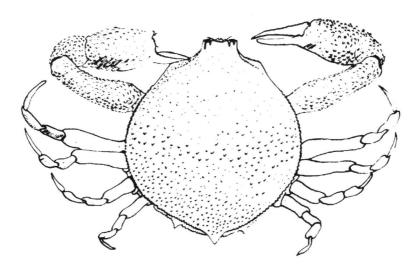

**FIGURE 3.44.** The purse crab, *Persephona aguilonaris.* (x1.5)

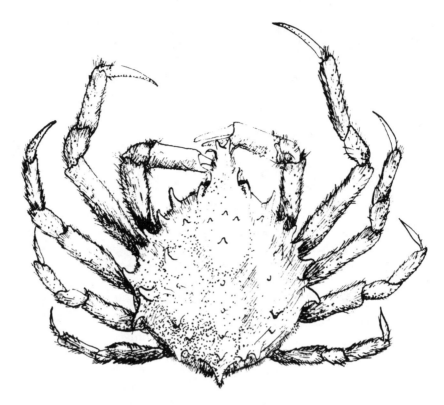

**FIGURE 3.45.** The spider crab, *Libinia dubia*. (x1)

ber of spines in the median row on the carapace. *Libinia emarginata* has more than seven spines (usually nine) in this row, and *Libinia dubia* has seven or fewer spines (usually six). Both species are slow moving and cryptic. Sexual maturity follows the terminal molt; thus, the females mate with a hardened carapace.

Young *Libinia* are commensal with the cabbagehead medusa, *Stomolophus meleagris*. They are often found riding in the bell of this large jellyfish. Adult *Libinia* can be found on pilings or in grass flats, where their unusual shape helps to camouflage them. They are most common during the summer months, which is their peak breeding season.

# CHAPTER FOUR

# Flotsam and Jetsam

The waves that wash up on the beach often carry organisms whose normal habitat is in deeper water on the continental shelf or adrift far at sea. Storm waves deposit the shells of numerous mollusks, including the heavy shells of the snail *Hexaplex fulvescens,* on the beach. Unfavorable winds often carry the Portuguese man-of-war, *Physalia physalis*; the by-the-wind sailor, *Velella velell*a; and the purple storm snails, *Janthina* spp., onto the beach. Most of these organisms are dead and badly battered by the time the beachcomber finds them, presenting a confusing array of broken shells and jellied blobs to the inexperienced collector. A little experience with intact specimens enables the average collector to identify most of these fragments.

Several species inhabit driftwood and other objects floating at sea. Among the more conspicuous of these are the stalked barnacles, *Lepas anatifera, Lepas anserifera,* and *Lepas pectinata,* which are commonly found on styrofoam floats and bottles as well as driftwood.

Like other barnacles, they are permanently attached to their substrate and obtain their food by filtering plankton from the water with their long, curved feet. *Lepas anatifera* (Figure 4.1) has a shell marked by very fine lines; the other two species have deeply grooved shells. *Lepas anserifera* has five or six pairs of filtering appendages, whereas the scaled goose barnacle, *Lepas pectinata*, has fewer than three pairs of filtering appendages.

FIGURE 4.3. Driftwood bored by *Bankia gouldi*. (x0.5)

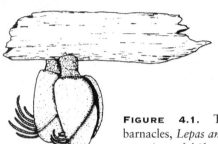

FIGURE 4.1. Two gooseneck barnacles, *Lepas anatifera*, attached to a piece of driftwood. (x1)

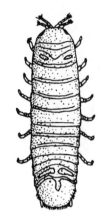

FIGURE 4.4. The wood-boring isopod, *Limnoria tripunctata*. (x5)

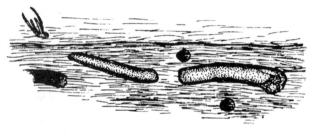

FIGURE 4.2. The wood-boring clam, *Bankia gouldi*. (x2)

Breaking open pieces of driftwood may expose the boring clams *Bankia gouldi* (Figure 4.2) or *Teredo bartschi,* or the boring isopod (or gribble), *Limnoria tripunctata*. The burrows taper toward the outside of the block of wood (as the clam bores into the wood, it grows and makes a wider burrow) and are the only evidence of boring clams usually found in the drift-wood (Figure 4.3). The burrows of *Bankia* have a calcareous lining. The shells of *Bankia* and *Teredo* are greatly reduced, and thus these clams appear more like worms. *Limnoria* (Figure 4.4) is a small isopod about 5mm long. It bores holes about 13mm deep in wooden structures such as pilings. *Bankia* tunnels most rapidly in hard, dry wood and usually avoids soft, rotten wood.

Once a piece of driftwood has settled on the beach and partially dried out, it may be inhabited by a variety of terrestrial creatures such as insects, scorpions and pseudoscorpions. Most of the marine species will be dead by this time, and their burrows provide ready-made places for the terrestrial invaders.

## Portuguese Man-of-War

One of the most conspicuous objects on the beach is the pale, purple float of the Portuguese man-of-war, *Physalia physalis* (Figure 4.5). But be careful not to handle it. Beneath the float and often stretched across the beach for several meters are dozens of nearly invisible tentacles armed with nematocysts. These nematocysts may be active long after the rest of the animal seems quite dead. Like bee stings and spider bites, contact with nematocysts produces different reactions in different people and may be fatal. *Physalia* is actually a colony of smaller animals called zooids, and each zooid is highly specialized for bearing the nematocysts, digesting food, or forming the float. The float is filled with a mixture of gases, similar to air and secreted by an oval disc at the base of the float. The Portuguese man-of-war usually floats in schools at the mercy of ocean currents and winds that occasionally drive them onto the shore. When driven into the bays, *Physalia* feeds primarily on anchovies and other small fish.

The upper portion of *Physalia*'s float is compressed into a small "sail" oriented diagonally on the float. Two forms have been found: a left-sailing form, with the sail extending from the upper left corner to the lower right corner (when viewing the *Physalia* along its long axis); and a right-sailing

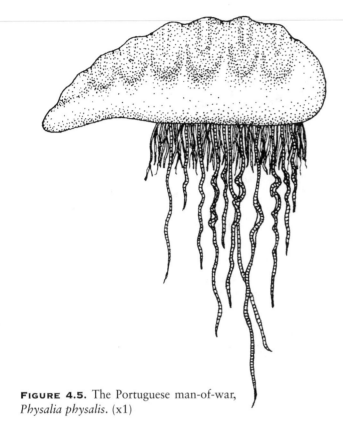

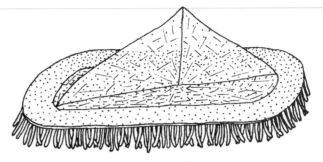

**FIGURE 4.6.** The by-the-wind sailor, *Velella velella.* (x1.2)

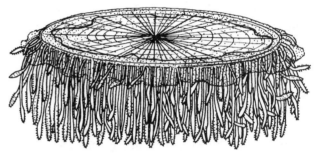

**FIGURE 4.5.** The Portuguese man-of-war, *Physalia physalis.* (x1)

**FIGURE 4.7.** *Porpita porpita.* (x1.2)

form, with the sail extending from the upper right corner to the lower left comer. The left-sailing form predominates in the Gulf of Mexico.

## Purple Sailors and Bubble Rafts

Two close relatives of *Physalia*, the by-the-wind sailor, *Velella velella* (Figure 4.6) and its cousin, *Porpita porpita* (Figure 4.7), may also be beached by onshore winds. *Velella*'s float is modified to form a sail, from which it gets its name, and a horizontal base across which the sail is mounted diagonally. Like *Physalia*, two forms exist, with the left-sailing form being the most common in the Gulf of Mexico. *Porpita*'s float is a round disk resembling the cross section of a tree trunk. It lacks a sail. Unlike that of *Physalia*, the floats of *Velella* and *Porpita* are chitinous and thus remain adrift long after the animal has died. These floats are valuable as substrates upon which some surface-dwelling animals lay their eggs and to which barnacles and hydroids attach. The floats are often all that is found of these species on the beach. The softer parts of the animals decay rapidly. The tissues of *Velella* and *Porpita* are usual-

ly bluish, and their floats are usually translucent white. *Porpita* is limited more to tropical waters than *Velella* and *Physalia* and hence is less often found in the northern Gulf.

Although an occasional Portuguese man-of-war falls prey to a sea turtle or a gooseneck barnacle, perhaps the most significant predators of *Physalia* and its kin are the purple storm snails, *Janthina* spp. Three species of *Janthina* are common to the northwestern Gulf of Mexico—*Janthina janthina*, *Janthina pallida*, and *Janthina prolongata* (Figure 4.8). These species can be distinguished by the shape of their shells. *Janthina janthina* is the largest species found locally, reaching a diameter of over 4 cm, and its shell is squatter and more angular than the other species. The shells of *Janthina prolongata* and *Janthina pallida* are smaller and more rounded, the lip of the former being slightly more slender and pointed than the latter. *Janthina* constructs a bubble raft by coating trapped bubbles of air with mucus. The raft and *Janthina*'s very thin shell enable it to stay afloat. Because the snail must be at the sea surface to trap air, a snail separated from its raft beneath the surface is doomed to sink and starve or be eaten.

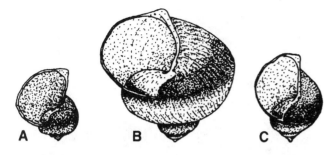

FIGURE 4.8. The purple storm snails, *Janthina prolongata* (A), *Janthina janthina* (B), *and Janthina unbilicata* (C). (x1.5)

FIGURE 4.10. The onion anemone, *Paranthus rapiformis,* inflated (left) and buried in the sand (right). (x1)

When it comes in contact with a *Physalia* or *Velella, Janthina* extends its proboscis to its prey and rasps away at its tissues. A pair of *Janthina* can consume a 10-cm long *Physalia* in less than one day. If its usual prey is scarce, *Janthina* may resort to cannibalism. These snails, particularly *Janthina janthina*, are countershaded. They are pale blue on top and deep purple underneath. However, they float upside-down, so that the pale side faces down. Seen from below, looking up, the pale side blends in with the silvery undersea surface reflecting the sky. Seen from above, looking down, the dark side blends in with the deep-sea surface.

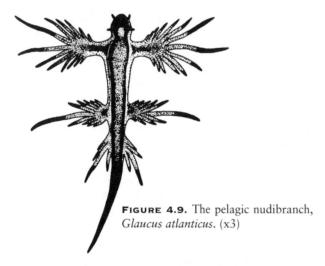

FIGURE 4.9. The pelagic nudibranch, *Glaucus atlanticus.* (x3)

A blue nudibranch, *Glaucus atlanticus* (Figure 4.9), also feeds on *Physalia* and its kin. *Glaucus* floats upside down at the sea surface with the aid of six frilled lobes containing gas-filled pockets. It may also catch a ride on its floating prey.

## Onions from the Sea

Occasionally the onion anemone, *Paranthus rapiformis* (Figure 4.10), will wash up on the beach. This anemone is so named because, when disturbed, it pulls in its tentacles and inflates itself with water. Its translucent white color with longitudinal white stripes gives it the appearance of a boiled onion. It usually lives in deeper water offshore, but if it is washed into shallow water, it will bury itself up to its tentacles in the sand and look right at home.

Unlike anemones that attach themselves to rocks or other hard surfaces, anemones like *Paranthus* that burrow into sand have a rounded base that can be everted into a bulblike structure called a physa. Burrowing is accomplished by first gaining a toehold with probing of the physa and weak contractions of the body. It then pulls itself further into the sand by a two-step digging process in which the physa is alternately everted and inverted. By swelling the body wall during extension of the physa, it anchors its upper portion so that the physa pushes downward. Then the base of the body wall swells to form a lower anchor, as strong longitudinal muscles pull the body further into the sand and at the same time cause inversion of the physa. This process of pushing, pulling, and anchoring is used by all soft-bodied burrowing forms, although the form of the digging organ and helping structures may vary.

## The Floating *Sargassum* Community

The Gulf Coast lacks the giant seaweeds or kelp that are common along the Pacific and North Atlantic coasts. Consequently, beach litter consisting of uprooted or broken fragments of seaweed are relatively scarce. One notable exception is the pelagic seaweed *Sargassum* spp. (Figure 4.11). *Sargassum* is buoyed by small air bladders and is transported by the same currents that bring *Physalia* and *Velella* to Gulf Coast shores. Hence, it washes up on Gulf Coast beaches sporadically

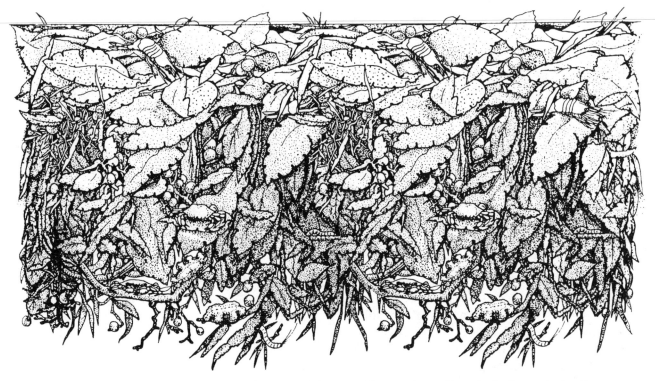

**FIGURE 4.11.** The Sargassum community: the sargassumfish, *Histrio histrio*; the nudibranch, *Scyllaea pelagica*; the sargassum crab, *Portunus sayi*; the sargassum shrimp, *Latreutes fucorim*; and the polychaete worm, *Platynereis dumerilii*. (x0.8)

and brings with it a fascinating community of specialized creatures. Many of these animals have shapes and colors that blend in with the *Sargassum*. Some of these animals, such as the hydroids and the sargassum anemone, *Anemonia sargassensis,* are sessile; others, such as flatworms, polychaetes, shrimps, and crabs, crawl about on the surface of the drifting seaweed. Still others, such as the sargassum fish, *Histrio histrio,* and the young of certain other oceanic fish, are free-swimming and use the rafts of *Sargassum* as a refuge from larger, predaceous fish.

Although *Histrio* can swim quite rapidly, it often crawls through the seaweed, using its pectoral fins like arms. *Histrio* is a member of the frogfish family but is much more ornate than its relatives. Its irregular outline and mottled coloration help it to blend in with its leafy environment. Similarly, the carnivorous nudibranch, *Scyllaea pelagica* (Figure 4.12), has large, leaflike lobes along its back and an orange-brown and yellow coloration that make it almost impossible to distinguish from its plant host. The sargassum crabs, *Portunus sayi* (Figure 4.13) and *Callinectes marginatus,* and the shrimp, *Latreutes fucorum,* also sport a mottled-brown disguise (Figure 7.29). The small sargassum flat-

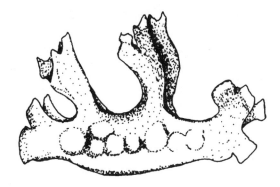

**FIGURE 4.12.** The nudibranch, *Scyllaea pelagica*. (x0.7)

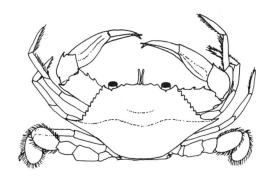

**FIGURE 4.13.** The sargassum crab, *Portunus sayi*. (x2.5)

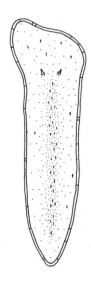

**FIGURE 4.14.** The flatworm, *Gnesioceros sargassicolor.* (x4)

worm, *Gnesioceros sargassicola* (Figure 4.14) is a tawny gray color flecked with reddish-brown spots.

The delicate appearance of the *Sargassum* is enhanced by the numerous fernlike hydroids and intricate bryozoans that grow over its surface. Some hydroid species have a high degree of fidelity to certain varieties of *Sargassum* and have been used as a means of classifying sargassum assemblages. Hence, the hydroid fauna found on *Sargassum* varies greatly, depending upon the variety of the plant. *Gonothyraea gracilis* and the ostrich plume hydroid, *Aglaophenia latecarinata* (Figure 4.15), are among the more common hydroids on *Sargassum* washed ashore along the northwestern Gulf Coast. The polychaete worms, *Platynereis dumerilii* and *Harmothoë aculeata,* are also common on the sargassum on these beaches. *Platynereis*

is a pale yellow worm with a bright red stripe running the length of its back. This stripe is actually a blood vessel, and the pulses of blood can be easily observed under a low-power microscope. *Harmothoë* is a scaleworm that is easily recognized by the 15 pairs of large, fringed plates or scales extending over its back.

The *Sargassum* fauna is closely related to and is undoubtedly derived from the littoral fauna. However, it is a dwarf fauna, the species found on *Sargassum* being generally smaller than its relatives living on the shore. It is also a warm-water fauna that is best developed in areas where the water temperature exceeds 18°C. Most of these animals abandon the *Sargassum* when it is washed in, or they die and are washed out of the seaweed in the surf. A few of the more tenacious species can be dislodged by vigorously shaking freshly beached *Sargassum*. A much better impression of this interesting fauna is gained by collecting fresh *Sargassum* from the sea with a dip net or bucket and examining it in detail.

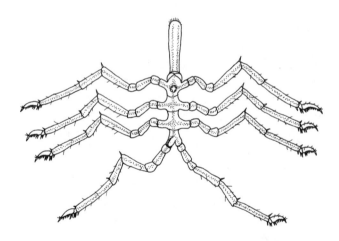

**FIGURE 4.16.** The sea spider, *Endeis spinosa.* (x12)

The sea spider, *Endeis spinosa* (Figure 4.16), is often observed crawling over sargassum clumps placed in a bucket of water. Not truly a spider, *Endeis* does not produce silk or poison, but it is equipped with a long proboscis with which it attacks bryozoans and hydroids found on the sargassum. Its long legs are adapted to clinging to its plant host; thus, it is much more sluggish than true spiders. Male *Endeis* have an extra pair of small legs, known as ovigerous legs, with which they carry egg clusters until the eggs hatch.

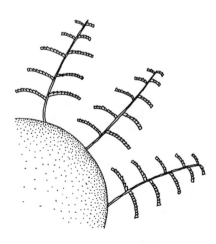

**FIGURE 4.15.** The ostrich-plume hydroid, *Algaophenia latecarinata,* attached to a Sargassum float. (x2.8)

## A Deep-Sea Castaway

Sometimes the lucky beachcomber will find what appears to be a tiny ram's horn. This is the shell of the mesopelagic cephalopod *Spirula spirula* (Figure 4.17). Although the shells are commonly found on many subtropical and tropical beaches of the world, the animal itself is rarely seen. Prior to 1922, only 13 animals had been found; with expanded sampling of the deep sea a few years later, *Spirula* was found often enough for its behavior to be observed.

Its normal position is vertical so that the shell is uppermost, and it often hangs suspended with its small tentacles enclosed by its mantle. Like other cephalopods, it moves by jet propulsion, and when disturbed, it discharges a cloud of grayish ink. It moves up and down in the water column by adjusting the gas contained in the chambers of its shell. This seemingly delicate shell has an inward-bending wall between each of the chambers and, in its entirety, can withstand pressures of several atmospheres.

Like many animals that live at depths below where light penetrates, *Spirula* has a light organ. Situated at the top of its mantle, this organ emits green light and seems to be usually "on," although it rests in a fold that can be extended to shut off the light. *Spirula* is thought to become mature at one year of age; females range in size from 31 to 37 mm—slightly smaller than males.

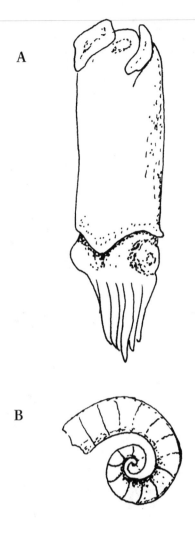

A

B

**FIGURE 4.17.** (A) *Spirula spirula* (x2) and (B) its shell. (x2)

# CHAPTER FIVE

# Offshore Bottoms: The Shrimp Grounds

Much of the continental shelf of the northern Gulf of Mexico, from just beyond the waves breaking on the beaches to a depth of about 200 meters, is intensively combed by shrimp trawlers in search of living gold. Large populations of commercial shrimp migrate vertically during the day between the bays and the Gulf as they mature and along the coast in search of food or some other requirement—perpetually keeping the fishermen on the move. So motile and elusive are these shrimp that as a boat crosses the bottom with two 75-foot-wide nets deployed, a second boat following the same path 15 minutes later can catch nearly as many shrimp as the first boat. Trawling at three knots, a shrimp boat may cover more than 500 acres (200 hectares) of bottom in an eight-hour tow.

Otter trawls catch many animals other than shrimp. Fish, crabs, lobster, snails, clams, squid, and sea stars are among the "cull" that must be isolated from the marketable shrimp catch. Sea turtles, too, frequent this habitat. Numerous other cohabitants are too small to be retained by the coarse-meshed nets. Among these are polychaete worms, the numerically dominant macroscopic animals throughout most of this habitat, and a major food resource of commercial shrimp. Polychaetes also make up a large portion of the diets of demersal fishes, such as porgies, batfish, flounders, and tonguefish.

Animal populations inhabiting this seemingly homogeneous seascape respond differently to subtle changes in the characteristics of this environment. Shrimp, crabs, and other animals living on the sediment surface are sensitive to differences in temperature, salinity, and water depth. Various worms, clams, and other animals that burrow are also sensitive to sediment texture. Shell fragments and sand grains are materials used in the construction of burrows. Particle sizes of the sediment affect the ease of burrowing and the durability of burrows. Grain- size patterns also reflect local currents that distribute the sediments and transport suspended food along the bottom.

Animals that construct permanent burrows generally prefer coarser sediments than species that move continuously. The motile species are also able to survive in offshore areas where food is not abundant and must be searched for, whereas sedentary species are generally plentiful in nearshore areas where high productivity and steady currents assure a supply of food for those that sit and wait. Most of the food consumed by offshore benthic animals is imported, either as organic matter carried to the Gulf by rivers or as plankton production near the sea surface. This food is mixed with less nutritious sediment particles as it rains on the sea floor. One common means of obtaining this food is by deposit-feeding, i.e., by simply swallowing sediment and extracting the nourishing components chemically in the gut. Undigested sediment is extruded as feces into small mounds. These mounds are a common sight on the bottom. Deposit-feeding may occur either directly by swallowing sediment while burrowing through it or indirectly by intercepting sediment with outstretched tentacles or a proboscis as it falls from the surface.

Filter-feeding, which usually involves extension of the tentacles vertically to intercept food drifting with currents across the bottom, is common among sedentary species. Occasional arrivals of larger bits of detritus and deaths of indigenous animals support the scavengers. Predators consume living residents.

Each of these feeding modes is represented among the polychaetes, the most abundant macroscopic animals living in soft bottoms in the Gulf. Polychaete dominance is challenged locally by brief blooms of amphipods, anemone, or surf clam populations, but the ecological importance of this diverse taxon is seldom diminished. Eighty-seven of the 100 most abundant macroinfaunal species in the eastern Gulf of Mexico are polychaetes.

## The Ubiquitous Fauna

The sedentary polychaetes, *Diopatra cuprea*, *Paraprioniospio pinnata*, and *Clymenella torquata*, and the errant polychaete *Glycera americana*, are among the most ubiquitous offshore species in the Gulf. *Diopatra* (Figure 3.12) is also one of the most colorful species. Its iridescent, reddish-brown body is often speckled with gray dots and is lined with yellow-brown parapodia speckled with green as a background for its bright red gills. Its durable tubes of shell fragments woven into a parchmentlike lining project like crude periscopes from the sea floor. Once abandoned, these tubes are eventually dug out from the ever-shifting sea floor and are washed onto Gulf beaches. The tube seems to function as a food-gathering device as well as a residence for its omnivorous inhabitant. *Diopatra* consumes algae, copepods, gastropods, cumaceans, and barnacle larvae, many of which are commonly found on the outer surface of the tube.

The bamboo worm, *Clymenella torquata* (Figure 5.1), inhabits a straight, vertical sand tube. The worm's 22 segments are long and slender, superficially resembling a bamboo stalk. *Clymenella* resides head down in its tube and uses the funnel-like anal segment characteristic of its family to plug the surficial end of the tube. This position enables it to ingest sediment at the bottom of its tube and excrete its wastes at the sediment surface, where they are readily swept away by currents or surge. Bamboo worms draw sufficient water into the tube from the top to irrigate the tube every 15 to 20 minutes, which enables them to survive in anoxic sediments. Unlike many other tube-

FIGURE 5.1. The bamboo worm, *Clymenella torquata*; (A) posterior end, (B) anterior end, and (C) entire worm in its tube. (x5)

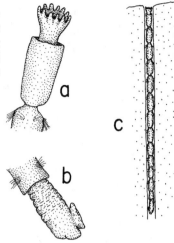

dwelling worms, *Clymenella* enjoys such a tight fit in its tube that it is unable to turn around. Because it must expose its tail to watchful predators during excretion, it has adopted unusual hastiness in this activity. However, should it miscalculate, it can regenerate the lost segments. *Clymenella torquata* is usually orange or green. The lesser bamboo worm, *Clymenella zonalis,* is always orange.

The bloodworm, *Glycera americana* (Figure 5.2), preys on other benthic invertebrates, particularly other polychaetes and amphipods. Juveniles typically construct burrows consisting of a network of waiting tubes from which they ambush passing prey. Adults are more motile but usually remain buried to avoid detection by shrimp or fish. Bloodworms detect their prey by sensing the pressure wave passing in front of a moving visitor. *Glycera*'s proboscis

FIGURE 5.2. Anterior end of the bloodworm, *Glycera americana,* with extended proboscis exposing its four teeth. (x3.75)

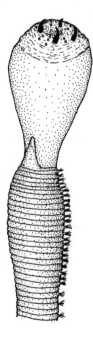

is rapidly everted to expose its four large jaws, which seize the hapless victim. Bloodworms swarm at the sea surface during their breeding season and die shortly after releasing their gametes.

*Paraprionospio pinnata* (Figure 5.3) is a polychaete related to the blister worm found in oyster shells. This worm lives in a highly branched burrow network. It is both a deposit-feeder and suspension-feeder. It gathers food particles from the sand by the action of cilia on its tentacles, which ferry captured particles to the mouth. However, when there is a lot of food suspended in the water, it simply raises its palps and, by lashing them rhythmically in the water, also captures particles that are similarly propelled to its mouth. Sometimes, it will hold one tentacle on the surface while lashing the other in the water. Large *Paraprionospio pinnata* have another feeding mode in which they arch both tentacles, deposit-feeding at the tips and suspension-feeding along the rest of the tentacle!

FIGURE 5.3. Anterior end of *Paraprionospio pinnata.* (x6.25)

Another ubiquitous wormlike species is the nemertean, *Cerebratulus lacteus* (Figure 7.13). Like *Glycera, Cerebratulus* captures its prey by everting its proboscis with surprising speed to snare unsuspecting passersby. The sharp-knobbed nassa *(Nassarius acutus),* the Atlantic abra *(Abra aequalis),* and the phoronid *(Phoronis architecta)* are also widely distributed in the northern Gulf.

Fish or crab remains rapidly attract numerous minute scavengers. *Nassarius acutus* (Figure 5.4) has a keen sense of smell that enables it to quickly locate decaying flesh. This response is easily observed by allowing several of these snails to burrow into the sand layer at the bottom of a small

**FIGURE 5.4.** Shell of the sharp-knobbed nassa, *Nassarius acutus.* (x8)

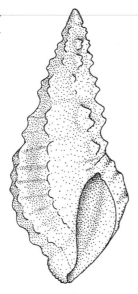

bowl filled with clean seawater and slowly adding a few drops of the liquor from clam, crab, or fish flesh homogenized in a blender. The detection range of these scavengers can be observed by replacing the bowl with a long trough and adding the liquor at one end. Hungry snails work best.

Usually quiescent and buried with only its proboscis probing through the sediment surface to test the passing water, *Nassarius* pops to the sand surface in startling abundance when the sediment is disturbed. Waving its proboscis, the snail seems to engage in a frantic search for some uncovered morsel lest the sea reclaim it as rapidly as it appeared. *Nassarius acutus* is apparently more resistant or resilient than most benthic invertebrates to the summer anoxia that develops off the Louisiana coast, and its abundance enables it to play a major role in disposing of the carcasses of less-fortunate organisms. It is commonly associated with shrimp-trawl discards, and turtle biologists often find it in gut contents of turtles that have dined on discards.

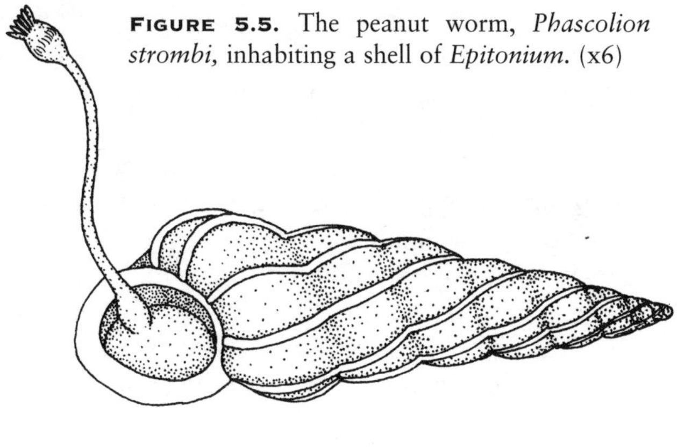

*Nassarius acutus* is more slender than its congener in the bays, *Nassarius vibex* (Figure 7.16), and, as its name suggests, the knobs on its white or yellowish shell are more pronounced. When rotting flesh is not readily available, *Nassarius* will attack live prey or eggs that it finds on the bottom.

Small shells of deceased snails such as *Nassarius* are often utilized by the tiny hermit crab, *Pagurus bonairensis,* or the peanut worm, *Phascolion strombi* (Figure 5.5). More sedentary than the hermit crab, *Phascolion* wedges its bulbous trunk into the shell and cements sand grains or shell fragments over the aperture, leaving only a small hole through which it can extend its long, necklike introvert and crown of feeding tentacles. As its name suggests, the introvert can be withdrawn into the trunk if disturbed, as may occur when a nearby hermit crab begins searching for a new shell. *Abra aequalis* (Figure 5.6) is also quite small (about 6 mm). This deposit-feeding clam has a very smooth shell, which is usually white but often with a yellowish cast.

**FIGURE 5.6.** Shell of the Atlantic abra, *Abra aequalis.* (x1.3)

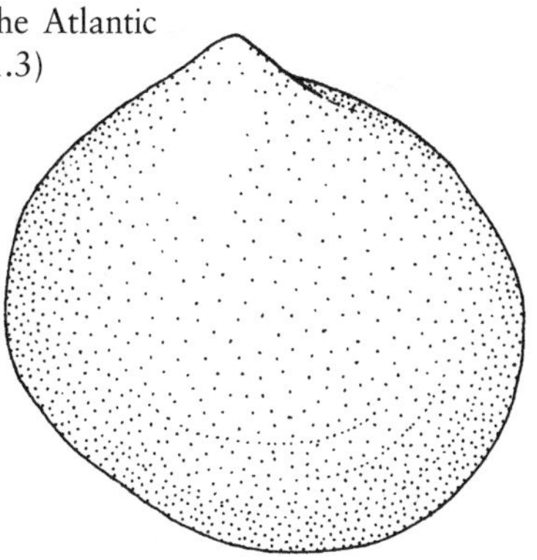

**FIGURE 5.5.** The peanut worm, *Phascolion strombi,* inhabiting a shell of *Epitonium.* (x6)

**FIGURE 5.7.** The phoronid, *Phoronis architecta.* (x0.9)

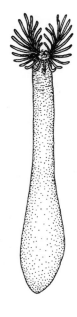

The phoronid, *Phoronis architecta* (Figure 5.7), is a small, wormlike animal that dwells in a vertical chitinous tube in the sea floor. Like the brachiopods and bryozoans, it has a spiralled crown of feeding tentacles called a lophophore. *Phoronis* is only about 10 to 15 mm long, and its narrow tube is about four times its length. The tube is flexible and is usually covered with a single layer of sand grains. Its lower end is rounded and closed. *Phoronis* has a U-shaped gut, bringing its anus back up to the single opening in the tube. The anterior two-thirds of *Phoronis* is flesh colored, and the posterior end is a dark yellowish-red, resulting from a concentration of hemoglobin in this end. Unlike most other phoronids, *Phoronis architecta* has separate sexes.

The brachiopod, *Glottidia pyramidata* (Figure 5.8), also lives in a vertical burrow and filters suspended food with a lophophore. However, *Glottidia*'s burrow is lined with mucus-impregnated sand, and except for its long pedicle, its body is encased in a bivalved shell composed of calcium phosphate. These shells rarely wash out of the burrows after the death of the brachiopods; they decay in the burrows and thus are seldom found by shell collectors. *Glottidia* typically remains in its burrow, which is easily identified by its slitlike opening, but it can rebury itself if displaced. The likelihood of such displacement may be reduced if it attaches the end of its pedicle to a buried shell. If completely covered by shifting sand, *Glottidia* can also dig itself out.

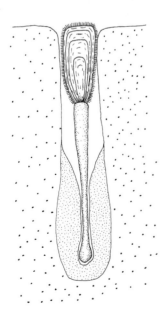

**FIGURE 5.8.** The brachiopod, *Glottidia pyramidata*, in its burrow. (x0.9)

*Glottidia* spawns about 10,000 eggs during a full or occasionally a new moon, when tidal flushing is great enough to carry the eggs seaward. Its larvae spend about three weeks in the plankton before settling as they are carried shoreward by tidal currents. Willits and moon snails are its major predators. The exposed edge of its shell is often exploited as an attachment site by hydroids and algae and by snails as deposition sites for their egg capsules.

## Nearshore Worms and Neighbors

Less widespread species are often characteristic of special environments to which they are particularly sensitive. Sensitivities to temperature and salinity generally constrain the distribution of marine species. Because these parameters are similar over large areas of ocean bottom, subtler variables often assume greater importance. Epifaunal species, i.e., species living on the surface of the sea floor, frequently respond to differences in water depth or distance from shore. Infaunal species, i.e., those burrowing into the sediments, are usually sensitive to sediment type. Organisms living nearshore must be more tolerant of variable temperatures, salinity, and high turbidity than those living offshore. However, food is frequently more abundant near to shore, and for several epifaunal species, proximity to nursery areas within the bays is an important asset of the nearshore environment.

In the fine sand that characterizes most of the nearshore sediments in the northwestern Gulf, the infauna is dominated by polychaetes such as *Magelona phyllisae, Mediomastus californiensis, Scoloplos rubra, Phyllodoce mucosa, Stenelais boa, Aglaophamus verrilli, Owenia fusiformis, Neanthes succinea, Lumbrineris tenuis,* and *Spiophanes bombyx.* The roofing worm, *Owenia fusiformis* (Figure 5.9), prefers to construct its long, flexible tube in areas of fairly clean sand. It selects flat, light-colored sand grains and arranges them like overlapping roof tiles with the free edges facing upward. In mature worms, this tube may be 15 to 20 cm long and 2 to 5 mm wide. *Owenia* is a versatile ciliary mucus feeder. Its feeding crown is drawn out into eight branching lobes that intercept and channel suspended food to its mouth, but it may also bend over to pick up larger food particles from the bottom near its tube. This crown may be light red, brown, or greenish in color and is infused with an elaborate network of blood vessels, which

FIGURE 5.9. Anterior end of the roofing worm, *Owenia fusiformis,* encased in its sand tube. (x9)

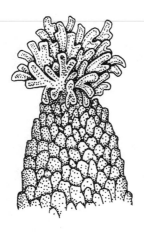

enables it to function as both a respiratory and feeding structure.

Like *Capitella capitata* (Figure 5.10), *Mediomastus californiensis* (Figure 5.11) has poorly developed parapodia and prostomium and thus may be mistaken for an oligochaete. Its head region, or prostomium, lacks eyes, tentacles, and palps. Its well-developed setae are typically much longer on the anterior 11 segments, the thorax, than on the rest of the body. Unlike *Mediomastus, Capitella* has only 9 thoracic segments and possesses genital spines on the eighth and ninth segments. *Mediomastus* is a very small, slender worm, about 10 to 12 mm long, which is commonly found in estuarine marshes as well as offshore.

*Scoloplos capensis* and *Scoloplos rubra* (Figure 5.12) also lack appendages or eyes on their heads. However, their heads are pointed and their parapodia are developed as gills. These gills, or branchiae, begin at about the fifth or sixth segment in *Scoloplos rubra,* but not until segment 13 or 14 in *Scoloplos capensis.* The thoracic region of these worms is somewhat flattened with dense clusters of short setae along the sides. The posterior portion of the worm is cylindrical with fewer setae. *Scoloplos capensis* usually has brown bars across its thorax beginning at the ninth segment, whereas *Scoloplos rubra* is reddish in color, as its name suggests. The paddleworm, *Phyllodoce mucosa* (Figure 5.13), uses its large, paddlelike parapodia to move rapidly through the sand. The scaleworm, *Stenelais boa* (Figure 5.14), is protected by a double row of overlapping plates along its back and captures its prey with a knobby eversible proboscis.

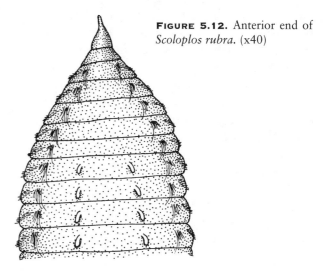

FIGURE 5.12. Anterior end of *Scoloplos rubra.* (x40)

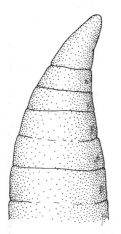

FIGURE 5.10. Anterior end of *Capitella capitata.* (x30)

FIGURE 5.13. Anterior end of the paddleworm, *Phyllodoce mucosa.* (x9)

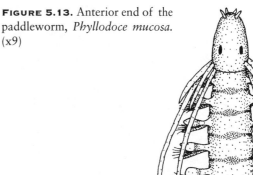

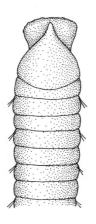

FIGURE 5.11. Anterior end of *Mediomastus californiensis.* (x20)

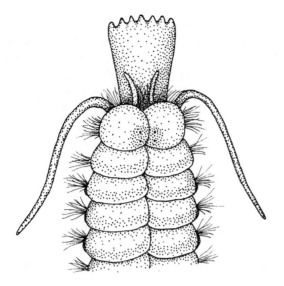

FIGURE 5.14. Anterior end of the scaleworm, *Stenelais boa*, with extended proboscis. (x11)

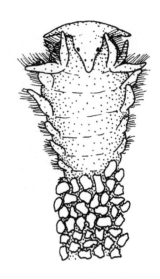

FIGURE 5.16. Anterior end of *Spiophanes bombyx*. (x23)

*Magelona phyllisae* (Figure 5.15) is also a non-selective deposit-feeder. It is easily distinguished from other genera of worms by its flattened, spadelike prostomium, which may spread beyond the width of its long, slender trunk. *Magelona* burrows through the sediment in search of food and does not construct substantial tubes. *Spiophanes bombyx* (Figure 5.16) constructs more durable tubes, from which it selectively ingests food particles. Its prostomium is marked by a pair of anterior horns. *Aglaophamus verrilli* (Figure 5.17) is an omnivore whose small prostomium belies the threat of its eversible pharynx. *Lumbrineris tenuis* (Figure 5.18) is a predator. Its simple, domelike prostomium lacks eyes, palps, or tentacles.

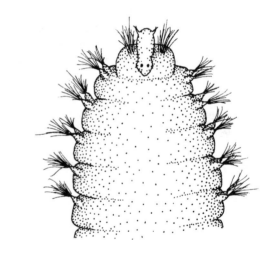

FIGURE 5.17. Anterior end of *Aglaophamus verrilli*. (x24)

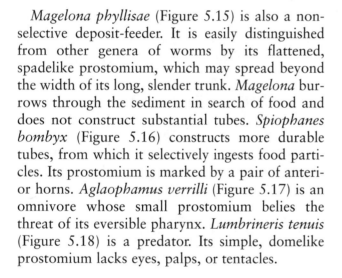

FIGURE 5.15. Anterior end of *Magelona phyllisae*. (x10)

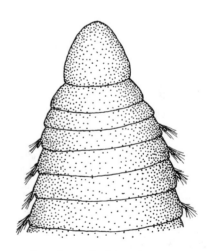

FIGURE 5.18. Anterior end of *Lumbrineris tenuis*. (x12)

Unlike its relative in the sand flats (Figure 7.20), the parchment worm, *Spiochaetopterus costarumi* (Figure 5.19), lives in a straight tube oriented vertically in the sediment. Rather than the constricted ends characteristic of *Chaetopterus* tubes, *Spiochaetopterus* tubes have perforated partitions across the buried end of the tube. These partitions help prevent tube collapse and maintain water pressure in the tube while permitting water to flow into the pore spaces between sand grains beneath the tube. This flow of water is maintained by cilia on modified parapodia in the middle body region. As this water passes the anterior portion of the body, suspended food is entrapped in mucous bags secreted by specialized parapodia. The long palps are equipped with ciliated gutters that probably functioned as a means of food capture in the ancestors of this worm, but that presently help to eject fecal pellets and other debris from the tube. The anteriormost segments are equipped with stiff setae, which anchor the worm within the tube, and a pair of larger cutting setae, which are used to remove partitions or slice open the tube when it must be enlarged to accommodate the growing worm.

These polychaetes share sandy habitats with other burrowing animals, such as the onion anemone, *Paranthus rapiformis* (Figure 4.10); the dwarf tellin, *Tellina versicolor*; and the fine-ribbed auger, *Terebra protexta* (Figure 5.20). The dwarf tellin is common on sandy bottoms. Its translucent shell is often marked with pink rays and is less than 2 cm long. This deposit-feeder is restricted to the surficial sediments by its short siphons. The shell of *Tellina versicolor* is more rectangular than those of other common tellins.

## Spring Bloomers

During spring, this sandy-bottom fauna is joined by the surf clam, *Mulinia lateralis* (Figure 7.5); the hermit crab, *Pagurus bonairensis*; the amphipod, *Corophium ascherusicum*; the cumacean, *Oxyurostylis salinoi*; and the lancelet, *Branchiostoma caribaeum*. *Oxyurostylis* (Figure 5.21), is easily recognized by its ovate body and slender, forked tail. It spends most of its time buried in the sand with only the tip of its head exposed. Burial is accomplished by excavating a hole with its hind legs and backing into it. A respiratory and feeding current is set up by movement of the epipodites of the anterior legs, forcing surface water over the gills and filtering mouthparts. The antennae are much longer in the active male than in the more sedentary female and usually are carried back over the carapace.

**FIGURE 5.19.** Anterior end of *Spiochaetopterus costarum.* (x2.2)

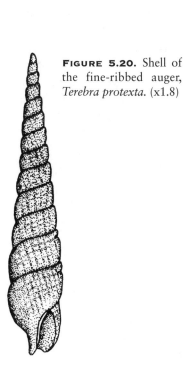

**FIGURE 5.20.** Shell of the fine-ribbed auger, *Terebra protexta.* (x1.8)

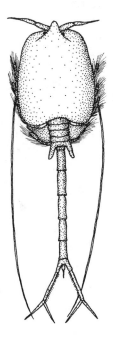

**FIGURE 5.21.** The cumacean, *Oxyurostylis salinoi.* (x15)

Patches of coarse, shelly sand are often inhabited by the lancelet, *Branchiostoma caribaeum* (Figure 5.22). Resembling a small fish, this primitive chordate lives partially buried in the sediment, where it filters suspended food borne by passing currents. It seems to prefer areas where there is moderate water movement from subsurface waves or tidal currents. Its feeding mechanism is similar to that of the sea squirt. Food-laden water is drawn into the pharynx and passes through two rows of narrow slits that retain the food but allow the water to escape to the sea. The mouth is protected by a circlet of tentacles that help to exclude unwanted debris and sand. Adults are about 5 cm long.

**FIGURE 5.22.** The lancelet, *Branchiostoma caribaeum*. (x3)

Several moon snails occur on the shrimp grounds. The familiar nearshore moon snail, *Neverita duplicata* (Figure 3.9), is also found to moderate depths, where it is joined by the colorful Atlantic natica, *Naticarius canrena* (Figure 5.23), and the miniature natica, *Tectonatica pusilla*. Unlike the shell of *Neverita*, *Naticarius*'s shell is usually marked by spiral stripes accented by dark brown bands, *Naticarius*'s operculum is calcareous with a white, exposed surface, in contrast to the thin, amber operculum of

*Neverita*. *Tectonatica* is less than 1 cm long but is easily distinguished from juveniles of the two larger species by its closed umbilicus. The miniature natica is fairly common near shore, but its small size hides it from the casual observer. Each of these snails preys on clams and other snails.

The fragile paraonid worm, *Aricidea fragilis* (Figure 5.24), prefers silty sand to coarser sediments. Its head has a single median antenna and its back is obscured by numerous pairs of antennalike gills. *Aricidea* is a nonselective deposit-feeder that is found in very shallow water as well as offshore.

**FIGURE 5.24.** Anterior end of *Aricidea fragilis*. (x25)

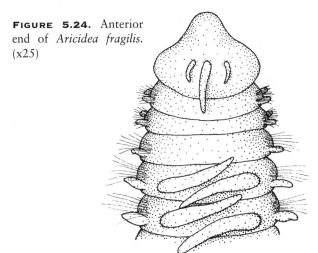

The reddish echiuroid worm, *Thalassema hartmani* (Figure 5.25), is often found near passes and in dredged areas. *Thalassema* is a deposit-feeder that lives with its proboscis extended over the sea floor to ensnare drifting particles of food. A small, fragile clam, *Paramya subovata* (Figure 5.26), and a pinnotherid crab, *Pinnixa lunzi*, are frequently caught with *Thalassema* and may be commensal with it, as is characteristic of several cohabitants of echiuroid worm burrows in California.

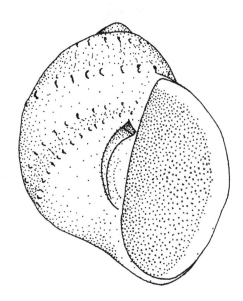

**FIGURE 5.23.** Shell of the Atlantic natica, *Naticarius canrena*. (x7)

**FIGURE 5.25.** The echiuroid worm, *Thalassema hartmani*. (x5.5)

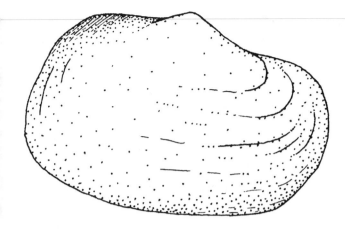

**FIGURE 5.26.** The commensal clam, *Paramya subovata*. (x7)

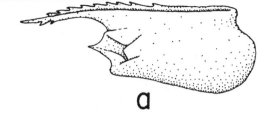

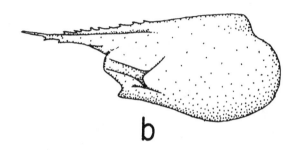

**FIGURE 5.28.** Carapaces of commercial shrimp: (a) *Penaeus aztecus* or *Penaeus duorarum*, and (b) *Penaeus setiferus*. (x0.9)

## Shrimp for the Table and Aquarium

Of the many species of shrimp that inhabit the shallow waters of the Gulf of Mexico, three species are sufficiently large and abundant to be fished profitably. These shrimp, members of the family Penaeidae, are the brown shrimp, *Penaeus aztecus*; the pink shrimp, *Penaeus duorarum*; and the white shrimp, *Penaeus setiferus* (Figure 5.27). These species differ from most similar shrimps in that the ventral surface of the rostrum is lined with teeth. They also have a deep groove along either side of the rostrum, which extends nearly to the posterior end of the carapace in brown shrimp and pink shrimp, but terminates near the base of the rostrum in white shrimp (Figure 5.28). Adult pink shrimp typically have a dark spot on each side of the abdomen, overlapping the third and fourth segments.

These shrimp are most active at night, often swimming to the surface in shallow water, where they can

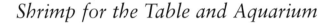

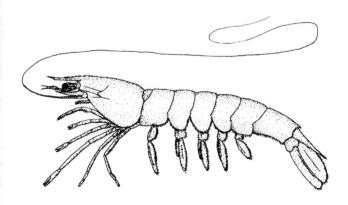

**FIGURE 5.27.** The white shrimp, *Penaeus setiferus*. (x0.25)

be caught in the surface-skimming butterfly nets used by many fishermen in Louisiana. During the day, pink shrimp and brown shrimp often burrow into the substrate. White shrimp seldom burrow and are usually caught while they are resting on the bottom during the daylight hours. Man is not the only shrimp predator. Fish such as sand perch and sea robins also enjoy this delicacy.

A commercial shrimp spends part of its life offshore and part of it in bays connected to the Gulf by passes. Mating and spawning take place offshore. *Penaeus aztecus* breed year-round at depths of 50 to 120 meters; individuals in shallower water do not breed in the coldest months, i.e., January and February. *Penaeus setiferus* inhabits shallower water (14 to 50 meters) and spawns mostly in the fall.

When these shrimp mate, a spermatophore, i.e., a capsule containing sperm, borne on the modified second pair of pleopods of the male, is transferred to the female's gonopores. These gonopores are found on the bases of her third pair of walking legs. When conditions are suitable, the female releases her one-half to one million eggs and they are fertilized as they pass through her gonopores. Twenty-four hours later, the drifting eggs hatch as nauplii and begin a planktonic existence. After five molts, the egg yolk is exhausted, and the nauplius transforms into a proto-zoea, then a mysis, and finally a postlarva, which enters a bay to become a bottom dweller. Postlarvae remain in the bays and estuaries along the coast until they are nearly mature. Then they migrate offshore, mature, and breed, thus completing the life cycle.

The sugar shrimp, *Parapenaeus longirostris* (Figure 5.29), can be readily distinguished from the commercial shrimps of the genus *Penaeus* in that it lacks teeth on the ventral edge of its rostrum. These teeth are replaced by a pronounced comb of setae. Its eyes are green and its tail is often tipped with red. It is not sought commercially in the Gulf of Mexico but is moderately abundant and undoubtedly mixed with catches of other species and thus is sold commercially. Individuals of this species in the Mediterranean Sea reach a much larger size than those in the Gulf and are exploited off the Tunisian coast.

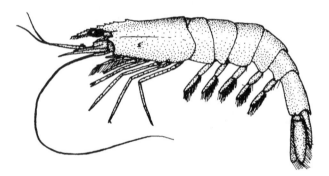

**FIGURE 5.29.** The sugar shrimp, *Parapenaeus longirostris.* (x0.5)

Three other species of shrimp supplement commercial catches in some portions of their ranges. The seabob, *Xiphopeneus krøyeri* (Figure 5.30), is commercially important in South America and can be immediately recognized by its long, upcurved rostrum. It is found near shore, although it does not enter the bays because it is apparently unable to tolerate low salinities. Two smaller shrimp, *Trachypeneus constrictus* (Figure 5.31) and *Trachypeneus similis,* are harvested off southern Florida. Like *Parapenaeus, Trachypeneus* lacks teeth on the lower surface of its rostrum but also lacks the fixed spines near the end of the telson characteristic of the former genus. The last three segments of *Trachy-peneus*'s abdomen have a sharp keel, or carina. In *Trachypeneus similis* these segments are covered by a pubescence, which is limited to the region of the carina in *Trachypeneus constrictus.*

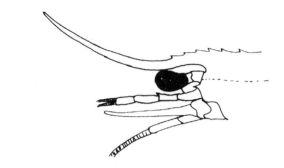

**FIGURE 5.30.** The seabob, *Xiphopeneus krøyeri.* (x0.5)

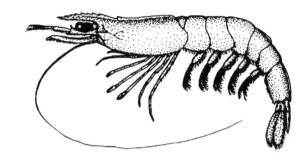

**FIGURE 5.31.** The shrimp, *Trachypeneus constrictus.* (x2)

The rock shrimp, *Sicyonia dorsalis* (Figure 5.32), is very common on soft bottoms at depths of 30 to 50 meters. It is easily recognized by the toothed keel that runs the length of its back. It gets its common name from the thick shell that has discouraged its use as a commercial species. The shells of old individuals are sometimes encrusted with the acorn barnacle, *Balanus amphitrite amphitrite.*

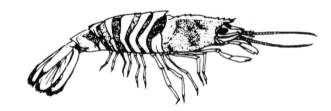

**FIGURE 5.32.** The rock shrimp, *Sicyonia dorsalis.* (x0.9)

Another creature frequently caught during trawling for commercial shrimp is the mantis shrimp, *Squilla empusa* (Figure 5.33). Unlike the penaeid shrimp, *Squilla* is dorso-ventrally flattened and armed with sharp spines on its telson and razorlike antennal scales. It lives on muddy and sandy bottoms and is very efficient capturing small fish and shrimp from ambush with its large, rapto-

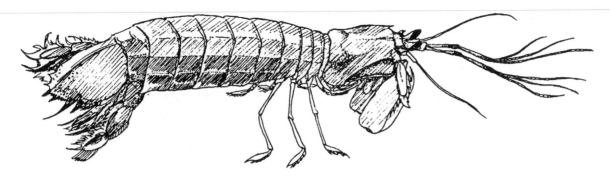

**FIGURE 5.33.** The mantis shrimp, *Squilla empusa*. (x1)

rial legs. These legs, which are equipped with long spines for holding its prey, give *Squilla* the appearance of a praying mantis, from which it gets its common name. *Squilla* also orients chemotactically to food through receptors in its antennules. Although *Squilla* has very good vision, chemoreception helps it to locate food in turbid water. *Squilla* is less aggressive than most other mantis shrimps. When one approaches another, it vibrates its walking legs. They threaten one another by lowering the raptorial legs and placing the toothed portion of these legs on the substrate surface. *Squilla* rarely strike one another in aggressive encounters and usually walk away without a serious altercation. Mating occurs after a minimum of courtship behavior. The eggs are spawned after mating and are bundled into a large mass and carried by the female in her maxillipeds for two to three weeks until they hatch. During this time, the female occupies a burrow and rarely feeds.

Schools of two small caridean shrimps, *Leptochela serratorbita* (Figure 5.34) and *Ogyrides limicola* (Figure 5.35), are common in the northern Gulf but are rarely recovered from commercial shrimp catches because the mesh of the nets used is too coarse. Both species have a short rostrum without teeth, although *Ogyrides* has serrations on its carapace just behind the rostrum. This small, smooth rostrum distinguishes them from other caridean shrimps commonly encountered in the northern Gulf. *Ogyrides* has very long eyestalks, reminiscent of the sergestid shrimp *Acetes americana* (Figure 5.36). Although typically residents of water strata near the bottom, *Leptochela* and *Ogyrides* move freely through the water column and are occasionally caught in the surface plankton.

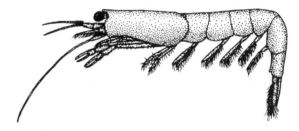

**FIGURE 5.34.** A caridean shrimp, *Leptochela serratorbita*. (x3)

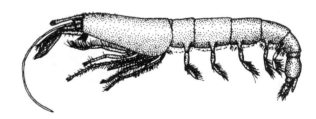

**FIGURE 5.35.** A caridean shrimp, *Ogyrides limicola*. (x3)

**FIGURE 5.36.** A sergestid shrimp, *Acetes americana*. (x3.5)

## Crabs—Like Hermits and Frogs

Not all inhabitants of the offshore shrimp grounds are as cryptic as worms or burrowing crabs nor as elusive as shrimp. The persistent diver will encounter siphonal tubes maintained by large bivalves such as the quahog, *Mercenaria campechiensis,* the giant cockle, *Laevicardium robustum,* and the false angel wing, *Petricola pholadiformis,* as well as trails of gastropods such as the moon snail, *Naticarius canrena,* and the dwarf olive, *Olivella minuta* (Figure 5.37). Large shells of the horse conch, *Pleuroploca gigantea,* and various shells occupied by colorful hermit crabs are a fascinating part of this seascape.

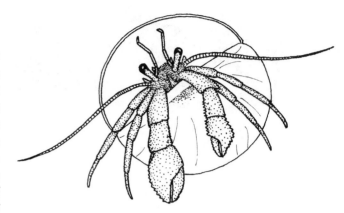

**FIGURE 5.38.** The hermit crab, *Pagurus impressus.* (x0.6)

**FIGURE 5.37.** The dwarf olive, *Olivella minuta.* (x6)

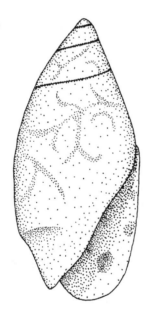

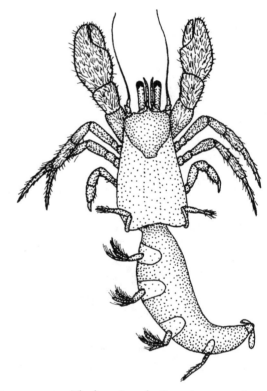

**FIGURE 5.39.** The hermit crab, *Paguristes puncticeps.* (x1)

The horse conch (Figure 3.22) is the largest marine snail in the northern Gulf, where its shell may attain a length of more than 20 cm. Juveniles may be found on oil platforms, but the adults are restricted to the bottom. *Pleuroploca* is a predator of clams and other snails. *Pleuroploca* shells and those of its gastropod prey are usually utilized by one of the populations of large hermit crabs, such as *Petrochirus diogenes, Pagurus impressus, Paguristes puncticeps,* and *Dardanus fucosus.*

*Pagurus impressus* (Figure 5.38) is easily recognized by its flattened, rust-colored claws with serrated margins. Its antennae are yellow, and its eyestalks have patches of brown, blue, and scarlet. *Pagurus impressus* occasionally wanders close to the beach, where it may be found around pier pil-

ings or in longshore troughs. *Paguristes puncticeps* (Figure 5.39) is also rust brown in color, but its claws are not nearly as flattened as those of *Pagurus impressus* and, unlike the latter species, are nearly equal in size. *Paguristes*'s carapace is also covered with white spots. It is typically found offshore near reefs and the bases of oil platforms.

The bar-eyed hermit crab, *Dardanus fucosus,* derives its name from the horizontal black bar that transverses its bluish cornea. Its heavy purple claw is highlighted by blue warts, and its walking legs are accented by brownish-orange bands. This colorful crab spends most of its time beneath offshore oil platforms or on natural reefs but seldom ventures near the shore in the northern Gulf.

The frog crab, *Raninoides louisianensis* (Figure 5.40), obtained its common name from its general appearance and the froglike posture that it assumes. It typically rests on the seafloor with its anterior end raised as if resting on the claws. Frog crabs usually bury themselves partially, similar to mole crabs.

The offshore mole crab, *Albunea paretii* (Figure 5.41), is readily distinguished from its littoral relative, *Lepidopa websteri* (Figure 3.6), by its narrow, triangular eyestalks and tapering carapace. *Lepidopa* has broad eyestalks and a broad, squarish carapace. *Albunea* may be found near beaches inhabited by other mole crabs, but it is the predominant species in deeper water. Like its kin, it uses its hind legs to burrow into the sand backwards, leaving only a portion of its head and its very setose antennae extended above the surface. *Albunea*'s antennae form a tube that permits a current of water to be drawn over its gills and filtering mouthparts.

**FIGURE 5.40.** The frog crab, *Raninoides louisianensis.* (x1.2)

**FIGURE 5.41.** The offshore mole crab, *Albunea paretii.* (x1.5)

Unlike many of its relatives, the longheaded porcelain crab, *Euceramus praelongus* (Figure 5.42), prefers a free-living existence among the shell rubble or coarse sand grains characteristic of submarine ridges and some beaches. Its cylindrical carapace gives it the appearance of a mole crab, but it lacks the spadelike telson and feathery antennae typically found on mole crabs. The dull greenish color of *Euceramus*'s carapace is often broken by fine gray or purple lines.

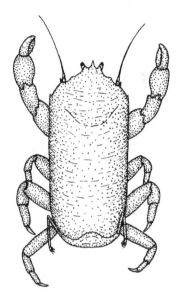

**FIGURE 5.42.** The longheaded porcelain crab, *Euceramus praelongus.* (x1.8)

Another animal preferring coarse sediments is the amphipod *Batea cartharinensis* (Figure 5.43). Its large rectangular eyes and the serrated posterior edge of its third abdominal plate help to distinguish this species from other subtidal amphipods, including *Synchelidium americanum* (Figure 5.44), *Ampelisca abdita* (Figure 5.45), and *Corophium acherusicum*. The latter three species generally prefer fine sediments. *Synchelidium* also has a relatively large eye, but it is located very close to its small, hooked rostrum. It is unusual among amphipods in that its first pair of claws are subchelate but its second pair are chelate. Its short, setose antennae are contrasted by its very long last walking legs. *Ampelisca* is easily recognized by its two pairs of small eyes. It lives in a long, narrow tube. Another tube-dwelling amphipod, *Corophium*, has a body whose slimness is emphasized by its lack of large coxal plates. Its stout antennae flank the blunt projections bearing its eyes.

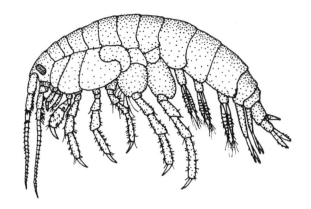

FIGURE 5.43. The amphipod, *Batea catharinensis*. (x8)

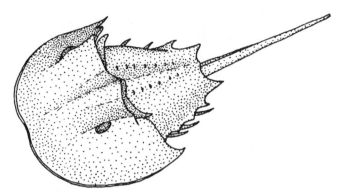

FIGURE 5.46. The horseshoe crab, *Limulus polyphemus*. (x0.25)

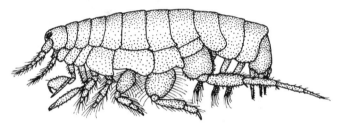

FIGURE 5.44. The amphipod, *Synchelidium americanum*. (x8)

true crabs, it lacks mandibles and must chew its food, consisting primarily of worms and mollusks, with the bases of its walking legs. Its long, rigid tail is used for balance and as an aid in burrowing. Females, which are much larger than the males, deposit their eggs in holes in the sand. The young hatch out in midsummer and swim off into deeper water, where they grow to adulthood in time for the following spring's migration.

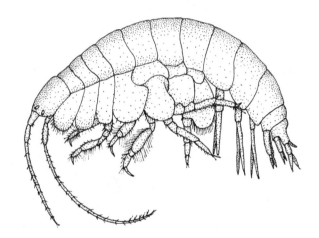

FIGURE 5.45. The amphipod, *Ampelisca abdita*. (x8)

## Creatures to Entice the Sea Lover

The horseshoe crab, *Limulus polyphemus* (Figure 5.46), is one of the most ancient and exotic marine animals in the Gulf. It is commonly encountered in the eastern Gulf in the spring when it moves inshore to spawn. In the western Gulf, its distribution is apparently limited to the coast of Yucatán and to Galveston Bay, where it has been accidentally introduced. *Limulus* is not actually a crab at all, but is related to the extinct trilobites of ancient seas. Unlike

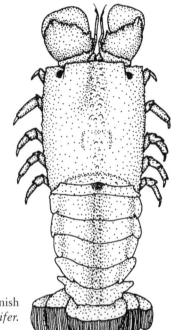

FIGURE 5.47. The Spanish lobster, *Scyllarides nodifer*. (x0.25)

The shovelnose or Spanish lobster, *Scyllarides nodifer* (Figure 5.47), has been tasted by relatively few Gulf Coast residents. Although it reaches a sufficiently large size and its flesh is reportedly flavorful, it is not sufficiently abundant, nor does it dwell close enough to shore to inspire harvesting on a commercial scale. Individuals that are snared in shrimp trawls are usually eaten on board by the fishermen or taken home to their families. This colorful lobster is more flattened than the familiar New England lobster and has short, stout claws held close to its body. *Scyllarides* is brownish-yellow with touches of red marking the carapace edges and many of the numerous tubercles on its shell. Its yellow underside offsets its red-and-purple-banded legs.

**FIGURE 5.49.** The brittle star, *Micropholis atra* (arms truncated). (x4)

**FIGURE 5.48.** The brittle star, *Hemipholis elongata* (arms truncated). (x0.25)

Several brittle stars live on the shrimp grounds. *Hemipholis elongata* (Figure 5.48) typically has a mottled gray-and-white body, or disc, and banded arms. Each of its five arms has a pattern of four to eight dark segments alternating with one to two light segments. Each arm segment bears three conical spines on each side. *Micropholis atra* (Figure 5.49) resembles *Hemipholis* in that it is gray or dull lavender in color and has five arms bearing six conical spines per segment. However, its arms are not banded and its disc appears inflated or swollen. The scales on the upper surface of its disc are much larger than those on the lower surface, which extend slightly around the margin of the upper surface. Several of the scales on the disc's upper surface are darker than the others, giving the

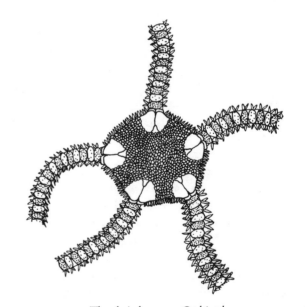

**FIGURE 5.50.** The brittle star, *Ophiophragmus moorei* (arms truncated). (x4)

disc a somewhat mottled appearance, but less so than in *Hemipholis*. *Ophiophragmus moorei* (Figure 5.50) has closely spaced bands on its arms and a row of spines around the margin of its disc. It is also rather drably colored. This species often extends into shallow water, where it can be found on sandbars in association with sand dollars.

Brittle stars typically lie buried in the sand with only the tips of their arms exposed. They shun light, and, if exposed, they usually move away or bury themselves with a rowing action of two arms. The arm tips are often waved over the sand surface, grasping food particles encountered, which are then transported to the mouth by podia or by retraction of the arm. Large pieces of decaying flesh may be sensed 10 to 20 cm away, stimulating the brittle star to unbury itself to reach its food.

## The Elusive Octopus

The cephalopod, *Octopus vulgaris* (Figure 5.51), occurs offshore. It inhabits crevices, large shells, or empty cans and is nocturnal in its habits. *Octopus* has a larger brain than any other invertebrate and can learn to discriminate among objects of different sizes and shapes for a reward, retaining the memory for at least three weeks. Along the underside of its right legs, *Octopus* has two rows of suckers that can grasp objects securely. Its mouth lies in the center of the web of tentacles. The eyes are well developed and image-forming. When orienting to its prey, the octopus only uses one eye. In estimating the distance of the object, it raises and lowers its body. An octopus stalks its prey by gliding over the bottom and stopping within 15 or 20 cm of it. It then gathers itself together and leaps on the prey, trapping it beneath the web of tentacles.

*Octopus* exhibits a variety of colors and can change the surface texture of its skin. It responds to the color of its environment and exhibits the same color changes even when blinded. This behavior is protective; when the octopus is moving and changing colors at the same time, it confuses potential predators. During mating, the male octopus deposits a spermatophore in the female's mantle cavity. This capsule breaks open, releasing the spermatozoa, which enter the oviduct and fertilize

**FIGURE 5.51.** The common octopus, *Octopus vulgaris*. (x0.4)

the eggs. The eggs are attached in strings to the roof of the octopus's burrow. As many as 150,000 eggs may be produced over a week's time. The female cares for them, cleaning and aerating them with spurts of water from her siphon. The young hatch in approximately six weeks, when they are nearly 1 mm long. The diminutive octopuses then spend weeks or months in the realm of the plankton and settle to the bottom when they have grown to a length of 5 mm or more.

CHAPTER SIX

# The Bay Shore: Salt Marshes

S tands of the cordgrass, *Spartina alterniflora*, are a prominent feature of the bay shore. Many animals seek refuge on and among its sturdy stalks during tidal highs and daylight hours (Figure 6.1). One of the most abundant animals in this habitat is the marsh periwinkle, *Littorina irrorata* (Figure 6.2), a small, grayish yellow-brown snail that grows to a height of 23 mm. Faint lines on the shell, similar to the venation of the *Spartina leaves* and the shape of its shell and reminiscent of a bent leaf, effectively camouflage it when viewed from above. *Littorina* climbs the *Spartina* stalks to escape the rising tide and while on the stalk secretes mucus around the perimeter of its shell lip. This permits the snail to withdraw into its shell and prevent desiccation by closing the aperture with its operculum, which is carried on the back of its foot.

When the tide recedes, the snail descends the stalk and crawls about on the mud, grazing on plant matter and other detritus as it glides along. This snail has a bipedal foot, i.e., the foot is divided into left and right halves that are alternately extended and contracted for locomotion.

Like most other prosobranch snails, the sexes are separate in *Littorina* and reproduction is accomplished by internal fertilization. Unlike most prosobranchs, *Littorina* releases its eggs into the water in single capsules. These planktonic eggs develop into trochophore larvae within the capsules and hatch as free-swimming veliger larvae. During this stage, small shells are developed as they transform into miniature adults, settling on

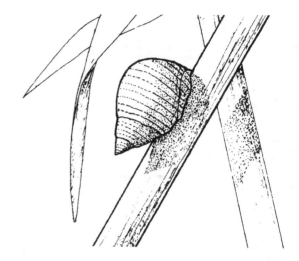

**FIGURE 6.2.** The marsh periwinkle, *Littorina irrorata.* (x1.5)

**FIGURE 6.1.** The salt marsh community: hermit crab, *Clibanarius vittatus*; the fiddler crab, *Uca rapax*; the marsh periwinkle, *Littorina irrorata*; the horn shell, *Cerithidea pliculosa*; the pulmonate snail, *Melampus bidentatu*s; and the amphipod, *Gammarus mucronatus.*

the nearest *Spartina* stalks. During the summer and early fall months, many young snails are present, but not all survive to adulthood due to physical hazards and predation by stone crabs.

If one looks closely around the bases of the *Spartina* stalks, one may find fragments of shells of *Littorina*, other gastropods, and clams. These fragments are remnants of meals of the stone crab, *Menippe adina*. These formidable crabs have massive, strong claws that are capable of cracking open clams, snails, and hermit-crab shells. They live in short burrows, excavated among the *Spartina* roots and usually open at both ends. *Menippe* is not as pugnacious as the blue crab and will withdraw into its burrow and wedge itself against the walls when disturbed.

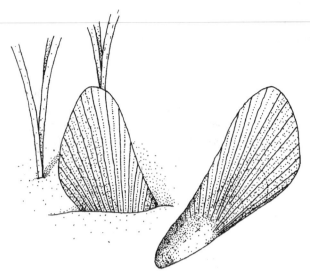

**FIGURE 6.4.** The ribbed mussel, *Geukensia demissa granosissima*. (x0.5)

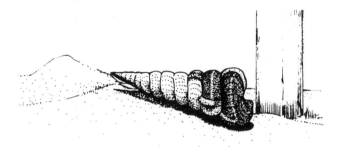

**FIGURE 6.3.** The horn shell, *Cerithidea pliculosa*. (x1.5)

Another snail, *Cerithidea pliculosa* (Figure 6.3), is common on the mud at the bases of the *Spartina* stalks. This turret-shaped snail has a thickened lip that forms a small, whitish ridge (or varix) on the shell as the snail grows. Populations of *Cerithidea* on Galveston Island, Texas, are heavily parasitized by a number of trematodes. The cercariae of these parasites attack the gonad and hepatopancreas of the snail. Parasitism of the hepatopancreas probably results in impaired digestion; parasitism of the gonad impairs reproduction. A snail whose gonad is parasitized may grow to an abnormally large size. because the energy usually allotted to reproduction is instead shunted into growth. *Cerithidea* grazes on the filamentous algae that grow on the mud at the base of the grass stalks.

## Mussels and Worms in the Mud

At the roots of the *Spartina* growing in less saline parts of the bay and near the mouth of small creeks, clumps of the ribbed mussel, *Geukensia demissa granosissima* (Figure 6.4) may be found. Like most mussels, *Geukensia* anchors itself in the

substrate with the aid of a heavy byssus; adults are usually burrowed up to their siphons in the mud. Like the foot of the pen shell *Atrina*, the foot of *Geukensia* is greatly reduced. Although the young crawl freely until locating their kind and attaching, adults are relatively stationary because they have small feet and are only capable of feeble movements. This mussel is eurythermal, surviving temperatures from -22°C to 40°C; and euryhaline, surviving salinities from 5 to 100 parts per thousand and osmotically conforming in waters of 9 to 43 parts per thousand. When *Geukensia* is exposed during low tide in the summer, the evaporative cooling of the wet mud reduces the mussel's temperature by as much as 5°C to 10°C. Frequently, the valves gape when the mussel is exposed, cooling the body by allowing water to evaporate from the tissues. *Geukensia* is photosensitive and, as a possible predator defense, responds to shadows by closing its valves both when submerged and exposed. In some areas, raccoons prey upon *Geukensia*.

Reproduction occurs in the spring, with the number of recruits to the populations being greatest in March and April. The shell grows throughout the year, especially in small and medium-sized individuals, although growth is most rapid during the warm months. It takes approximately two years for a young mussel to reach maturity. The greatest mortality occurs during the summer and fall, with virtually no population losses during the winter. The smallest *Geukensia* suffer the greatest mortality throughout the year.

One of the most common polychaetes in the muddy sand of the salt flats is *Laeonereis culveri*, which ranges in color from pinkish-red to yellowish-green. Because it burrows rather deeply in the mud, it is relatively resistant to short periods of low salinity and extreme temperatures as well as droughts. However, after prolonged periods of rain, many *Laeonereis* may be found exposed on the mud surface, relatively immobile due to osmotic stress.

## Fiddler Crabs and More Fiddler Crabs

The fiddler crab, *Uca* (Figure 6.5), is one of the most common crabs in the salt marsh. The common name of this genus of crabs refers to the oversized claw of the male; females can be recognized by their equal-sized small claws. The male uses his large claw mainly in social interactions. In contrast to subtidal crabs such as *Callinectes* and *Arenaeus*, semiterrestrial crabs rely less on chemical clues to find suitable mates. Thus, in most terrestrial species, visual and acoustic signals are highly developed as communicative devices. Male *Uca* attract females by waving the major cheliped in a certain pattern and producing sounds by tapping the ground and rubbing their legs together. Having attracted a female, a male without a burrow mates with her on the surface. A male with a burrow entices the female into the burrow and mates with her there. As with other semiterrestrial crabs, mating occurs with the female's carapace hard. This adaptation not only reduces the chance of mechanical injury but also reduces the risk of dehydration.

A female *Uca* carries the eggs beneath her abdomen and releases the larvae at the water's edge. The larvae undergo five zoeal stages and a megalops stage, metamorphosing into an adultlike form as they settle on the shore. They then pass through five crablike stages before assuming the adult form completely. Fiddlers form very large colonies, with the younger crabs usually living closer to the water's edge than older individuals.

The depth of the burrows of these crabs depends upon the water level within the sand. The upper portion of the burrow is usually straight, extending down at a steep angle for the first 30 cm or so. It then abruptly angles downward, terminating in a small chamber at the water table. This chamber is usually partially filled with water. As high tide approaches, *Uca* plugs the burrow entrance with packed sand and spends high tide sitting in the chamber. When the tide recedes, the fiddler crab emerges from his burrow and feeds or attends to other business. Burrows in current use may be immediately recognized by small sand pellets around the entrance.

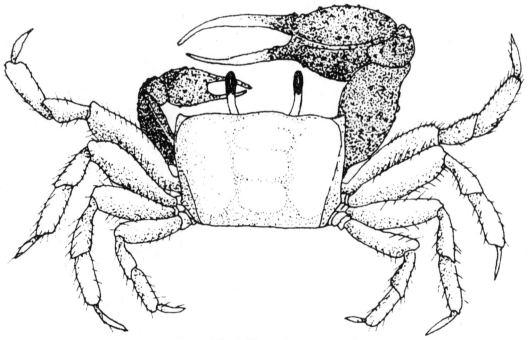

**FIGURE 6.5.** The fiddler crab, *Uca rapax*. (x2)

*Uca* usually feeds by sifting through a "clawful" of sand with its mouthparts for edible matter, which it locates, apparently chemotactically, by first probing the sand with its minor chela. The male uses only the small claw in feeding, although the female employs both claws. The sand surface is scraped and a dab is passed between the outermost mouthparts (third maxillipeds). Water from the gill chambers floods the mouth cavity, floating the lighter edible particles which are then caught by setae on the mouthparts and held by capillary action of the water. The unsuitable material drops to the bottom of the buccal cavity. Species that feed in sand have more sorting setae on their mouthparts than those that feed in fine, silty mud. Because water is necessary for feeding and branchial water is used in the process, *Uca* must periodically refill its gill chambers, even though some of the water is recycled. As *Uca* sifts through continuously augmented mouthsful, a small drop of sand begins to form at the bottom of the mouthparts. When it grows to "pellet" size, it either drops to the ground or is wiped away with a claw. With this feeding habit, *Uca* may harvest up to 40 percent of the suitable food in the substrate. *Uca* also scavenges from beached fish and other dead animals. During low tides, especially at night, *Uca* emerge in hordes to feed and wet their gills at the water's edge. At this time, the less fleet-footed may fall prey to wading birds and *Callinectes* lurking in the shallows.

The color of *Uca* differs during daylight and nighttime. During the day, the dark pigment spots (melanophores) are dispersed and the white chromatophores (leucophores) are contracted so that the crab is dark in color. At night, conversely, the melanophores are contracted and the leucophores are dispersed, giving it a light color. The change in carapace color is an endogenous rhythm, for crabs kept in total darkness will exhibit the same color changes as those under natural conditions. However, crabs kept in total light soon lose the rhythmical color change, indicating that the endogenous rhythm is influenced by photoperiod. Thus, crabs whose burrows are closer to the shore are submerged for longer periods, causing them to exhibit a slightly different color rhythm than crabs whose burrows are more supratidal and therefore submerged for shorter periods of time.

Of the 59 species of this genus that are recognized in the world, seven species occur on the northwestern Gulf coast: *Uca subcylindrica, Uca longisignalis, Uca spinicarpa, Uca rapax,* a western Gulf form of *Uca pugilator* which has recently been named *Uca panaceae* (Salmon, in press), *Uca minax* (Figure 6.6), and *Uca vocator. Uca minax,* however, is a brackish-water form that is seldom found west of the Mississippi Delta. *Uca vocator* only occurs in colonies near Brownsville, Texas. The males of the other five species may be distinguished by the following characteristics; unfortunately, females of these species are less distinct.

## Key to the Fiddler Crabs of the Northwestern Gulf Coast

1. If there is a presence of tubercles on the palm of the major chela. refer to statement 3.

   In the absence of tubercles on the palm of the major chela, refer to statement 2.

2. Carapace in lateral view cylindrical; abdomen of male broad     *Uca subcylindrica* (in the Laguna Madre only in Texas; ranges to Mexico)

   Carapace in lateral view more flattened than cylindrical; abdomen of male narrower     *Uca panaceae*

3. Spine present on inner median ridge of major cheliped carpus (turn claw upward to see it); tubercles on palm of major chela in right angle     *Uca spinicarpa* (ranges from west coast of Florida to Mexico)

   If no spine present on inner face of carpus of major cheliped and tubercles on palm not in right angle, refer to statement 4.

4. Rostrum (carapace margin between eyes) squarish; red chromatophores present, especially on walking legs and carapace; merus of walking legs not very setose     *Uca rapax* (ranges from Gulf of Mexico to Brazil)

   Rostrum rounded; no red chromatophores; walking legs setose     *Uca longisignalis* (brackish to freshwater; not in Laguna Madre; ranges from the west coast of Florida to Brownsville, Texas)

A

B

C

D

E

**FIGURE 6.6.** Major chelipeds and carapaces of male fiddler crabs: (A) *Uca subcylindrica* (body shown in profile); (B) *Uca panaceae* (body shown in profile); (C) *Uca spinicarpa*; (D) *Uca rapax*; and (E) *Uca longisignalis*.

## Life in the Marsh Debris

*Sesarma reticulatum* and *Sesarma cinereum* (Figure 6.7), two other species of small crabs, also inhabit the marsh. *Sesarma reticulatum* lives in large communal burrows in the muddy part of the marsh, emerging during midtide to feed on the oldest, outermost leaves of the *Spartina* or any *Uca* it can catch. Their burrows are approximately 70 cm deep and are usually filled with water. *Sesarma reticulatum* can be distinguished from *Sesarma cinereum* by the presence of a second tooth on the front side of the former's carapace (Figure 6.8). It is more robust than *Sesarma cinereum*, although less active. This is partially due to the greater gill area of *Sesarma cinereum*. The wood crab, *Sesarma cinereum*, lives high in the marsh in abandoned bird nests and under debris. Like *Uca, Sesarma* are primarily nocturnal in their habits and exhibit a color-change rhythm. A female may carry from 5,000 to 13,000 eggs at a time and may breed up to five times during her lifetime.

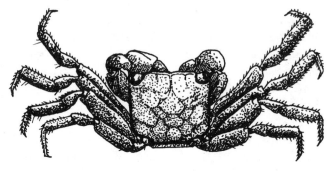

**FIGURE 6.7.** The wood crab, *Sesarma cinereum*. (x1.5)

A

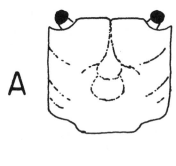

B

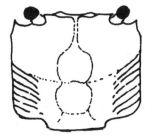

**FIGURE 6.8.** Carapace of *Sesarma cinereum* (A) and *Sesarma reticulatum* (B). (x1.5)

Another supralittoral animal found in similar shaded refuges is the pulmonate snail, *Melampus bidentatus* (Figure 6.9). Lacking gills, this snail respires across its highly vascularized mantle cavity wall and will drown during prolonged submergence. During their six-week reproductive period, occurring from late May to early July, the snail's behavior is synchronized with the lunar cycle and the occurrence of biweekly high tides. These hermaphroditic snails aggregate at this time and mate. Oviposition occurs at each spring tide (every two weeks) over a period of four days. Over all these periods, each individual deposits approximately 40 egg masses; each egg mass contains an average of 850 eggs.

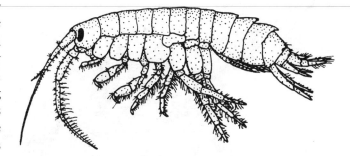

**FIGURE 6.10.** The amphipod, *Gammarus mucronatus.* (x7)

This species ranges from the Gulf of St. Lawrence to the Gulf of Mexico and occurs in a variety of estuarine habitats.

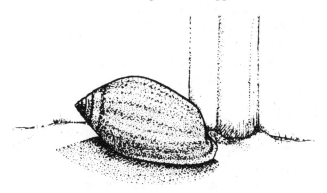

**FIGURE 6.9.** The pulmonate snail, *Melampus bidentatus.* (x3.5)

The *Melampus* eggs are deposited in a single continuous strand enclosed in two tubular gelatinous layers. The eggs develop in 10 to 11 days and are protected from desiccation during this time by tidal deposition of detritus. The eggs hatch into veligers at the next spring tide and enter the plankton, where they spend two to six weeks. Settlement of the young also occurs on a high spring tide. Growth is slow during the winter and greatest in the spring and summer. *Melampus* attain sexual maturity at approximately 5 mm in length and live for three to four years, reaching a maximum length of 10.5 mm. *Melampus* is most active at night, during the morning and evening twilight hours, and on cloudy, sultry days. On warm, sunny days it usually takes refuge under debris or in *Uca* burrows. Its diet consists chiefly of diatoms and other algae, although it also consumes tissues of higher plants and decayed animal matter.

*Gammarus mucronatus* (Figure 6.10) is a large, reddish-brown amphipod that utilizes the debris trapped in the marsh for both food and shelter. Ovigerous females occur from April to September.

## Land Crabs

One of the largest crabs living along the Texas coast is the great land crab, *Cardisoma guanhumi* (Figure 6.11). Adult males may weigh 500 gm at carapace widths of 10 to 11 cm. These crabs have inflated epibranchial chambers that aid in respiratory exchange by increasing the volume of air to which the gills are exposed. Although *Cardisoma* can survive three days without water, they frequently moisten their gills with the groundwater that wells up in the bottom of their burrows. These herbivorous crabs burrow in muddy sand at varying depths, depending on the water table, and may be found up to eight kilometers from the sea along canals and irrigation ditches. *Cardisoma* also commonly burrows beneath mangroves growing along bays.

The upper part of the *Cardisoma* burrow extends at a 25° to 50° angle from the surface, then descends steeply to the water table, increasing slightly in width. At the bottom, the burrow is expanded into a chamber one to two liters in volume. Dirt is excavated with the large claw and carried to the surface held between the major cheliped and the body. During the winter, the burrow mouth is plugged and the crab remains below the surface. New burrows may be constructed in the summer months.

Juveniles are tan or brown in color and usually weigh 5 gm or less. Maturing crabs have purple spots on the carapace and weigh up to 40 gm. The adults are bluish-gray with whitish chelipeds. Females may exhibit the adult coloration before they reach sexual maturity. Crabs weighing 80 to 90 gm are usually mature. The spawning season

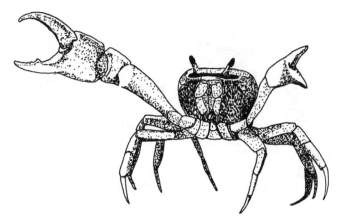

**FIGURE 6.11.** The great land crab, *Cardisoma guanhumi*. (x0.3)

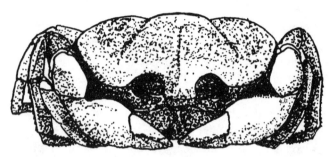

**FIGURE 6.12.** The black land crab, *Gecarcinus lateralis*. (x1)

extends from June or early July to December, with a peak in October and November. The number of eggs carried per female ranges from 200,000 to 700,000, although the average number borne is 370,000. The freshly attached eggs are black and turn brown over the 10 to 12 days of development. When they are ready to spawn, the females mass and migrate to the sea, which appears to occur on a bimonthly lunar rhythm. The larvae are released by fanning the abdomen, and they spend approximately five months in the plankton before metamorphosing and returning to land. In Central America, *Cardisoma* is an important protein source for lower economic groups. In the United States, man is less a predator than raccoons, which appear to be important consumers of *Cardisoma*.

The black land crab, *Gecarcinus lateralis* (Figure 6.12), is another terrestrial crab found in this region. It only occurs in the extreme southern portion of Texas where it constructs burrows on the back side of the dunes. It is a nocturnal feeder and thus is not often encountered.

## Invisible Grass Shrimp

Returning to the water's edge, one can find some animals that frequent the *Spartina* but that also exist elsewhere in the bay. The transparent grass shrimp, *Palaemonetes pugio* (Figure 6.13) and *Palaemonetes vulgaris*, take refuge from predators among the *Spartina stalks* at high tide. Young commercial shrimp, such as *Penaeus aztecus*, may also share this refuge. These two genera represent the two major groups of shrimp, Caridea and Penaeidea. These groups may be distinguished in the field by the shape of the tail. Caridea are often nicknamed "broken-back" shrimp because the covering of the fourth abdominal segment is capped over the fifth segment. Thus, the tail of a caridean shrimp will have a noticeable hump when viewed from the side, in contrast to the smooth line of the tail of a penaeid shrimp.

*Palaemonetes*, like *Penaeus*, is a scavenger. These shrimp are most abundant in areas ranging in salinity from 10 to 20 parts per thousand. Males and females may be distinguished by the shape of the second pair of abdominal appendages, modified as copulatory organs in the male. Female *Palaemonetes* attach their fertilized eggs to their pleopods. The eggs are aerated by the rhythmic beating of the pleopods and are kept free of detritus by frequent cleaning. The number of eggs carried per female depends upon her size but ranges from 100 to 700. Spawning occurs in July and October. Those young spawned in the summer grow to maturity in two to three months; those spawned in the fall require four to six months. Grass shrimp live for one year, although hapless individuals may be consumed sooner by redfish and speckled trout.

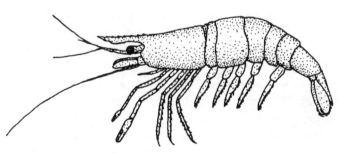

**FIGURE 6.13.** The grass shrimp, *Palamonetes pugio*. (x3)

# CHAPTER SEVEN

# The Bay Shore: Mudflats

Extensive portions of the shallow Gulf Coast bays are covered by only a few inches of water at low tide and may be exposed during extreme low tides and northers. These mudflats are too low for the development of salt marshes and, far from being flat, they are finely sculptured by currents, waves, and burrowing animals. Like the sandy beach, the mudflat is a habitat best suited for burrowing species or very motile species. The substrate varies depending upon the location, being somewhat sandier near the passes and in channels cut by currents. This, in turn, influences the fauna that are found on the mudflat.

## Razors, Jackknives, and Boring Clams

Two species of razor clam, so called because of their elongate shape, are common burrowers in sandy mud. The stout razor, *Tagelus plebeius* (Figure 7.1), is a deposit feeder like the tellin clams.

**FIGURE 7.1.** The stout razor, *Tagelus plebeius*. (x1)

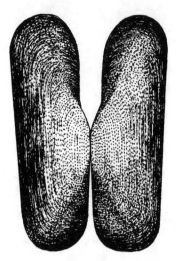

**FIGURE 7.3.** The angel wing, *Cyrtopleura costata*. (x1)

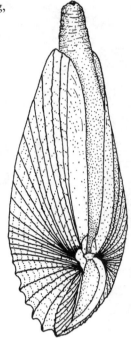

*Tagelus* lives in habitats in which the salinity may be less than 10 or greater than 30 parts per thousand. However, it lives in deep burrows in which the variation in salinity is not nearly as great. The stout razor has numerous enemies, including the drill, *Stramonita haemastoma*; the blue crab, *Callinectes sapidus*; the hermit crab, *Clibanarius vittatus*; and various shorebirds. The shells of dead *Tagelus* often rise to the mud surface, where they stand erect like small monuments.

The slimmer, more elongate jackknife clam, *Ensis minor* (Figure 7.2), is a filter-feeder. Despite its fragile appearance, this greenish clam has a powerful foot with which it can dig itself into the mud in seconds. The foot extends down into the sediment and swells with water, widening the hole.

**FIGURE 7.2.** The jackknife clam, *Ensis minor*. (x1.5)

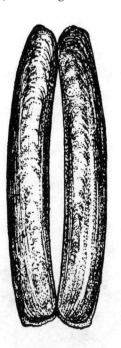

The tip of the foot then anchors itself at the bottom of the hole and contracts, yanking the rest of the clam after it. *Ensis* is a favorite prey of the whelks *Busycon pulleyi* or *Busycotypus plagosus*, either of which may nearly bury itself in search of this slender clam. *Ensis* differs from *Tagelus* in that the hinge, or point of attachment, of its valves is located at the end rather than in the middle of its shell.

Another burrowing clam usually found in stiff mud is the fragile angel wing, *Cyrtopleura costata* (Figure 7.3), a relative of the boring clams often found in wood or oyster shells. This clam burrows 30 cm or more beneath the surface, depending on its size. Its long, fused siphons protrude about 1 cm above the mouth of the burrow and circulate water and suspended matter below to the gills. The clam cannot completely close its shell or withdraw the siphons into the shell; thus, it is susceptible to extremes of temperature and salinity. The musculature holding the valves together is quite weak, and it depends upon the stiff mud for support. If one is patient enough to carefully dig up a *Cyrtopleura* intact, it will survive longer if one ties a string around the valves. Old *Cyrtopleura* shells are often found projecting upright from the mud. The gaping valves of these shells provide a refuge for small mud crabs, such as *Rithropanopeus harrisii* and *Panopeus* spp.

## Clams for Food, Roads, and Barter

With the possible exception of the oyster, the common rangia, *Rangia cuneata* (Figure 7.4), is often the most common bivalve in the low-salinity bays. A truly estuarine species, it is found well into the mouths of the rivers and bayous and grows to its maximum size in brackish water. *Rangia* shells have been used as a road-surfacing material in areas where they are particularly abundant. The outer surface of these thick shells is covered by a chocolate brown periostracum and its smooth surface is broken only by thin growth lines. *Rangia* is found from Chesapeake Bay to Texas. It reproduces once per year (in the spring) in the northern part of its range and twice per year (spring and autumn) in the Gulf of Mexico.

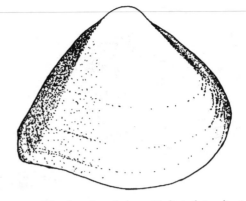

**FIGURE 7.5.** The dwarf surf clam, *Mulinia lateralis*. (x4)

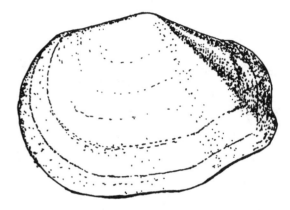

**FIGURE 7.6.** The constricted macoma, *Macoma constricta*. (x1.1)

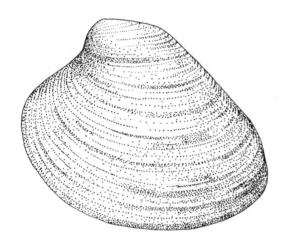

**FIGURE 7.4.** The common rangia, *Rangia cuneata*. (x1.1)

The dwarf surf clam, *Mulinia lateralis* (Figure 7.5), lives in clayey mud in the bays. It is tolerant of a wide range of salinities; hence, it is common in both low-salinity bays and the hypersaline lagoons, such as the Laguna Madre. *Mulinia*'s small, cream-colored shell is nearly triangular in shape. This abundant clam is an important food item for bottom-feeding fish.

The constricted macoma, *Macoma constricta* (Figure 7.6), is a common deposit-feeding bivalve in northwestern Gulf Coast bays. It is about 4 to 6 cm long and is very tolerant of temperature and salinity extremes. *Macoma* buries itself in the mud by rocking its shell back and forth so that it cuts into the mud. A smaller relative, *Macoma mitchelli*, is found in the mud in brackish water near the mouths of rivers.

The southern quahog, *Mercenaria campechiensis texana* (Figure 7.7), seems an unlikely mudflat resident. Its heavy shell is reminiscent of clams living in more turbulent waters. This clam lives in soft mud 3 to 4 cm beneath the surface. It is closely related to the Atlantic quahog, *Mercenaria mercenaria*, which is commonly used in clam chowder. The shell of the southern species lacks the purple border present on the valves of the Atlantic quahog. The shells of the latter species were used as currency by Atlantic seaboard Indians. Further inspection of the shell of *M. campechiensis* or *M. mercenaria* will reveal the presence of so-called lateral teeth on the hinge line. These ridges help to reduce the shear on the cardinal teeth—the most apparent triangular-shaped structures of the hinge—during burrowing. The shells of small *Mercenaria* differ from those of older, heavier individuals in having a surface sculpture of small ridges to help anchor them in the substrate. The weight of the shell of the large clams keeps them buried. Young *Mercenaria* are bisexual and become male

FIGURE 7.7. The southern quahog, *Mercenaria campechiensis texana* (x0.8)

or female at about ten months of age, reaching maturity about two months later.

*Mercenaria campechiensis texana* frequently falls prey to large *Menippe* and *Callinectes,* as suggested by the shell fragments littering the grass flats at low tide. Young *Mercenaria* are also a common prey of whelks. Due to the lack of large waves and the heavy weight of *Mercenaria*'s shell, this shell often remains on the mudflat long after the clam's death. Here it fills with mud and is frequently inhabited by a mud crab, a mud shrimp, or a ribbon worm.

## Mud Crabs and Mud Shrimp

The smallest mud crab living on the mudflat is *Rithropanopeus harrisii* (Figure 7.8). It can be distinguished from the other mud crabs and from small stone crabs by the pale tips of its claws; other similar crabs have black-tipped claws. It is usually less than 15 mm wide and prefers sheltered locations—clam

FIGURE 7.8. The mud crab, *Rithropanopeus harrisii.* (x2)

shells, oyster reefs, tin cans, and clumps of vegetation.

The common mud crabs, *Panopeus obesus* or *P. simpsoni,* may also be found in old *Mercenaria* shells or in tin cans on the mudflats. These species may be distinguished by the shape of the carapace and the form of the large claw (Figure 7.9). *P. obesus* is mainly associated with the margins of salt marshes and *P. simpsoni* with oyster beds. In some areas they may occur together. They have a large tooth on the moveable finger of the large claw, which can be used to chip pieces off of the shells of small oysters and barnacles. The flat mud crab, *Eurypanopeus depressus* (Figure 7.10), is smaller

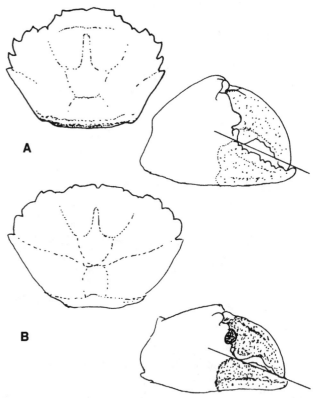

FIGURE 7.9. (A) Carapace and major chela of *Panopeus stimpsoni.* (x1.3) (B) Carapace and major chela of *P. obesus.* (x1.3) Note relative shape of dentition in relation to guideline.

FIGURE 7.10. The flat mud crab, *Eurypanopeus depressus.* (x1.3)

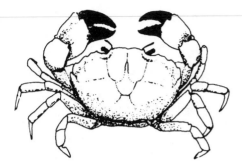

**FIGURE 7.11.** The mud crab, *Neopanope texana texana.* (x1)

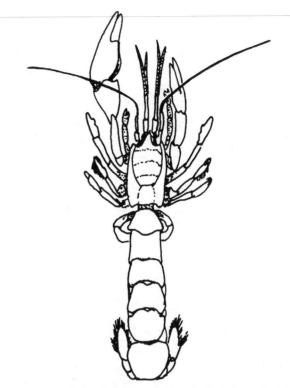

**FIGURE 7.12.** The mud shrimp, *Callianassa louisianensis.* (x2)

**FIGURE 7.13.** The ribbon worm, *Cerebratulus lacteus.* (x4)

than *Panopeus* (about 20 mm wide) and lacks the large tooth on its claw. It is usually mottled grayish-olive to dark olive brown in color and has a red spot on the concealed side of its claw. *Neopanope texana texana* (Figure 7.11) is a slightly larger mud crab (27 mm wide) that lacks both the tooth and the red spot on its claw.

The stone crab, *Menippe adina* (Figure 2.14), is a member of the same family as the mud crabs and often shares their mudflat habitat. Small stone crabs live primarily in crevices on the jetties and oyster reefs, but large ones dig burrows on the mudflat and along the edge of the marsh. These burrows play an important role in the ecology of the mudflat, because they often contain most of the water remaining there at low tide. Mud crabs, hermit crabs, grass shrimp, snapping shrimp, worms, and several species of fish may find shelter from the drying sun and foraging shorebirds in stone-crab burrows. During cold weather, *Menippe* may plug up the entrance to its burrow. Young *Menippe* often play dead when cornered and may autotomize legs that are caught. Old stone crabs occasionally carry the acorn barnacle, *Chelonibia patula,* on their carapaces.

The mud shrimp, *Callianassa louisianensis* (Figure 7.12), sometimes builds its burrow in mud that has collected in a large *Mercenaria* shell. It is a small, delicate shrimp with one oversized claw. *Callianassa* typically burrows into the mud near vegetation and sometimes shares its burrow with the small commensal crab, *Pinnixa chaetopterana.*

## Delicate Ribbon Worms

The ribbon worm or nemertean, *Cerebratulus lacteus* (Figure 7.13), is an inhabitant of the soft mud and can sometimes be found in the mud

inside old clamshells or in abandoned tubes of the polychaete, *Diopatra cuprea.* This pale yellow worm is a voracious predator on other worms and small crustaceans. *Cerebratulus* may reach lengths greater than one meter on the East Coast, but it rarely grows that large on the Gulf Coast. It is sometimes called a proboscis worm because of its long proboscis that can be shot out to capture prey some distance away. *Cerebratulus* also uses its proboscis quite effectively in burrowing. After it is everted, the tip is widened and hooked to form an anchor; successively, the head is narrowed and pushed into the burrow by contractions of the body wall and then expanded to form an anchor. As the proboscis is retracted, a wave of contraction passes down the body. Successive anchors form along the wave so that the posterior portion of the body is pulled into the burrow. The rapid burrowing of *Cerebratulus* results from repeating this process before the previous contraction wave reaches midworm. The name "ribbon worm" applies to its long, slender, flattened body.

A bright red nemertean, *Micrura leidyi*, lives in the sandier sediment near the passes. *Micrura* may attain a length of 20 cm, but it is very fragile and thus difficult to obtain intact. It lacks eyespots, and its anterior end is marked by a small, whitish mouth.

## Augers, Drills, and Moon Snails

The moon snail, *Neverita duplicata,* which also inhabits the sandy beach, can be found gliding along just below the surface, especially near the passes where the substrate is somewhat sandy. These snails lay their minute eggs in a capsule called a sand collar (Figure 7.14), in which the eggs are interspersed among sand grains in a mucous matrix. *Neverita* has an enormous foot, which expands to about twice the area of the shell. This foot is expanded by an internal vascular system; when the animal retracts into its shell, the fluid is drained from this system and the foot is folded into the shell.

A member of the naticid family, *Sinum perspectivum* (Figure 7.15), has a shell that is only partially exposed. Its shell is usually called a baby's ear by shell collectors, and it resembles a miniature abalone shell. *Sinum* also burrows beneath the sand surface and is highly modified for this habit. Unlike *Neverita*'s foot, *Sinum*'s foot is not retractable. *Sinum* glides through the sand by muscular action, aided by a copious secretion of mucus.

The common mud snail, *Nassarius vibex* (Figure 7.16), is found along the bay edges and subtidally. It is a scavenger with a highly developed chemoreceptive capability. The shells of these little snails provide homes for tiny hermit crabs that have recently settled from the plankton.

The common Atlantic auger, *Terebra dislocata* (Figure 7.17), can often be found near the passes. It crawls just under the sand surface, occasionally

**FIGURE 7.16.** The common mud snail, *Nassarius vibex.* (x2)

**FIGURE 7.17.** The common Atlantic auger, *Terebra dislocata.* (x1.5)

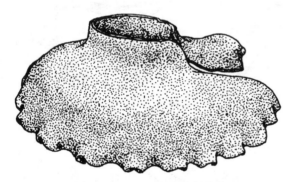

**FIGURE 7.14.** A sand collar: the egg case of the moon snail, *Neverita.* (x1)

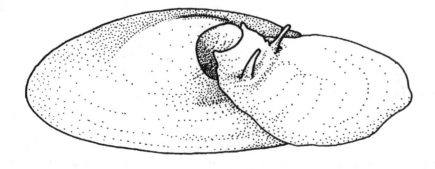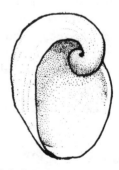

**FIGURE 7.15.** *Sinum perspectivum,* (A) live snail (x1) and (B) ventral view of shell (x1.5).

leaving a bulge in the surface. For an unknown reason, *Terebra* occasionally crawls out onto the surface in large numbers, and its white shell is very conspicuous. This carnivorous snail apparently has a venom that it uses in the capture of its prey.

The oyster drill, *Stramonita haemastoma,* can be found in great numbers during the spring breeding season laying eggs in capsules just beneath the waterline on almost any available hard surface, such as pier pilings and other *Stramonita.* These long, rectangular capsules turn yellow if laid on surfaces that are left dry when the tide recedes.

## Hermit Crabs on the Bay Shore

Three species of hermit crabs are common in the bays: *Pagurus longicarpus* (Figure 7.18), *Pagurus pollicaris,* and *Clibanarius vittatus.* The latter is most abundant and appears to be the most tolerant of water temperature and salinity fluctuations. All three species are scavengers, and they compete with one another for suitable shells. *Pagurus* is frequently

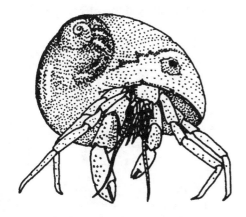

**FIGURE 7.18.** The hermit crab, *Pagurus longicarpus.* (x1.5)

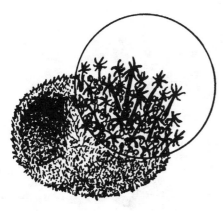

**FIGURE 7.19.** The commensal hydroid, *Hydractinia echinata,* with a magnification of the polyps. (x1)

found in shells encrusted with colonies of the hydroids *Hydractinia echinata* (Figure 7.19) and *Podocoryne selena. Clibanarius* appears unable to inhabit shells encrusted with living colonies of these hydroids, whose protective zooids seem to sting this hermit crab. The stinging zooids apparently do not harm *Pagurus,* either because *Pagurus* inhibits the firing of the nematocysts or because it is immune to the sting. Thus, the less-abundant *Pagurus* are afforded some protection from *Clibanarius* during shell fights. *Clibanarius,* easily recognized by its striped legs, is the most abundant intertidal hermit crab during the summer. In winter it migrates into the shallow subtidal zone, where it aggregates and frequently buries itself in the mud. It is quite rare along the shore during January and February. The long-armed hermit crab, *Pagurus longicarpus,* has longer and more slender claws than does the thumb-clawed hermit crab, *Pagurus pollicaris,* whose short, flat claws can be used to plug the aperture of its shell when molested. Both species of *Pagurus* are more common nearshore during the winter, when they apparently move into shallow water to breed. Many of the females are carrying eggs at this time. *Pagurus longicarpus* is the most common species on the eastern U.S. coast, where it is usually found nearshore during the summer. It migrates into deeper water during the winter.

## Worms and Their Neighbors

Another inhabitant of soft, sandy mud is the parchment tube worm, *Chaetopterus variopedatus* (Figure 7.20). This worm is a good example of modification of the parapodia and body segments to a tube-dwelling existence. It lives in a U-shaped tube, with a parchmentlike lining, with the ends protruding above the mud. *Chaetopterus* never leaves its tube to feed, as do some predacious species, but filters plankton from the water by a unique method. Modified parapodia near the anterior of the worm secrete mucus along their interior margin; this mucus flows back to form a sack as a water current is set up in the tube by the fans (other modified parapodia). When it is full of food particles, this mucous sieve is formed into a bolus, which is passed forward to the mouth by rows of cilia and swallowed. All of the similar segments on the posterior section of the body are nearly completely filled with gonad. *Chaetopterus* is a stenohaline species rarely found where the salinity drops below 20 parts per thou-

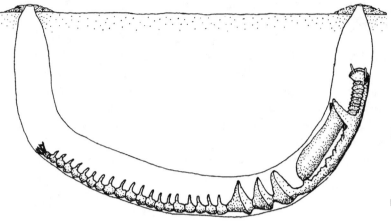

FIGURE 7.20. The parchment tube worm, *Chaetopterus variopedatus,* in its burrow. (x0.3)

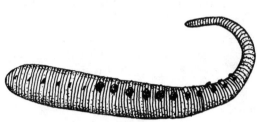

FIGURE 7.21. The lugworm, *Arenicola cristata.* (x1)

sand. Hence, it is usually found near the passes. It is a volume-regulating osmoconformer, meaning that it adjusts to salinity changes by swelling or shriveling until its internal salt concentration is nearly the same as that of its environment.

*Chaetopterus* frequently harbors a number of other animals in its tube. The crab, *Pinnixa chaetopterana,* is a common boarder; usually a male and a female can be found in the same tube. These elongate little crabs enter and leave the tube at will, biting a hole in the chimney if the end of the tube is too small. These crabs filter-feed by sweeping their very setose-feeding legs (maxillipeds) through the water. The fringe of setae is then cleaned by the other mouthparts to collect the food. *Pinnixa* probably takes advantage of the water current in the *Chaetopterus* tube for its filter-feeding and thus does not steal food directly from its host.

The lugworm, *Arenicola cristata* (Figure 7.21), is one of the mudflat's more interesting residents. It lives in an L-shaped burrow consisting of a mucus-lined horizontal gallery and a vertical tail shaft. *Arenicola* is a thick, dark green worm with eleven pairs of reddish gills near the center of its body. Water is drawn down the tail shaft, bringing oxygen to the gills, and is then forced up through the sediment at the blind end of the gallery. Because *Arenicola*'s gallery is often located in the black, sulfur-rich sediment layers, the stream of freshwater results in the oxidation of the sediment, changing its color to yellow. The lugworm is a direct deposit-feeder, i.e., it swallows this oxidized sediment and digests any organic matter in it as it passes through the worm's gut. It then backs up the tail shaft to defecate. Its tail is most vulnerable to attacks by shorebirds. *Arenicola* is well adapted to low-oxygen environments. If the tide stays out too long, *Arenicola* will retrieve bub-

bles of air from the surface and pass them to the gills. The gills can use atmospheric oxygen as long as they remain wet.

There are many other common species of polychaete worms in the bays, among which are *Eteone heteropoda* (Figure 7.22), *Laeonereis culveri, Neanthes succinea* (Figure 7.23), *Ceratonereis irritabilis* (Figure 7.24), and *Capitella capitata floridana* (Figure 5.10). *Eteone* and *Capitella* lack jaws and are probably deposit-feeders. *Eteone* is a

FIGURE 7.22. Anterior end of *Eteone heteropoda.* (x25)

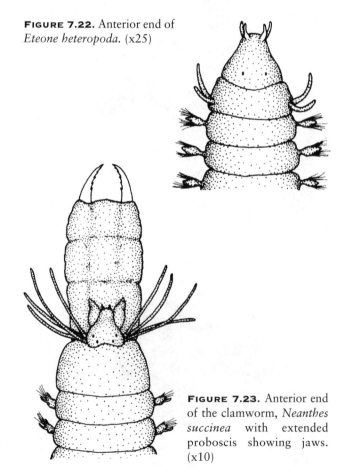

FIGURE 7.23. Anterior end of the clamworm, *Neanthes succinea* with extended proboscis showing jaws. (x10)

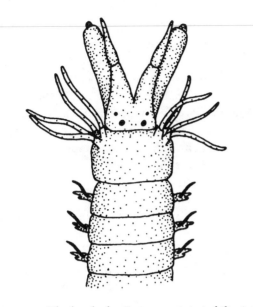

**FIGURE 7.24.** The head of a *Ceratonereis irritabilis*. (x10)

pale yellow or greenish worm about 50 to 90 mm long, usually found intertidally in sandy mud. *Capitella* differs from the other species in that it has very few parapodia; thus, except for its eyes, it looks like a blood-red earthworm. The red color is due to the blood that can be seen through its skin. *Capitella* is approximately 100 to 120 mm long and usually lives in vertical burrows in mud or fine sand. *Capitella* is often one of the first organisms to reinvade areas damaged by oil spills; thus, its presence is occasionally interpreted as an indication of oil pollution.

*Laeonereis, Neanthes,* and *Ceratonereis* are all members of the family Nereidae. They are active predators equipped with a pair of horny jaws with teeth along their inner edges. *Neanthes* is the largest of these worms; it reaches a length of 190 mm. It is a cosmopolitan species and is found in a great variety of habitats—on pilings, among oysters, in sandy or muddy sediment, under stones, and among barnacles. It is tolerant of a wide range of salinities, from brackish water to marine water. *Laeonereis* is a very common species on mudflats and in salt marshes, where it constructs deep, vertical burrows. It is about 30 mm long and varies in color from pink to red to bright yellow to green.

*Ceratonereis* has a light gray anterior region, a bluish midregion, and a brass-colored posterior region, and the bases of its parapodia are green. It reproduces through a process known as epitoky. The posterior end of the body, which contains the gonads, differs markedly from the anterior end. As the gonads mature, the worm transforms from a nonsexual individual, or atoke, into a sexual individual, or epitoke. The epitokes then swim up into the water. This activity is synchronized so that numerous epitokes enter the plankton at the same time. These swarms of epitokes release their gametes into the water, where fertilization takes place.

*Platynereis dumerilii* (Figure 4.11) is another predaceous nereid worm that is common nearshore. It constructs a pliable tube composed of several layers of fine threads held together by an adhesive secretion. Specialized anterior parapodia secrete the threads and adhesive. Bits of debris are often incorporated into the tube wall. Bundles of threads anchor the tube to the substratum, often a seagrass blade or old shell. Like most other nereids, *Platynereis* seldom tolerates direct contact with other worms, except during courtship, and quickly chases intruders from its tube. Sense organs on the anterior cirri, palps, and tentacles are used to identify worms of other species or sexes. Rapid biting thrusts of the proboscis accompany pursuit of unwelcome visitors to the burrow's exit.

Aggressive encounters between nereid worms are easily observed in sections of glass or clear plastic tubing. Introducing various combinations of species, sexes, or sizes into opposite ends of the tubing yields interesting behavioral experiments. A long-stemmed glass funnel can be used to manipulate stubborn worms. Try letting one of the worms make itself "at home" before adding its adversary.

## Life in the Seagrass Meadow

Bays along the coasts of Alabama, Florida, and Texas are structured by underwater meadows of vascular plants generically known as seagrasses. Seagrasses have tropical affinities and form lush beds at low latitudes. In the northern Gulf, the erect blades, or turions, die back during the winter and are broken off by storm waves, leaving a live network of rhizoidal roots to regenerate new turions in the spring.

The most common Gulf species are turtle grass, *Thalassia testudinum*, and shoal grass, *Halodule wrightii* (Figure 7.25). As its name implies, shoal grass is often found in shallow water and may be exposed at low tide. Widgeon grass, *Ruppia maritima,* also inhabits shoal areas but prefers a lower salinity than that tolerated by *Halodule*.

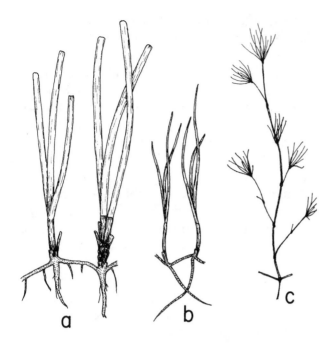

**FIGURE 7.25.** Common seagrasses: *Thalassia testudinum* (A), *Halodule wrightii* (B), and *Ruppia maritima* (C). (x0.3)

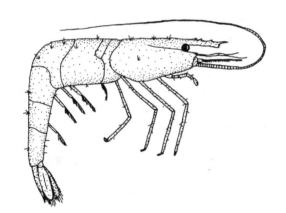

**FIGURE 7.26.** *Hippolyte pleuracantha.* (x6)

Seagrasses help to stabilize the physical environment and provide cover for numerous small organisms. Their meadows form nursery areas for major Gulf of Mexico shrimp and crab populations. Juvenile blue crabs and juvenile penaeid shrimp exploit the cover provided by these plants to pass the numerous molts required by rapid growth in early life. Each molt is accompanied by a vulnerable soft-shelled stage.

Juvenile pink, brown, and white shrimps share this habitat with several other species, some of which spend their entire lives in the meadow. Perhaps the most ubiquitous of these species is the broken-back shrimp, *Hippolyte pleuracantha* (Figure 7.26). *Hippolyte* is somewhat of a chameleon, ranging in color from a bright kelly green to a speckled reddish-brown, depending on the color of the grass to which it is clinging.

The arrow shrimp, *Tozeuma carolinensis* (Figure 7.27), is so named because of its long rostrum (the spine at the front of the carapace) and its elongated body. It, too, can match its color to its background by responses of color organs called chromatophores imbedded beneath its integument. In Florida, *Tozeuma* is bluish purple on gorgonians of the same color and green on grass. Its ability to flatten itself against the grass blade also conceals its presence.

The snapping shrimp, *Alpheus estuarensis* (Figure 7.28), is usually found under debris or in discarded cans within the grass beds. It prefers sheltered locations in quiet, shallow water and is sometimes common on oyster reefs. The major claw of this shrimp has a small disk on which a circular "hammer" closes when muscular tension reaches a release point. The closure of this disk produces a loud pop, stunning small crustaceans

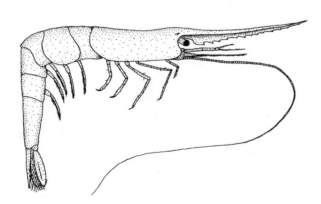

**FIGURE 7.27.** The arrow shrimp, *Tozeuma carolinensis.* (x6)

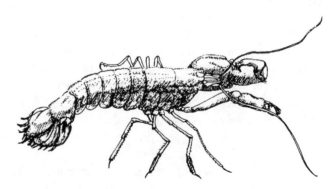

**FIGURE 7.28.** The snapping shrimp, *Alpheus estuarensis.* (x1.5)

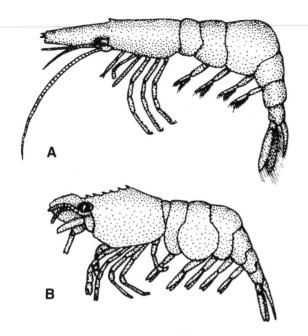

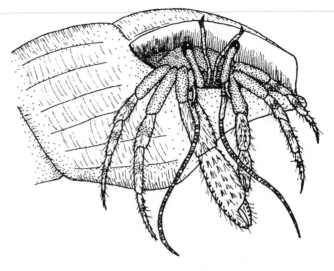

**FIGURE 7.30.** The hermit crab, *Pagurus annulipes*. (x5)

**FIGURE 7.29.** Sargassum shrimps, *Latreutes fucorum* (A) and *Latreutes parvulus* (B). (x2.5)

upon which *Alpheus* feeds. Males and females are usually found together, the female being about twice the size of the male. Females carry their green eggs on their pleopods, like *Palaemonetes*. *Alpheus* will do well in capitivity, provided it is given a piece of pipe or small jar in which to hide.

The grass shrimp, *Palaemonetes pugio* (Figure 6.13) and *Palaemonetes vulgaris,* are characteristic residents of seagrass meadows. The sargassum shrimps, *Latreutes parvulus* and *Latreutes fucorum* (Figure 7.29), are less common and may be occasional invaders rather than residents. *Latreutes fucorum* is typically brownish-green or greenish-yellow with white spots, but this pattern is quite variable in that this shrimp often blends well with its environment. *Latreutes parvulus* is much stockier than *Latreutes fucorum* and has a very short rostrum. It is also found associated with sponges in the eastern Gulf.

Young blue crabs, mud crabs *(Neopanope texana texana)* (Figure 7.11), spider crabs *(Libinia dubia)* (Figure 3.45), and several hermit crab species are commonly seen in seagrass beds. The striped hermit crab, *Clibanarius vittatus* (Figure 2.8), is a common migrant in Texas, moving confidently between the meadow and the adjacent exposed seafloor under the protection of its borrowed shell. Minute hermit crabs, *Pagurus bonairensis* and *Pagurus annulipes* (Figure 7.30), are abundant in Florida seagrass meadows.

Dove snails, *Anachis semiplicata* (Figure 2.10), may be seen dangling from grass turions by slender mucous threads. Brittle stars, *Ophiothrix angulata* (Figure 8.22) and *Ophiactis savignyi* (Figure 8.21), are sometimes entangled around the plant bases, particularly in the eastern Gulf. Sediment within the meadow is often inhabited by phoronids, *Phoronis architecta* (Figure 5.7), and worms such as *Diopatra cuprea* (Figure 3.12), *Owenia fusiformis* (Figure 5.8), and *Polydora ligni*.

## Clams and Scallops of the Grass Beds

The pale orange shells of *Lucina pectinata* (Figure 7.31) are a common sight on beaches near passes and along bay margins. This medium-sized bivalve is found in the grass flats but is not restricted to them. Occasionally, a shell is found with the distinctive boring of a naticid snail (probably *Neverita duplicatus*), suggesting that *Lucina* is found in the more open areas patrolled by this predator. *Lucina* is tolerant of a broad salinity range, enabling it to exist in the hypersaline lagoons of southern Texas as well as in the brackish bays of northern Texas.

The whitish shell of the cross-barred venus, *Chione cancellata* (Figure 7.32), is characterized by its high, bladelike, concentric ridges superimposed on numerous radial ribs, giving it a latticed appearance. These ridges are often curved toward the apex, so they offer less resistance during burrowing than during removal of the clam from the sediment by currents or by predators such as the

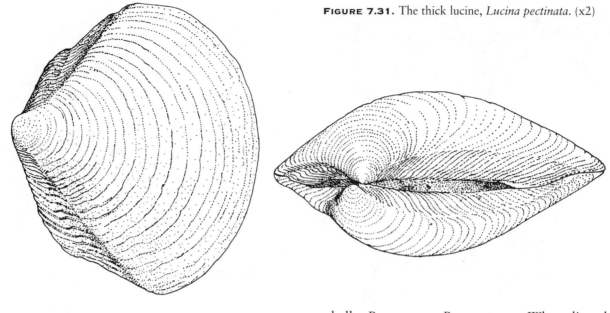

**FIGURE 7.31.** The thick lucine, *Lucina pectinata.* (x2)

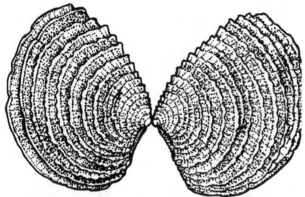

**FIGURE 7.32.** The cross-barred venus, *Chione cancellata.* (x1.4)

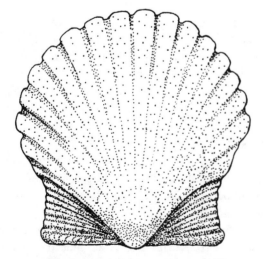

**FIGURE 7.33.** The bay scallop, *Argopecten irradians amplicostatus.* (x1.2)

whelks *Busycon* or *Busycotypus*. When disturbed, *Chione* begins to wander, usually leaving a telltale furrow in the sand. It is usually found in the upper 15 cm of sand and is usually more abundant in the grass than in bare areas. It often burrows quite shallowly, leaving its posterior uncovered. This habit accounts for the encrustations of polydorid polychaetes and algae that one often sees on their shells. This clam can tolerate salinities down to 18 parts per thousand. Individuals reach maturity at a length of about 15 mm and become either males or females. Females and males are equally abundant in populations.

The bay scallop, *Argopecten irradians amplicostatus* (Figure 7.33), is another bivalve that is found both on the grass flats and on the adjacent bay bottom. It is unusual among bivalves in that it moves by swimming in short spurts just above the bottom. This is accomplished by opening its valves and then quickly closing them, forcing out a stream of water that propels the scallop in the opposite direction. The margin of the mantle has numerous eyes among a fringe of short tentacles. These eyes are very sensitive to sudden changes in light intensity, and a passing shadow may cause the scallop to take flight.

Young bay scallops have a row of small teeth, the ctenolium, near the anterior "ear" of the right valve, over which the threads of the byssus pass that attach the young scallop to the substrate. When the scallop withdraws its small foot on which the byssal gland is located, the byssus is pulled tight, raising the lower margin of the scallop up so that the shell is at an angle to the substrate. The ctenolium thus separates the byssal threads, increasing their effective strength and preventing twisting of the shell on its anchorage. This structure becomes overgrown in older scallops around 50 to 75 mm in length, which lie free on the sand, and is also only found in members of the family Pectinidae.

## The Inconspicuous Cucumber

The sea cucumber, *Thyone mexicana* (Figure 7.34), is a sluggish member of the fauna that is found in and around the grass flats. It is rather small (2 to 3 cm long) as sea cucumbers go, so it is easily confused with a small rock or bit of debris. *Thyone*'s body resembles a distorted football, with a mouth at one end and an anus at the other. The mouth is surrounded by ten short, branching tentacles that retract when the animal is disturbed. The body is covered with short tube feet or podia, more or less uniformly distributed over its surface. The podia on the bottom of the sea cucumber have suckers; those on top lack suckers. *Thyone* usually lives buried in the mud with both ends of its body extended to the surface. If uncovered, it may require several hours of slow burrowing to rebury itself. *Thyone* eats plankton, which it entangles in mucus on its tentacles as they are waved through the water. When severely disturbed, *Thyone* may undergo a process known as evisceration, during which its anterior end and gut are discarded. The wound quickly heals and a new mouth, tentacles, and gut are slowly regenerated. A sea cucumber may be stimulated to eviscerate if overcrowded or if kept in an aquarium without adequate circulation.

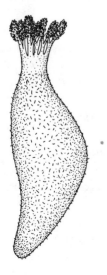

**FIGURE 7.34.** The sea cucumber, *Thyone mexicana*. (x2.5)

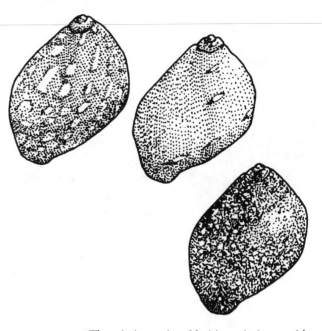

**FIGURE 7.35.** The virgin nerite, *Neritina virginea*, with several shell patterns. (x3)

The virgin nerite, *Neritina virginea* (Figure 7.35), is one of the most colorful grass-flat snails on the northwestern Gulf Coast. Its shell pattern and color are extremely variable. It may be white, gray, yellow, olive, red, purple, or black, and its pattern may consist of stripes, waves, large or small triangular dots, or fine lines. Live *Neritina* may be found crawling over the mud surface or on the grass stalks at night or on cloudy days, but its shells are most conspicuous when inhabited by the more active hermit crabs. It is most common along the South Texas coast. It lays eggs during the winter in yellow gelatinous capsules on its own shell or that of another mollusk.

## The Carnivorous Whelks

Two species of large whelks, *Busycon pulleyi* and *Busycotypus plagosus* (Figure 7.36), are common in the bay, although their occurrence in shallow water may be seasonal. The former species is the more common one. They are easily distinguished by the direction of coiling of the shell. *Busycon pulleyi* has a "lefthanded" shell and *Busycotypus plagosus* coils to the right, as do most snails. One may determine the "handedness" of a shell by trying to insert one's hand into the aperture while holding the thumb on the apex of the shell. The hand that curls naturally in the same direction as the shell is coiled indicates the hand-

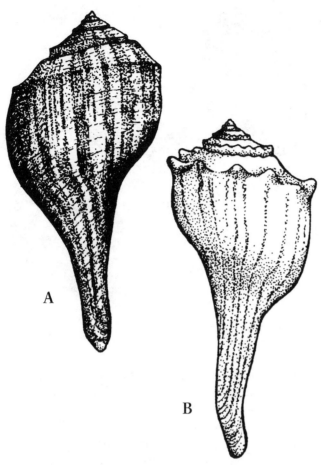

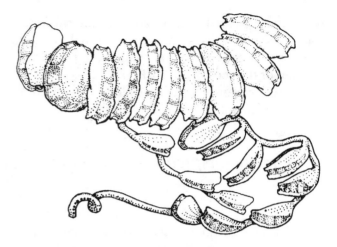

**FIGURE 7.37.** Egg capsules of *Busycon pulleyi*. (x1)

**FIGURE 7.36.** The whelks, *Busycotypus plagosus* (A) (x1) and *Busycon pulleyi* (B). (x0.8)

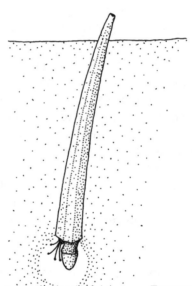

**FIGURE 7.38.** The Texas tusk shell, *Dentalium texasianum*, in a feeding position. (x2.5)

edness. The two species of whelks can also be distinguished by the color of their flesh. *Busycon* has a black body, and *Busycotypus* has a pale orange body with black tentacles. Both of these species feed on small bivalves such as *Ensis minor* and small *Mercenaria campechiensis*. The clams are grasped by the foot and may be forced open by wedging the edge of the lip between the clam's valves. Once the valves are opened, the whelk rasps the flesh away with its radula. The abundance of large whelk shells occupied by hermit crabs attests to the snails' longevity.

Both species lay their eggs in disklike capsules. *Busycon* produces 50 to 175 capsules in a string (Figure 7.37) and lays up to 200 eggs in each capsule. *Busycotypus* produces a smaller string with fewer eggs per capsule. The proximal end of the string is anchored in the sand, and the last few capsules added to the string are usually small and devoid of eggs. Strings of these sculptured capsules that become unmoored can occasionally be found washed up on the shore. The young pass through all of their larval stages within the capsule, emerging as miniature snails.

## Tusks and Bubbles

The Texas tusk shell, *Dentalium texasianum* (Figure 7.38), also lives in inlet-influenced portions of Gulf bays. It is easily recognized by its slender tapering, curved shell, which is hexagonal in cross-section. *Dentalium* is not a snail, as might be suspected, but rather a member of the related class Scaphopoda. It burrows into the sediment by

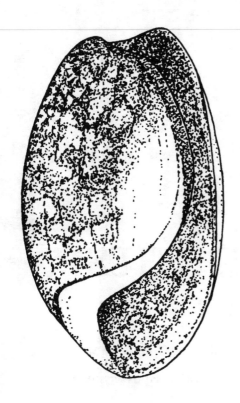

**FIGURE 7.39.** The bubble shell, *Bulla striata*. (x4.5)

extending its muscular foot out of the large end of the shell as a digging tool. Only the tip of the small end of its shell is left protruding above the surface. A respiratory current is maintained through the hole in this exposed tip. When buried, *Dentalium* uses probing motions of its foot to pack the sediment away from the buried end of the shell, forming a feeding cavity. Knobbed, tentaclelike structures called captacula arise from near the mouth and scour the surface of this cavity for bits of detritus that are collected and passed to the mouth. When this feeding cavity has been exhausted, *Dentalium* pushes itself up through the sediment and moves to a new site to begin the process again. The shells of Pacific Coast species of *Dentalium* were once used as currency by Indians.

The bubble shell, *Bulla striata* (Figure 7.39), is a small, carnivorous opisthobranch that burrows in the mudflat. Its shell is very thin and has an aperture that extends along the entire length of the shell. *Bulla* completely envelopes its shell in its mantle, much like *Neverita* and *Sinum*. It remains buried during the heat of the day; thus, it is most readily found at night or on overcast days.

CHAPTER EIGHT

# Artificial Reef Habitats

Since completion of the first successful oil well in the Gulf of Mexico in 1938, approximately 900 major platforms and thousands of support structures have been constructed in the Gulf. In an environment where such habitat is rare, each of these structures provides habitat for numerous organisms dependent on a hard substrate for attachment. A typical major platform in 20 meters of water may provide more than one-half acre (0.2 ha) of hard substrate. The average existing platform is older than 16 years, and several are nearly 30 years old, offering ample time for the development of a rich community.

Such long-time intervals are not required, however. Although the process may be delayed slightly by the use of antifouling paints, populations of bacteria and diatoms may reach densities of several thousand individuals per square centimeter within 24 hours after a new surface becomes available.

This bacterial slime favors subsequent colonization of the new habitat by protistans, algae, barnacles, and numerous other organisms. Depending on the time of year and the proximity to other structures or shipping lanes, a thick coat of organisms may develop in less than a fortnight.

As might be expected, this biota is very similar to that which encrusts the hulls of ships; thus, many common species are cosmopolitan in distribution. These "fouling" organisms add a rough texture to the submarine surfaces of the structure, providing a maze of crevices in which crabs, shrimp, worms, and other motile animals can take refuge from wave forces and predatory fish. This is especially true of structures encrusted by the giant barnacle *Balanus tintinnabulum,* which often grows atop others of its species to form a honeycombed layer 10 to 5 cm thick.

Oil-field structures are not the only artificial reef habitats in the Gulf of Mexico. Many sunken ships serve the same function. A dozen Liberty ships have been sunk intentionally off the Texas coast in recent years in hope of attracting game fishes for recreational fishing and diving. Such reefs may last more than 100 years before their ultimate destruction by marine corrosion.

## Barnacles Upon Barnacles

Probably the most significant event in the colonization of an artificial reef by fouling organisms is the arrival of barnacles. Usually more numerous than oysters or mussels, their longevous shells greatly increase the size of the colonizable surface and the number of refuges for more cryptic cohabitants. The barnacle species most prevalent on oil platforms are the giant barnacle, *Balanus tintinnabulum* (Figure 8.1), and various members of the *Balanus amphitrite* complex of species. The latter group includes *Balanus reticulatus,* which is common off Louisiana under the influence of Mississippi River runoff.

*Balanus tintinnabulum* is a cosmopolitan species often found encrusting ship hulls and, consequently, wharf pilings in ports around the world. They are also found on the rocky shores of western Africa and the eastern and western coasts of North America. It is primarily an intertidal species and thus reaches its maximum abundance near the sea surface on Gulf of Mexico oil platforms. However, it is a dominant structural feature as deep as 10 m below the surface,

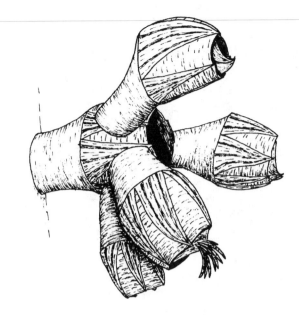

**FIGURE 8.1.** Clusters of giant barnacles, *Balanus tintinnabu-lum.* (x0.3)

and scattered individuals may be found deeper than 20 m. Its large shell is not only shared by dozens of species while the barnacle lives, but is inhabited by various crabs, shrimp, and fish after its death. One curious inhabitant is the crested blenny, *Hypleurochilus geminatus,* whose demonic appearance and aggressive antics have delighted many alert divers. One of these little fish seems to be nestled in each empty barnacle shell, poised to dart forth to challenge all trespassers or to graze algae, hydroids, and amphipods found on the shell surface.

Barnacles growing too near the sea surface or attached to other barnacles in unstable hummocks are often easily dislodged by storm waves or grazing fish. Even then, they contribute to the development of the reef-associated biota. Snails and hermit crabs aggregate at the bases of platforms to consume the dislodged food. The empty shells continue to serve as shelter for mud crabs and young octopuses. Clusters of *B. tintinnabulum* shells are also prized as coffee-table conversation pieces. The shell's color can be preserved by coating it with an artist's varnish. Cleaning the shell of unwanted sponge, algae, and hydroids is an arduous task that may be lightened with the aid of garden pests such as ants and pillbugs. A successful association with these scavengers requires soaking the shell in freshwater to leach as much salt as possible out of the unwanted tissues before placing the shell in a shad-

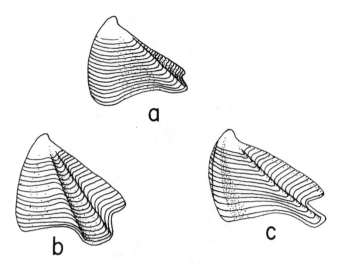

**FIGURE 8.2.** Tergal plates of *Balanus venustus* (A), *Balanus amphitrite* (B), and *Balanus reticulatus* (C). (x15)

ed part of the garden. Too much salt will preserve the tissue; too much sun will bleach the shell.

*Balanus tintinnabulum* is apparently a longevous barnacle that does not reproduce as readily as other barnacle species in the Gulf. Young individuals are rarely observed; small barnacles with reddish stripes, which may appear to be young *B. tintinnabulum,* frequently belong to the *Balanus amphitrite* complex of barnacle species. Like *B. tintinnabulum, B. amphitrite* is an extremely variable species with a worldwide distribution in temperate and tropical waters. Several of the *B. amphitrite* subspecies have been elevated in rank to species, now belonging to the *B. amphitrite* "complex."

Three of these species commonly found in the Gulf of Mexico are *B. amphitrite amphitrite, B. venustus niveus,* and *B. reticulatus* (Figure 8.2). *Balanus amphitrite amphitrite* is an intertidal species that apparently invaded the Gulf of Mexico during the first half of this century with the aid of foreign shipping. *Balanus venustus niveus* is a predominately subtidal species, which is apparently more common in the eastern Gulf than west of the Mississippi Delta. *Balanus reticulatus* is reported as common on oil structures off the Louisiana coast, but its distribution extends to Japan, where it fouls cultured oysters.

## Add Soft Colors and Textures

Barnacles are often disguised by one or more layers of other organisms, among the most colorful of

which are sponges. The abundance of sponges on artificial reefs, particularly those that reach the sea surface, such as oil platforms, is typically obscured by algae, hydroids, and bryozoans growing on their exposed surfaces.

Among the most common species in the Gulf are encrusting sponges of the genus *Haliclona,* which spread over the substrate in a mat ranging from a little over 1 mm to nearly 20 mm in thickness. Their growth form varies considerably. Some individuals have their oscula, or excurrent pores, raised on pinnacles resembling tiny volcanos, as is typical for *Haliclona loosanoffi* (Figure 8.3). Other individuals are so smooth that they are easily mistaken underwater for a coat of paint. Color is also variable. *Haliclona rubens* is characteristically brick red, and *H. viridis* is usually yellowish-green. The color of *H. permollis* ranges from lavender to deep purple; that of *H. loosanoffi* is usually tan or cream but may appear to be dingy gray because of the adhesion of other organisms and detritus. *Haliclona permollis* may also be gray when growing in shade.

*Haliclona rubens* and *H. viridis* are common in the West Indies, where they form massive and branching colonies in addition to the encrusting form familiar in the Gulf. *Haliclona permollis* and *H. loosanoffi* have more northern affinities, the latter species being found along the Atlantic Coast to Connecticut, where it commonly inhabits eelgrass beds. Its planktonic larvae are negatively phototactic and thus typically settle on the undersurface of submerged objects. *Haliclona permollis* inhabits the littoral zone (at 0.5 m above MLLW) in Oregon.

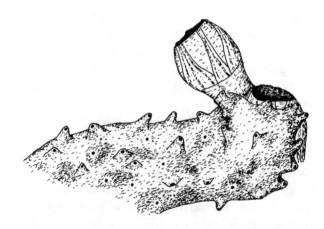

**FIGURE 8.3.** Colony of the sponge *Haliclona loosanoffi* growing over a barnacle cluster. (x0.5)

Yellow or beige colonies of *Halichondria bower-banki* are often found among colonies of *Haliclona*. *Halichondria* colonies superficially resemble those of *Haliclona loosanoffi* and cannot usually be distinguished without microscopic examination of the spicules. *Halichondria* spicules are 0.2 to 0.4 mm long, two to three times the size of *Haliclona loosanoffi* spicules. Adjacent colonies of *Halichondria* often fuse as they grow into one another. This species generally prefers habitats where strong currents are experienced.

The boring sponge, *Cliona celata*, is also found on oil platforms in the shells of oysters and barnacles. Perhaps the least conspicuous sponge found on artificial reefs is a small calcareous sponge, *Scypha barbadensis* (Figure 8.4). Seldom higher than 8 mm and appearing like a tiny puffball, this sponge is most easily observed when it colonizes portions of the substrate that have been denuded by the removal of a barnacle cluster or oyster. Its single osculum is ringed by long, slender spicules, and smaller spicules bristle from the body wall.

Its sponge fauna is severely limited by a variety of the northern Gulf's most prominent characteristics. Low winter temperatures discourage many species common in the Caribbean, southern Florida, and Yucatán. Numerous rivers add millions of tons of sediment that smother sponges growing too near the bottom or on horizontal surfaces off the bottom. Rapid summer algal growth also smothers sponges growing too near the sea surface. Thus, the northern Gulf's sponges thrive best on submerged reefs far from shore, where the water is clearer, or on the vertical surfaces of artificial reefs at intermediate depths. Unfortunately, such habitats are not uniformly distributed in the Gulf

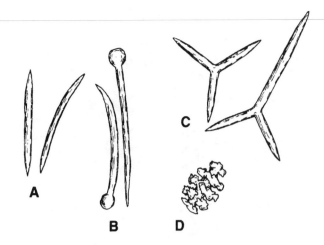

**FIGURE 8.5.** Sponge spicules (A-C) and gorgonial spicule (D). (x50)

region, and the planktonic larvae of sponges are short-lived, making it difficult for them to colonize the new habitats that do appear.

Sponges cannot be identified reliably on the basis of shape or color. Determination of the size and shape of the spicules and microscopic examination of the tissue are usually required. Spicules can be easily extracted by dissolving a piece of tissue in a solution of sodium hypoclorite (Clorox), leaving the spicules behind. Addition of a weak acid will demonstrate the nature of the spicules: calcareous spicules (as in *Scypha*) will dissolve; siliceous spicules (as in *Haliclona* and *Cliona*) will not. Some spicule shapes commonly found in Gulf of Mexico sponges are illustrated in Figure 8.5.

## Serpentine and Mossy Forms

Sponges provide not only a secondary substrate for other fouling species, but a refuge for several motile species. Among those refugees with the greatest fidelity are the polychaetes *Haplosyllis spongicola* and *Trypanosyllis gemmipara*. These are omnivorous worms that feed through an eversible proboscis. When extended, the proboscis is tipped with a circlet of ten knobs. The tentacles and cirri of these cosmopolitan species have a beaded appearance. *Haprosyllis spongicola* (Figure 8.6) is a small, pale, yellowish-orange worm; *T. gemmipara* (Figure 8.7) is pale yellow with reddish-brown to purple cirri and matching thin bands on the anterior dorsal surface. The southern clamworm, *Neanthes succinea* (Figure 7.23), is another omnivorous

**FIGURE 8.4.** The calcareous sponge, *Scypha barbadensis*. (x10)

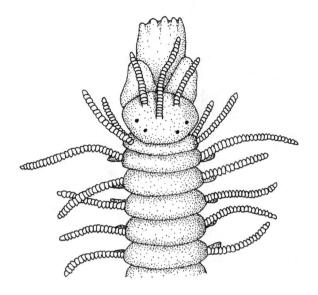

**FIGURE 8.6.** Anterior end of *Haplosyllis spongicola* with extended proboscis. (x15)

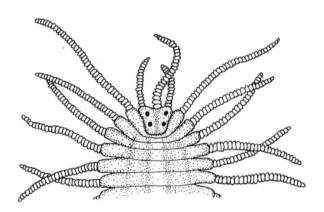

**FIGURE 8.7.** Anterior end of *Trypanosyllis gemmipara*. (x10)

resident of this sponge-barnacle habitat. During the breeding season, and occasionally for migration, adult *Neanthes* leave this habitat and swarm to the sea surface. Such swarming has been observed in midwinter in the northern Gulf.

Algae, hydroids, and bryozoans grow over the sponges, as well as over portions of the habitat not occupied by sponges. Among the most conspicuous of these are the bryozoans *Bugula neritina* and *B. rylandi* and the hydroid *Tubularia crocea*, which often grow in colonies several centimeters in diameter and 2 to 5 cm thick. As its name suggests, *T. crocea* (Figure 8.8) resembles a cluster of flowers on long stems, making it difficult to remember that they are actually animals. Upon closer examination, each "flower" is seen to consist of two rows of tentacles, between which are located numerous

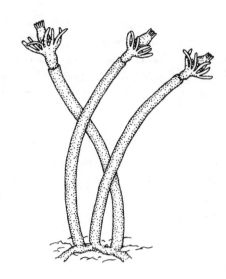

**FIGURE 8.8.** Colony of the hydroid *Tubularia crocea*. (x3)

gonozooids. The inner row of tentacles surrounds the mouth. *Tubularia* is neither a good invader nor resistant to the invasions of other species. It relies on its tolerance of low temperature and its rapid growth rate to bloom briefly during the winter and early spring.

*Bugula neritina* (Figure 8.9) initially resembles a coarse, reddish-brown alga, but once identified,

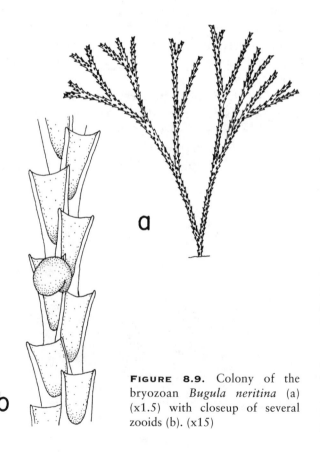

**FIGURE 8.9.** Colony of the bryozoan *Bugula neritina* (a) (x1.5) with closeup of several zooids (b). (x15)

**FIGURE 8.10.** Portion of *Bugula rylandi* colony.(x15)

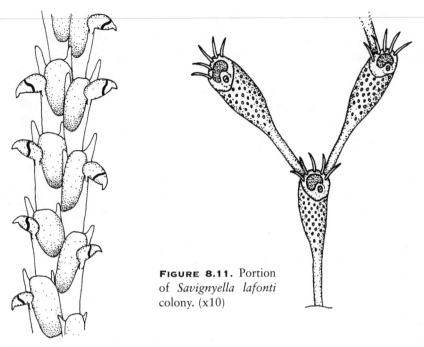

**FIGURE 8.11.** Portion of *Savignyella lafonti* colony. (x10)

the confusion vanishes. Subtle differences—its rough texture, frequent branching, and large size—catch the eye. Each colony consists of a succession of individual zooids attached to one another in a zigzag pattern, as if in continual doubt as to which way to turn. Each zooid is encased in a chitinous box equipped with a long aperture through which the zooid can extend its tentacles to feed. *Bugula's* eggs are brooded in a spherical chamber known as an ovicell, which develops during the reproductive season. *Bugula neritina* can be found in harbors around the world. Its congener, *B. rylandi* (Figure 8.10), can be easily distinguished by its lack of significant color and its remarkable avicularia, which are lacking in *B. neritina*. Located approximately in the center of each zooid, these avicularia protect the colony from its encrusting and predatory neighbors. They function as small claws, pinching intruders that come within range. Each of these three species appears seasonally on Gulf of Mexico oil platforms. The bryozoans are more common during the summer, and *Tubularia* is most abundant during the winter months.

Several other bryozoans are common on artificial reefs. Of two common erect species, *Savignyella lafonti* (Figure 8.11) and *Aetea anguina*, the former is more easily seen due to its larger size and ornate branching structure. *Savignyella* is more brittle than *Bugula* and thus typically lives in sheltered areas. It can be found on exposed sur-

faces but does not attain its magnificently delicate and complex growth form unless protected from surge and current stresses. *Aetea* can be found by carefully examining bits of shell or sponge under a microscope. Unlike most other bryozoans, its zooids are not attached directly to one another, but are interconnected through a vinelike stolon. At first glance, the *Aetea* colony (Figure 8.12) often appears to be a tangled mass of stalks from which delicate hydranths or zooids have broken off. However, the right-angle bend in these "stalks" provides the first clue to *Aetea's* identity. Closer examination reveals its scalloped orifice.

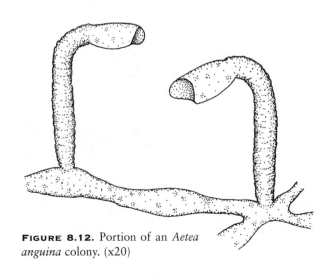

**FIGURE 8.12.** Portion of an *Aetea anguina* colony. (x20)

Encrusting bryozoans grow as a single layer of tightly packed zooids, each of which is attached to the substrate. Colonies on large, flat surfaces are typically circular and up to 6 cm in diameter, but they conform to the topographies of small, irregular surfaces. Species common in the northern Gulf of Mexico are *Schizoporella errata, Membranipora savartii, Membranipora tenuis,* and *Parasmittina trispinosa.*

As its specific name suggests, *Parasmittina* (Figure 8.13) is easily recognized by the three oral spines located just above its orifice. Numerous small pores can be seen around the periphery of the exposed upper surface of each zooid. Three small teeth, the center one largest and flattened, can usually be seen along the lower margin of the orifice. *Schizoporella* (Figure 8.14) has small pores, each sunk in a small pit and distributed rather uniformly over its upper surface. Like

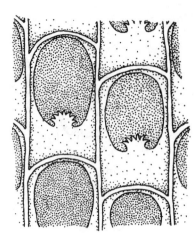

FIGURE 8.15. Portion of a *Membranipora savartii* colony. (x40)

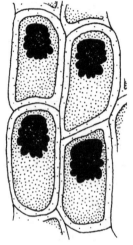

FIGURE 8.16. Portion of a *Membranipora tenuis* colony. (x40)

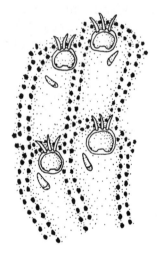

FIGURE 8.13. Portion of a *Parasmittina trispinosa* colony. (x40)

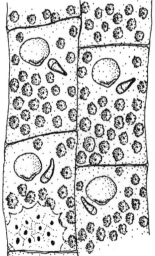

FIGURE 8.14. Portion of a *Schizoporella errata* colony. (x40)

*Parasmittina,* each *Schizoporella* zooid may be protected by a single avicularium located near its orifice. Appearing somewhat like an ice-cream cone, the tapered end of the avicularium is a hinged mandible, often with a terminal fang, which can snap shut on potential bryozoan predators. *Membranipora* has a quite variable aperture, which may extend over most of the zooidís exposed surface. This aperture is typically protected by jagged dentition around its lip, which is concentrated on a basal tooth in *M. savartii* (Figure 8.15) and more dispersed in *M. tenuis* (Figure 8.16). *Membranipora* lacks avicularia.

Several hydroids other than *Tubularia* are found on artificial reefs, the most common species being *Obelia dichotoma* (Figure 8.17) and *Clytia cylindrica.* Colonies generally appear as a whitish fuzz less than 1 cm high, but old *Obelia* colonies often develop a shrublike structure several centimeters tall. *Clytia* colonies (Figure 8.18) typically have few branches, with most zooids arising directly from a common stolon. Its hydrothecae are at least

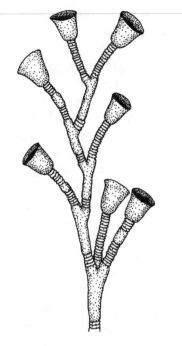

**FIGURE 8.17.** Portion of an *Obelia dichotoma* colony. (x10)

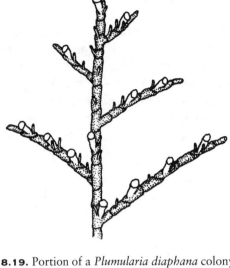

**FIGURE 8.19.** Portion of a *Plumularia diaphana* colony. (x8)

directly to the upper surfaces of the branches rather than on annulated stalks. Interspersed among these sessile cups are clublike defensive structures called nematophores, which bear clusters of nematocysts. Like *Obelia*, its hydrothecae have a smooth margin. More intriguing yet is *Syncoryne eximia* (Figure 8.20), in which the hydranths are naked, lacking the protective hydrothecae. Moreover, the hydranths are covered with 20 to 30 tentacles, which are tipped with knobs packed with nematocysts. This is a primitive arrangement that has given way to the more familiar circlet of tentacles on most modern species. *Syncoryne*'s hydranths arise from a stem that typically possesses numerous wrinkles or sloppy annulations.

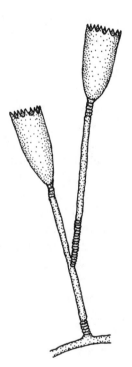

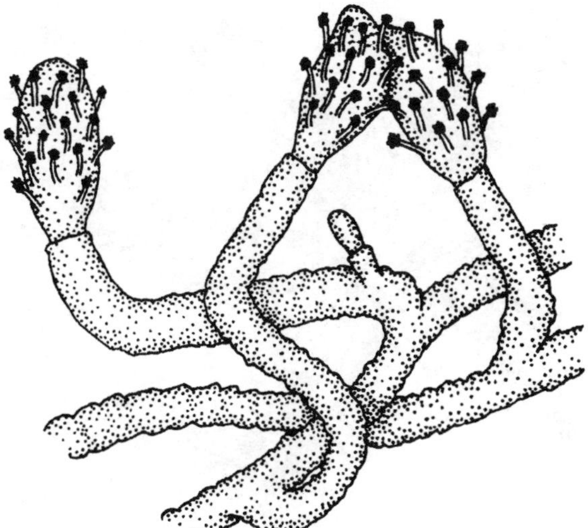

**FIGURE 8.18.** Two zooids of the hydroid *Clytia cylindrica*. (x12)

twice as long as they are wide and have a serrate margin bearing 10 to 12 teeth. *Obelia*'s hydrothecae are about 1.5 times as long as they are wide, and they have a smooth margin, which is often slightly flared. Its stems are often amber in color, particularly in older colonies.

The sea feather hydroid, *Plumularia diaphana* (Figure 8.19), is easily distinguished from *Obelia* and *Clytia* by the attachment of its hydrothecae

**FIGURE 8.20.** Portion of a *Syncoryne eximia* colony. (x25)

## Denizens of the Crevices

Among the motile animals associated with the sponge-barnacle complex are the brittle stars *Ophiactis savignyi* (Figure 8.21) and *Ophiothrix angulata* (Figure 8.22). *Ophiactis* is often very abundant on offshore oil platforms and on large sponges living on coral reefs, such as the Flower Garden Bank off Texas. Juveniles typically have six or seven arms, and adults typically have five arms.

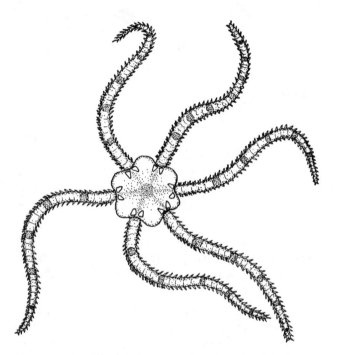

**FIGURE 8.21.** The brittle star, *Ophiactis savignyi*. (x6)

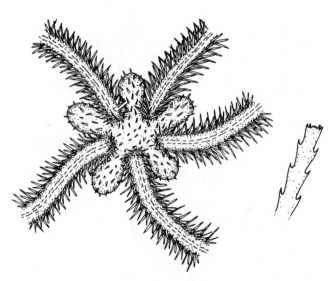

**FIGURE 8.22.** The brittle star, *Ophiothrix angulata* (arms truncated) and a closeup view of an arm spine. (x6)

It is usually yellowish-brown or yellowish-green, with darker bands along the arms. *Ophiactis savignyi* is a cosmopolitan species inhabiting tropical and subtropical seas. Elsewhere in the world, it is found in mangrove and rocky intertidal habitats. *Ophiothrix* is common in shallow water from North Carolina and Bermuda to Panama. It has five arms, and individuals from the Gulf area are maroon or reddish-purple on the upper surface and paler underneath. A pair of maroon stripes extends along each arm. The glassy arm spines, which are slightly longer than the width of the arm, are equipped with rows of thornlike teeth pointing outward. Similar teeth are also found on the largest spines covering the central disk. Brittle stars are occasionally eaten by spadefish and filefish grazing on the fouling fauna of oil platforms.

Brittle stars share crevices with a variety of amphipods. The most commonly encountered species include *Jassa falcata*, *Erichthonius brasiliensis*, and *Leucothoë spinicarpa*. Each of these species is widely distributed and quite variable in form. *Jassa* and *Erichthonius* are sexually dimorphic, the males being most easily recognized by claws with exaggerated features. Amphipod claws are typically located on the second and third pairs of legs and are usually subchelate, i.e. formed by folding the terminal leg segment back over the next segment to form a grasping appendage, such as is found on the praying mantis. In most amphipods, the claws on the third legs are larger than those on the second legs. In male *Jassa* (Figure 8.23), the former claws are extremely large, and the next to the last segment has a spurlike "thumb" that extends out to meet the claw. *Jassa* is frequently darkly pigmented by an abundance of crimson spots.

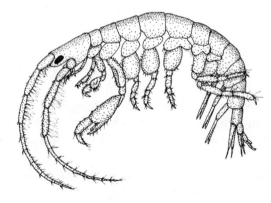

**FIGURE 8.23.** The amphipod, *Jassa falcata* (male). (x15)

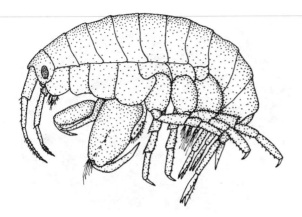

FIGURE 8.24. The amphipod, *Leucotheë spinicarpa*. (x15)

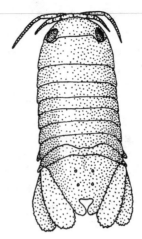

FIGURE 8.26. The squat isopod, *Dynamene perforata*. (x12)

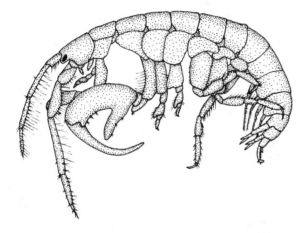

FIGURE 8.25. The amphipod, *Erichthonius brasiliensis*. (x15)

FIGURE 8.27. The sea spider, *Tanystylum orbiculare*. (x20)

*Leucotheë* (Figure 8.24) is also characterized by an oversized second claw, which is not restricted to the males, however. Its first, and smaller, claw is the more exotic, having its subterminal segment overlapped by both the terminal claw and a spur extending from the third most terminal segment (the carpus). *Leucotheë* is the largest common amphipod on Gulf offshore oil platforms and is pale in color.

Like the closely related *Corophium*, *Erichthonius* is a tube-building amphipod. Its tubes are typically attached to hydroids or filamentous algae. Male *Erichthonius* (Figure 8.25) have an elongated second claw, which superficially resembles the unusual first claw of *Leucotheë*: the carpus has a long spur that extends parallel to the subterminal segment. Its color is brownish to dull orange, distributed among numerous dots. *Erichthonius* has been found throughout the Atlantic coastline from Rio de Janeiro to Norway and in the North Pacific near San Francisco.

## Pillbugs, Crabs, and Sea Spiders

Careful examination of algal masses just below the sea surface for amphipod tubes should reveal several other fascinating creatures. Among these are the skeleton shrimp, *Caprella equilibra* (Figure 2.20); the squat isopod, *Dynamene perforata* (Figure 8.26); and the sea spider, *Tanystylum orbiculare* (Figure 8.27). *Dynamene* somewhat resembles its close relative, *Sphaeroma* (Figure 2.6) but possesses a pronounced cleft in its telson, which resembles a heart-shaped hole in some individuals. It lives around the bases of barnacles in shallow water, where it has access to the algae upon which it grazes.

*Tanystylum* is not actually a spider, but belongs to a related group of arthropods known as pycnogonids. Its understandable confusion with spiders, which do not inhabit the sea, arises from its eight long, slender legs. A pycnogonid has four eyes mounted in a short pinnacle on its back, giving it a remarkable 360-degree view of its world. *Tanystylum* ingests its food, consisting largely of hydroids, bryozoans, and sponges, through a proboscis and digests it in a gut whose branches extend nearly to the tip of each leg. Segments of food-packed gut can often be seen through the slender legs of this pale animal. Male sea spiders have an additional pair of legs, used to hold clusters of eggs that the male broods until they hatch.

A considerably larger resident of the littoral zone on oil platforms is the shore crab, *Pachygrapsus transversus* (Figure 8.28). Once a common resident of Texas jetties, this charming scavenger is now seldom seen nearshore. Even on oil platforms, its choice of habitat keeps it out of the view of most observers. It is restricted to the barnacle zone, where it can get a foothold against wave stresses, and it seldom ventures below the intertidal zone. Few divers or fishermen come close enough to the platforms at the waterline to espy this active crab.

Stone crabs, *Menippe adina* (Figure 2.14), are abundant below the littoral zone. Juveniles (Figure 8.29) are particularly common on oil platforms and may be easily recognized by the arrays of chartreuse spots covering their dark brown carapaces. *Menippe* is in the company of several other crabs

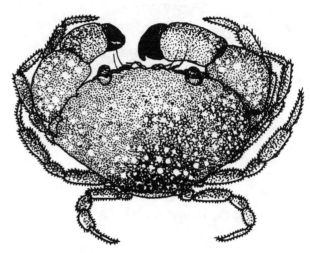

**FIGURE 8.29.** Juvenile stone crab, *Menippe adina*. (x1.2)

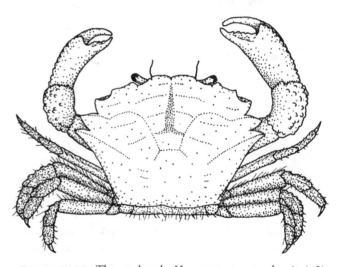

**FIGURE 8.30.** The mud crab, *Hexapanopeus paulensis*. (x3)

belonging to the family Xanthidae in this habitat. These crabs include *Panopeus turgidus*, *Pseudomedaeus agassizi*, *Hexapanopeus paulensis*, *Pilumnus dasypodus*, and *Pilumnus pannosus*.

The mud crab, *Panopeus turgidus*, is distinguishable from its congener in the bays, *Panopeus herbstii*, by its lack of a large blunt tooth near the base of the moveable finger of its large claw. *Hexapanopeus* (Figure 8.30) also has such a tooth but is distinguishable from *Panopeus herbstii* by the presence of 10 to 15 granulated tubercles on the carpus ("elbow") of its large claw. On *Pseudomedaeus* (Figure 8.31), this coarse granulation is distributed over much of the carapace. These small mud crabs often take refuge within shells of deceased barnacles. Crabs that shun such precautions often fall prey to sheepshead and triggerfish.

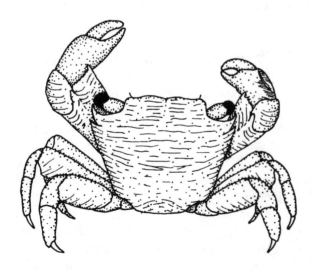

**FIGURE 8.28.** The shore crab, *Pachygrapsus transversus*. (x1.1)

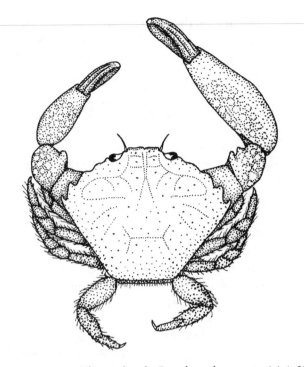

**FIGURE 8.31.** The mud crab, *Pseudomedaeus agassizi*. (x3)

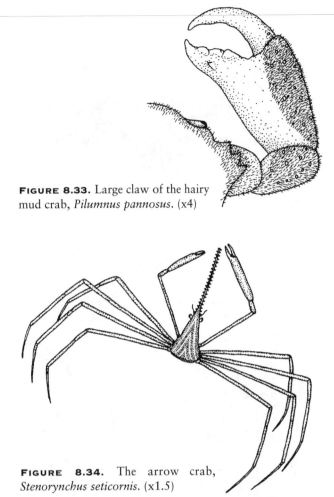

**FIGURE 8.33.** Large claw of the hairy mud crab, *Pilumnus pannosus*. (x4)

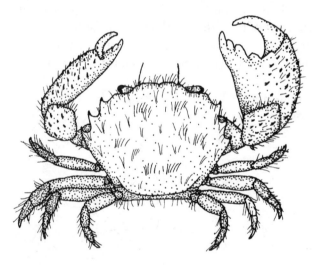

**FIGURE 8.34.** The arrow crab, *Stenorynchus seticornis*. (x1.5)

**FIGURE 8.32.** The hairy mud crab, *Pilumnus dasypodus*. (x2.5)

The hairy mud crabs, *Pilumnus* spp., bear a pubescence over most of their bodies. The hair of *Pilumnus dasypodus* (Figure 8.32) is longer and less dense than that of *Pilumnus pannosus* (Figure 8.33). These *Pilumnus* also have small spines on the upper surface of claws and carpi, with those on *Pilumnus dasypodus* being sharp and those on *Pilumnus pannosus* being blunt.

The arrow crab, *Stenorynchus seticornis* (Figure 8.34), crawls over the reef on extremely long, slender legs. Its long, jagged rostrum extends from a pear-shaped carapace, which is marked with black,

brown, and white stripes. The decorator crab, *Dromidia antillensis* (Figure 8.35), is less flashy. It further disguises its already drab carapace by carrying a sponge blanket on its back. This sponge is held in place by the crab's hindmost legs, which are raised over its carapace for this function. The sponge is contoured to the crab's back by a combination of sponge growth and pruning by the crab. A secondary coat of hydroids, algae, and bryozoans over the sponge usually completes the disguise.

The red crab, *Cronius ruber* (Figure 8.36), can often be found in or near large crevices on the reef. It is recognized as one of the swimming crabs by its paddlelike posterior legs. However, its maroon color is distinctive, as is the alternating pattern of large and small spines on the sides of its carapace.

Among the most abundant crustaceans on offshore oil platforms is the snapping shrimp, *Synalpheus fritzmuelleri* (Figure 8.37). Unlike *Alpheus*, the snapping shrimp commonly encountered in the bays, *Synalpheus* lacks epipodites,

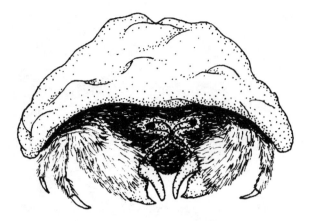

**FIGURE 8.35.** The decorator crab, *Dromidia antillensis*, with its sponge overcoat. (x4)

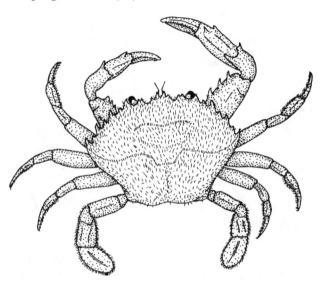

**FIGURE 8.36.** The red crab, *Cronius ruber.* (x0.5)

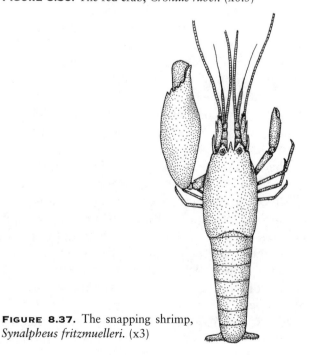

**FIGURE 8.37.** The snapping shrimp, *Synalpheus fritzmuelleri.* (x3)

which are outgrowths from the first segment of the walking legs. Mature *Synalpheus* have a reddish body and green claws, which become darker toward the tips of the fingers.

## Clams, Oysters, and Mussels

Offshore oil platforms are inhabited by a variety of bivalves. Some of them cement themselves directly to the substrate *(Ostrea equestris, Chama macerophylla)*, some attach themselves via byssal threads *(Pteria colymbus, Brachidontes exustus, Isognomon bicolor)*, and others bore into the shells of other bivalves and barnacles *(Lithophaga bisulcata, Lithophaga aristata)*. The horse oyster, *Ostrea equestris* (Figure 8.38), is among the largest of these bivalves, and its heavy oval shell may reach 7 to 8 cm in diameter. Unfortunately, it is not sufficiently abundant to warrant commercial interest. The leafy jewel box, *Chama macerophylla* (Figure 8.39), is often more abundant but too small to harvest. The surface of its upper shell is covered with scalelike plates, making it one of our most ornate bivalves. A thin coating of orange or red sponge often enhances its natural beauty.

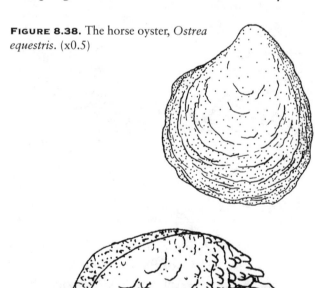

**FIGURE 8.38.** The horse oyster, *Ostrea equestris.* (x0.5)

**FIGURE 8.39.** Shell of the leafy jewel box, *Chama macerophylla.* (x1)

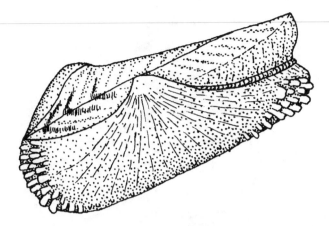

**FIGURE 8.40.** Shell of the mossy ark, *Arca imbricata*. (x1.4)

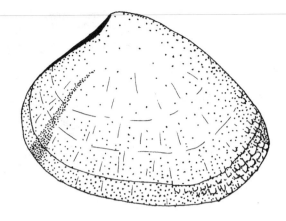

**FIGURE 8.42.** Shell of the pygmy venus clam, *Chione grus*. (x10)

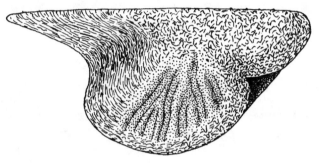

**FIGURE 8.41.** Shell of the Atlantic wing oyster, *Pteria colymbus*. (x1)

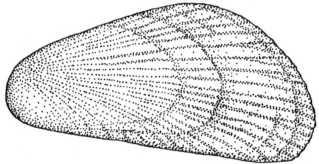

**FIGURE 8.43.** Shell of the scorched mussel, *Brachidontes exustus*. (x4)

The mossy ark, *Arca imbricata* (Figure 8.40), and the Atlantic wing oyster, *Pteria colymbus* (Figure 8.41), dwell within deep recesses formed by joints of the oil platforms. Clinging by byssal threads provides them the flexibility and mobility to face environmental changes produced by wave stresses or encroachment by neighboring barnacles. Secreted within a groove in the bivalveís foot, byssal threads can be replaced or repositioned to enable an effective, although extremely slow, mode of locomotion. Both of these species are filter-feeders. In sheltered areas they may survive to reach lengths up to 10 cm.

The pygmy venus clam, *Chione grus* (Figure 8.42), also attaches its shell within crevices on the reef. This tiny filter-feeder is less than 1 cm long. Its shell is grayish-white and often has a dark band along the posterior edge. This color is typically hidden by a layer of sponge or hydroids.

Hidden among hydroids and sponges are juvenile scorched mussels, *Brachidontes exustus* (Figure 8.43). They also use byssal threads to attach themselves to barnacles or other bivalves. Some-

what more demanding in its choice of habitat is the two-toned tree oyster, *Isognomon bicolor* (Figure 8.44). It usually resides within the shells of deceased barnacles or within narrow crevices between barnacles. However, it can often be found sharing the shells of living barnacles. The shape of its shell is extremely variable, but it usually appears quite flattened and fragile. Its valves converge on a relatively straight hinge bounded by a row of four to eight square teeth. Both *Brachidontes* and *Isognomon* are filter-feeders.

Clusters of large barnacles broken from the reef will often display short tunnels excavated in their bases by boring clams or mussels. Among the most common of these borers are the mahogany date mussel, *Lithophaga bisulcata,* and the scissor date mussel, *Lithophaga aristata* (Figure 8.45). Both of these mussels are about 3 cm long, mahogany in color, and shaped like a torpedo or slender bread date. The scissor date mussel is easily distinguished by the crossed posterior tips of its shell, which resemble exaggerated tips of a pair of scissors.

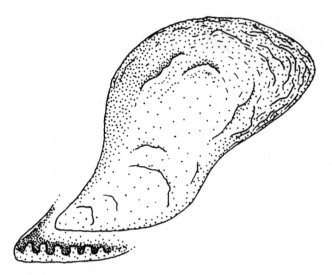

FIGURE 8.44. Shell of the two-toned tree oyster, *Isognomon bicolor*, with a view of its square teeth. (x1.5)

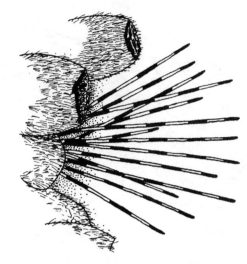

FIGURE 8.46. A juvenile long-spined urchin, *Diadema antillarium*, hidden within a barnacle cluster. (x0.6)

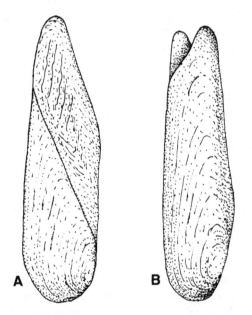

FIGURE 8.45. Shells of the mahogany date mussel, *Lithophaga bisulcata* (A), and the scissor date mussel, *Lithophaga aristata* (B). (x3)

These mussels also bore into rocks along the jetties, which is undoubtedly more difficult but more stable than boring into barnacle shells.

The purple sea urchin, *Arbacia punctulata* (Figure 2.18), is a common predator of many fouling species. Its grazing on algae, hydroids, bryozoans, and various incidental species frees substrate for new colonists. Although its numerous tube feet adequately attach it to oil-platform legs at moderate depths, it seldom finds shelter from wave stresses near the sea surface. Hence, the intertidal and shallow subtidal fauna usually enjoys freedom from urchin grazing. Juvenile long-spined urchins, *Diadema antillarium* (Figure 8.46), are occasionally seen on oil platforms. Unlike *Arbacia*, the long-spined urchin is a tropical species usually associated with coral reefs. Adult *Diadema* are deep purple—almost black—in color, although white individuals occur sporadically. Juveniles have purple-and-white- banded spines, which are much longer and more slender than those of *Arbacia*.

Calcareous tubes of serpulid polychaetes are a common sight on barren substrate created by urchin or fish grazing or by physical damage to barnacles. These tubes belong predominately to the serpulid worm, *Eupomatus protulicola* (Figure 8.47), and the feather duster worm, *Spirobranchus giganteus* (Figure 8.48). *Eupomatus* tubes are typically less than 3 cm long and are much more abundant than the large tubes of *Spirobranchus*. Each of these worms is equipped with an operculum, which is used to plug the tube's aperture in time of stress. These opercula are armed with spines to discourage pursuit by potential predators. *Eupomatus* possesses a circlet of spines that curve outward from the center. *Spirobranchus* possesses a branching, antlerlike spine in the center of its operculum. The feather duster worm is well known as a decorative, but shy, inhabitant of coral heads. Its elaborate feeding structure, from which it derives its generic and common names, consists of three concentric rings of radioles borne on paired stalks. These radioles are usually colorfully

**FIGURE 8.47.** The serpulid worm, *Eupomatus protulicola,* within its calcareous tube. (x5)

**FIGURE 8.48.** Anterior end of the feather duster worm, *Spirobranchus giganteus*, within its calcareous tube. (x1.6)

banded, making them a favorite subject of underwater photographers. This feeding structure traps suspended food particles and directs them to the worm's mouth through a series of ciliated grooves.

Although changes in the biota-fouling surfaces of offshore oil platforms occur frequently, predictable patterns of change are seldom found. Change is assured by the short life spans of most fouling species. With the possible exception of the barnacle *Balanus tintinnabulum,* fouling species rarely persist for as long as a year. Thus, substrate is frequently relinquished. Colonists generally arrive as planktonic larvae being carried past the structure. The composition of this larval assemblage varies greatly in both time and space. Once established, most colonists have mechanisms for resisting further colonization. Arriving larvae are either physically attacked or simply included in the diets of resident species. This is not always successful, as demonstrated by the multilayered community that develops in the northern Gulf of Mexico. However, it does contribute to the sudden blooms and disappearances of species commonly observed on oil platforms. Whereas this unpredictability often frustrates one's attempts to understand the processes involved in the development of fouling communities, it greatly enhances the pleasure that can be derived from repeated visits to the same artificial reef.

# CHAPTER NINE

# Oyster Reefs

The common eastern oyster, *Crassostrea virginica,* is a sessile bivalve that attaches permanently to almost any firm substrate below mean tide level. It is actually a fouling organism, but its commercial importance spares it that title. It can be found on jetties, pilings, boats, and shells of other mollusks. But it is its affinity for other oysters that makes it ecologically as well as commercially important.

The oyster's planktonic larvae prefer shell to rock, glass, or other hard substrates, although many of them must settle for a second choice. As the young oysters (spat) grow, they cement their shells to those of their neighbors, forming a cluster. If this cluster forms on a site where passing currents bring more oyster larvae and a steady supply of planktonic food, it will continue to develop into a reef. As the oysters die, new larvae settle on their shells, eventually producing a structure that may be several feet thick and miles long.

Oyster reefs are typically elongate structures that are usually perpendicular to the prevailing currents. Exceptions are found among small reefs, or where currents are very strong, or where the bottom topography has a dominant influence. Oysters nearest the current, and thus nearest the incoming food, grow most rapidly and are encountered first by settling larvae. Thus, the reef tends to spread along a leading edge perpendicular to the current.

Oyster reefs are ecologically important as oases of solid substrate in the midst of a vast muddy terrain that is otherwise unsuitable for the survival of many species, such as barnacles and anemones, that require a firm base of attachment. Consequently, the reef fauna is similar to the jetty fauna. Oysters are filter-feeders. Particles are strained from the water current as it passes through the gills. These particles are passed along ciliated grooves to the mouth, where they are sorted by a pair of palps. The desired food is ingested; the rejected particles are wrapped in mucus and discarded as a by-product called pseudofeces. The oyster shell is asymmetrical: the right valve is flatter than the left valve. The left valve not only provides a natural bowl for the raw-oyster fancier, but also helps to keep the lip of the shell above the sediments. *Crassostrea* may change sex several times during its lifetime. This ability is a safeguard against the accidental formation of a cluster of only one sex.

## Reef Inhabitants

Some oyster-reef inhabitants compete with the oysters for food and attachment sites. Prominent among these competitors are the hooked mussel, *Ischadium recurvum*; a small anemone, *Aiptasiomorpha texaensis*; the acorn barnacle; the common Atlantic slipper shell, *Crepidula fornicata*; and the serpulid worm, *Hydroides dianthus* (Figure 9.1).

**FIGURE 9.1.** The oyster community: the common eastern oyster, *Crassostrea virginica*; the hooked mussel, *Ischadium recurvus*; the anemone, *Aiptasiomorpha texaensis*; the stone crab, *Menippe mercenaria*; the barnacle, *Balanus eburneus*; and the serpulid worm, *Hydroides dianthus.* (x1)

The hooked mussel is common on low-salinity reefs, where it attaches by byssal threads. It is a small bivalve (2 to 6 cm long) with pronounced ribs and a sharply hooked beak. The acorn barnacles *(Balanus improvisus, Balanus eburneus,* and *Balanus amphitrite amphitrite)* are common on the high-salinity reefs. *Hydroides* secretes a calcareous tube on the surface of a mollusk shell. Only the head and its crown of filtering tentacles protrude from this tube. When disturbed, *Hydroides* withdraws into the tube and plugs the opening with its operculum.

Oysters are molested by a number of organisms that attack their shells and thus much of the oyster's energy is consumed for repair of the damaged shell. These species include the blister worm, *Polydora websteri;* the boring sponges, *Cliona celata* and *Cliona truitti;* and the oyster piddock, *Diplothyra smythii.* When young *Polydora* settle on an oyster shell, they begin to etch out a shallow groove that is slowly expanded into a deep pit, where the worm lives curled like a horseshoe. The space in the center of the pit is filled with mud and detritus that have been cemented together with mucus. This forms the mud blister often seen on the insides of oyster shells. The worm can be detected in living oysters by the presence of its two long, slender tentacles that wave freely in the water.

The boring sponges, *Cliona* spp., also etch holes in oyster shells. These holes, which are small (less than 2.5 mm in diameter) but numerous, are usually part of an extensive network of tunnels beneath the shell's surface. This network may be expanded until the shell is completely destroyed. The sulfur sponge, *Cliona celata,* prefers habitats where the salinity is higher than 15 parts per thousand at least half of the time and higher than 10 parts per thousand at least three-fourths of the time. It produces relatively large holes (1.5 to 2.5 mm in diameter) from which bright yellow tufts of sponge extend. In addition to oysters, the sulfur sponge is also destructive to coral, gastropod shells, and calcareous rock. It is especially destructive to limestone breakwaters in England. *Cliona truitti* is more euryhaline than *Cliona celata* and is able to withstand habitats where the salinity drops to 10 parts per thousand or less about half the time. It is characterized by smaller holes than those of *Cliona celata.* It also produces gemmules, which are clusters of sponge cells surrounded by a protective shield that is resistant to drying and to extreme temperatures. These gemmules ensure the propaga-

**FIGURE 9.2.** The oyster piddock, *Diplothyra smythhii.* (x5)

tion of the species. Gemmules are typical of freshwater sponges.

The oyster piddock (Figure 9.2) is a boring clam that both bores into the oyster's shell and competes with it for food. Its boring activities weaken the oyster's shell, and it may occasionally break through the shell, requiring the oyster to secrete additional layers of shell over the intruder.

## Oyster Predators

Many of the animals inhabiting oyster reefs are oyster predators, such as the drill, *Stramonita haemastoma,* and the stone crab, *Menippe adina.* *Stramonita* bores a hole through the oyster's shell, usually between the lips where it is weakest, and extends its flexible proboscis through the hole to remove the oyster's flesh. The proboscis may be as long as the snail's shell. It contains the radula, which rasps off bits of oyster tissue, and the mouth and esophagus, which ingest these bits and transport them back to the snail's stomach.

The stone crab has powerful claws with which it chips off successive small fragments of the oyster's shell until it gains entry to the meat. A large stone crab may simply crush the shell of a small oyster. Two other crabs that are common reef inhabitants may be destructive to small oysters. The blue crab, *Callinectes sapidus,* and the common mud crab, *Panopeus simpsoni,* become large enough to chip small oyster shells. *Panopeus* eats barnacles *(Balanus eburneus)* as well as small oysters. The flat mud crab, *Eurypanopeus depressus,* attacks oyster spat, but it is too small (2 cm wide) to be considered a serious threat to larger oysters. Another mud crab found on the oyster reefs, *Rithropanopeus harrisi,* is also too small (1.5 cm wide) to prey on most oysters.

Among the least conspicuous oyster predators are the flatworms, *Stylochus ellipticus* and *Stylochus*

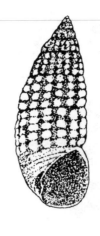

**FIGURE 9.4.** *Bittolium varium.* (x8)

*frontalis,* which are called "oyster leeches" by oystermen. These wafer-thin animals are able to slip between the open valves of an oyster. The oyster may be able to blow the intruder out by rapidly expelling water from its shell, but persistence usually pays off for the flatworm. If it is unable to force the flatworm from its shell, the oyster may try to isolate it by building a wall around it. Unfortunately, the oyster must often leave a breach in this wall if it is to avoid cementing its valves together. The successful flatworm extends its proboscis to ingest the oyster's tissues.

*Stylochus* has numerous eyes, some of which are located on the tentacles and many of which are distributed in a band along the margin of the dorsal surface. In *Stylochus ellipticus* (Figure 9.3), this marginal band of eyes is limited to the anterior third of its body; in *Stylochus frontalis,* the band completely encircles the dorsal surface, although it is wider at the anterior end. *Stylochus ellipticus* grows to a maximum length of about 25 mm; a large *Stylochus frontalis* may be twice that long. The color of the former species is quite variable, ranging from yellow to brown to gray. *Stylochus ellipticus* preys on both oysters and barnacles, while *Stylochus frontalis* eats primarily oysters.

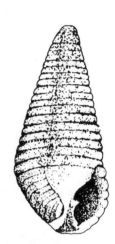

**FIGURE 9.5.** The parasitic snail, *Odostomia impressa.* (x10)

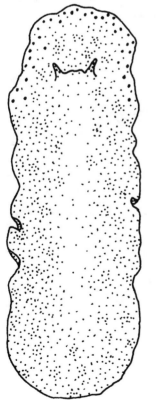

**FIGURE 9.3.** The flatworm, *Stylochus ellipticus.* (x4.3)

## Oysters as Shelter

Two small snails, *Bittiolum varium* (Figure 9.4) and *Odostomia impressa* (Figure 9.5), are commonly found crawling on the oysters. *Bittiolum* is slightly larger and darker than *Odostomia* and has a siphonal notch in the outer lip that *Odostomia* lacks. *Odostomia* is an ectoparasite that sits on the lip of the oyster and extends its proboscis inside to feed on mucus and tissue fluids. *Bittiolum* is apparently not harmful to the oysters. Similarly, the porcelain crab, *Petrolisthes armatus,* apparently uses the oyster reef primarily as shelter.

The sea squirt, *Molgula manhattensis* (Figure 9.6), attaches itself to oysters, pilings, boat bottoms, submerged grass stalks, and occasionally hermit-crab shells. It resembles a small (1 to 2 cm in diameter) gelatinous sphere with two short siphons attached to the upper surface. Seawater is drawn into the sea squirt through an inhalant siphon, passed through a fine mesh that removes the suspended food particles and forces out the water through an exhalant siphon. A stream of water may be expelled several centimeters into the air when the animal is exposed at low

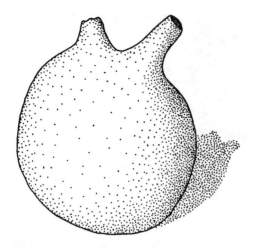

**FIGURE 9.6.** The sea squirt, *Molgula manhattensis*. (x3)

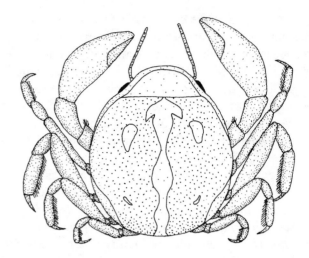

**FIGURE 9.7.** The commensal crab, *Pinnotheres maculatus*. (x4)

tide (or stepped on); hence, the name "sea squirt." *Molgula* is usually pale green or olive, but it may be covered with pieces of detritus or shell. This species is relatively tolerant of water pollution and is one of the few species of sea squirt that tolerates reduced salinities.

The oyster-au-naturel fancier may find a small soft crab nestled up against his delicacy. This is *Pinnotheres ostreum*, the oyster crab. These commensal crabs enter the oysters as larvae and become permanent residents. They usually live among the oyster's gills and steal food that the oyster has strained from the water. A related crab, *Pinnotheres maculatus* (Figure 9.7), is commensal with the pen shells, *Atrina* spp. Its carapace is covered with short brown hairs that are interrupted by a varied pattern of light spots. Although the carapace of *Pinnotheres ostreum* is similar in shape, it lacks the dense covering of hair. Both of these species are also found living commensally with other species of bivalves and with the worm *Chaetopterus variopedatus*.

# CHAPTER TEN

# Shell Habitats

Shells are a very common feature of shallow marine habitats. They provide support and protection from abusive surf, desiccation, and predators. Organisms are more buoyant in seawater than in air and hence require less skeletal support. However, intertidal species are periodically exposed to the air and thus need additional support. These species are also subjected to abrupt changes in pressure caused by waves passing overhead or shifting sand. Thus, snails, barnacles, oysters, clams, and hermit crabs make use of protective shells.

These shells also function as a substrate for dozens of small species that require a firm attachment. These species undoubtedly evolved from rocky-shore species whose planktonic larvae found the shells an acceptable substitute for a rock, but most of them have become specialists in using a shell substrate.

Some of these species, particularly anemones and hydroids, offer the host some protection from potential predators in return for a place to live. Most of them, however, compete with their shelled hosts for food, impede the feeding or burrowing actions of the hosts, or erode the shell so that it is more easily broken.

Shell-inhabiting organisms appear to be most successful at invading shells used by hermit crabs. However, these shells are older than those still possessed by the original owner. Thus, they have had a greater opportunity to encounter settling larvae of encrusting organisms. In addition, hermit-crab shells are often found in habitats where other solid substrates are rare. A planktonic larva that has been carried by currents onto a mudflat rather than onto a jetty may have little choice of substrates. Traveling with a hermit crab has certain advantages—the shell is usually kept free of sediment and is well aerated, and food is generally plentiful. But there are also disadvantages—the shell may be abandoned by the crab, or handled roughly or carried into unfavorable environments, such as up onto the beach.

Some invertebrates have defenses against settling larvae. Filter-feeding organisms, such as barnacles and oysters, simply include these larvae in their diets. Certain snails, such as the moon snail, *Neverita duplicata*, and the lettered olive, *Oliva sayana*, extend the mantle over much of the exterior of their shells and then bury themselves in the sand, probably preventing the settling of larvae. Sea urchins, starfish, and bryozoans have minute claws scattered over their surface that pick off larvae as they settle.

## Shell Inhabitants

The most conspicuous inhabitants of shells along the northwestern Gulf Coast are the hermit crabs, *Clibanarius vittatus*, *Pagurus longicarpus*, *Pagurus pollicaris*, and *Isocheles wurdemanni*; the barnacles, *Balanus improvisus* and *Balanus amphitrite amphitrite*; the white slipper shell, *Crepidula plana*; the encrusting bryozoan, *Membranipora commensale*; the amphipod, *Corophium louisianum*; the tanaid, *Leptochelia dubia*; the serpulid worm, *Hydroides dianthus*; young oyster drills, *Stramonita haemastoma*; the hydroids, *Hydractinia echinata* and *Podocoryne selena*; spat of the oyster, *Crassostrea virginica*; the boring sponges, *Cliona celata* and *Cliona truitti*; the boring polychaete, *Polydora websteri*; and the anemone, *Calliactis tricolor*.

**FIGURE 10.1.** The slipper shell, *Crepidula plana*, dorsal and ventral views. (x1)

## Slipper Shells

Slipper shells can be found on most shells occupied by hermit crabs. Though not permanently attached to its host's shell, this snail stays in one place and its shell conforms to the shape of the host shell as it grows. They are filter-feeders who lift their shells slightly to permit a current of plankton-laden water to flow underneath. Reproduction presents a problem for these sessile creatures, however. The males release their sperm into the water to seek out a mature female. Even with two slipper shells on the same host shell, the chances are 50-50 that they will be the same sex. *Crepidula* improves these odds through protandry, a sex reversal. All of these snails mature first as males, then become females. The male's metamorphosis into a female is retarded if there is another female nearby. The female broods the eggs under her shell until they hatch.

*Crepidula plana* (Figure 10.1) is a white slipper shell usually found inside shells occupied by hermit crabs. Because it must often grow in a curved shape to fit snugly into the shell, it sometimes gives the appearance of being turned inside out. Its shell shape is as variable as the contour of its host. The common Atlantic slipper shell, *Crepidula fornicata*, can sometimes be found on the outer surface of lettered olive *(Oliva sayana)* shells. Its shell is light brown and much deeper than that of *Crepidula plana*.

## Hydroids

Colonies of the hydroids, *Hydractinia echinata* and *Podocoryne selena*, are occasionally found on shells occupied by either species of *Pagurus*. *Clibanarius* are rarely found inhabiting shells covered by these hydroids because it appears to be more sensitive to the stings of the hydroids than is *Pagurus*. Thus, the hydroids provide a refuge for *Pagurus* from the more abundant *Clibanarius*. The hydroid colonies look like white or pink fuzz covering the shell. Each hydroid colony is polymorphic, like those of *Physalia* and *Velella*, consisting of individual zooids that are specialized for different functions: support, defense, feeding, and reproduction. These two hydroids can be distinguished by the nature of their skeletal spines: *Hydractinia*'s are jagged and *Podocoryne*'s are smooth. All of the reproductive zooids in each colony are the same sex. Reproduction is probably aided by interactions among the hermit crabs. Spawning is synchronized to the daily light-dark cycle and usually occurs about one hour after dawn.

The larvae of *Balanus improvisus* and *Balanus amphitrite amphitrite* often find hermit-crab shells a suitable spot to settle, and unfortunately for the crab, the latter species may also settle on its legs or eyestalks. It can also be found attached to other crustaceans, such as the rock shrimp, *Sicyonia dorsalis*. These barnacles grow very rapidly, probably a result of an abundant food supply. Adult barnacles can be found on crabs, indicating that they have grown to maturity since the crab's latest molt, because all of the barnacles on the crab's exoskeleton are shed with each molt. Because young crabs molt more frequently than older crabs, *Balanus amphitrite amphitrite* is more common on large, old crabs that have passed their terminal molt. This barnacle can usually be distinguished from *Balanus improvisus* by the purple marks on its shell.

The shells of dead barnacles and the deep umbilicus of *Neverita* shells are often inhabited by the amphipod, *Corophium louisianum*, or the tanaid, *Leptochelia dubia*. These minute crustaceans construct mud tubes in depressions. *Leptochelia* resembles an isopod, except that its second pair of legs have claws.

## Bryozoans, Sponges, and Scaleworms

Another rapidly growing shell inhabitant is the encrusting bryozoan, *Membranipora commensale* (Figure 10.2). A colony the size of a quarter can develop within a month, forming a delicate mat on the surface of the shell. Each individual zooid is encased in a small, coffinlike shell. Like most other shell-inhabiting species, bryozoans are filter-feeders. They trap food particles in minute tentacles extended through the opening in the top of the shell. Their intricate skeletons persist long after the host shell has dried out.

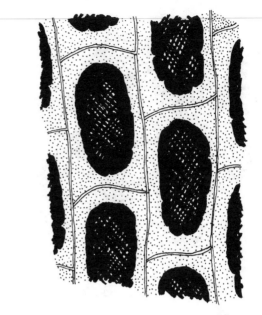

**FIGURE 10.2.** Portion of a colony of the bryozoan *Membranipora commensale*. (x30)

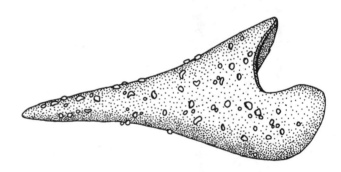

**FIGURE 10.3.** The boring sponge, *Cliona celata*, in an old *Busycon* shell fragment. (x1)

Occasionally, a shell is found that is pierced by dozens of small holes, usually filled with yellow tufts when fresh. These holes were bored by the early growth stage of the sulfur sponge, *Cliona celata*, or its smaller relative, *Cliona truitti* (Figure 10.3). These sponges chemically erode a network of tunnels within the shell, and their later stages completely dissolve the shell. The boring polychaete *Polydora websteri* also burrows into the shell, leaving a network of tunnels that weaken the shell. Unlike *Cliona*, *Polydora* may bore tunnels that are oblique to the surface of the shell so that several millimeters of the tunnel may be exposed. The serpulid worm, *Hydroides dianthus* (Figure 10.4), also dwells in tunnels, but it constructs its own calcareous tubes on the surface of the shell. The fanlike radioles of this worm may be extended from the tube if the shell is placed in a small dish of seawater and watched quietly for a short while.

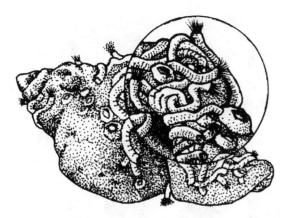

**FIGURE 10.4.** The serpulid worm, *Hydroides dianthus.* (x1)

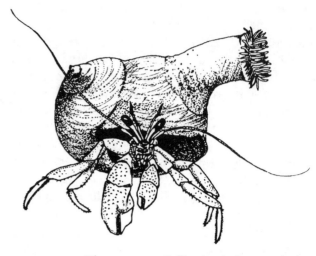

**FIGURE 10.6.** The anemone, *Calliactis tricolor,* attached to a *Neverita* shell inhabited by the hermit crab, *Pagurus pollicaris.* (x1)

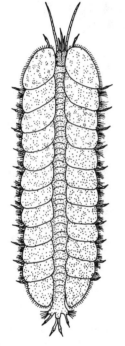

**FIGURE 10.5.** The scaleworm, *Lepidonotus sublevis.* (x2)

The scaleworm, *Lepidonotus sublevis* (Figure 10.5), is a common inhabitant of hermit-crab shells. Unlike *Polydora* and *Hydroides,* this polychaete does not construct a burrow but crawls about freely within the shell. When the hermit crab inhabits the shell of *Neverita duplicata,* the scaleworm is often found in the shell's umbilicus. It is easily recognized by the twelve pairs of large overlapping scales, or elytra, that cover its back. These scales are mounted on short pedicels, from which they readily break when handled. *Lepidonotus* probably lives on bits of food stolen from its host. This commensal worm is also found on sea pansies and starfish.

## Anemones and Flatworms

Occasionally, especially during the winter months, a hermit crab will be found with an anemone on its shell. This anemone is usually *Calliactis tricolor* (Figure 10.6), although the warty sea anemone, *Bunodosoma cavernata,* will also attach to shells if a better substrate is unavailable. *Calliactis* can readily be distinguished from *Bunodosoma* because it lacks the hundreds of minute bumps that cover the surface of *Bunodosoma.* Like its hermit-crab host, *Calliactis* has no lasting attachment for any particular shell and will readily abandon it if a more appealing surface comes along. Alhough this anemone is usually associated with hermit crabs of the family Paguridae, it is also found on the shells of live snails and on the carapaces of other crabs, such as the decorator crab (*Stenocianops furcata*) in Florida. *Calliactis* may also be found on other smooth surfaces, such as pieces of fiberglass or plastic, that are cast up on the beach.

*Calliactis* and its hermit-crab host seem to cooperate to move the anemone onto the crab's shell. The crab may tap at the base of the anemone with its claws, causing the anemone to loosen its grip on its current substrate. Then the crab may pick the anemone up in its claw and hold it against its own shell until the anemone attaches.

**FIGURE 10.7.** The flatworm, *Stylochus zebra.* (x5)

The flatworm *Stylochus zebra* (Figure 10.7) is another species that can sometimes be found in *Pagurus*-inhabited shells during the winter. It seems to prefer *Pagurus pollicaris* to *Pagurus longicarpus* as a host. This flatworm reaches a length of 3 to 4 cm and is flesh colored with conspicuous brown "zebra" stripes. It is apparently a cold-loving species and is more common along the New England coast, where it may be found on pilings as well as in shells.

# CHAPTER ELEVEN

# Plankton and Nekton

Nearly all of the marine invertebrates that have been discussed depend wholly or partially on plankton. Most planktonic organisms are microscopic, but a few are surprisingly large. The one characteristic they all share is an inability to swim faster than one knot. Thus, they are at the mercy of even moderate currents.

The planktonic fauna of the Texas bays is highly seasonal. Many of the species are sensitive to relatively minor changes in temperature, salinity, oxygen level, or toxin in the water. The species composition may change markedly during a heavy rain or drought. Moreover, the larvae of most marine animals are planktonic, and these are usually seasonal in their appearance. Such organisms, which spend only a portion of their life cycles in the plankton, are collectively called meroplankton; those that are planktonic during their entire lives are called holoplankton.

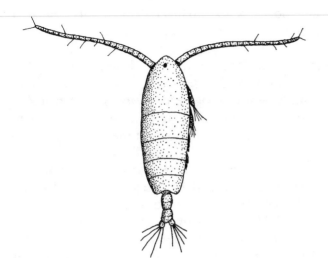

**FIGURE 11.1.** The copepod, *Acartia tonsa.* (x55)

**FIGURE 11.2.** The chaetognath, *Sagitta tenuis.* (x8.5)

The most frequently encountered forms of holo-plankton in the bays are copepods, medusae, ctenophores, chaetognaths, mysids, and sergestid shrimp.

Perhaps the most common holoplanktonic species are the copepods of the genus *Acartia. Acartia tonsa* (Figure 11.1) is the best known of these copepods. It is a small, short-lived filter-feeder. During the summer, when the water is warmest, it completes its life cycle in less than two weeks. Its swimming motion is very jerky—it flits through the water propelled by its long antennules. It is a euryhaline species, i.e., it can tolerate a wide range of salinities. It is found in habitats ranging from the lower ends of the bayous to the hypersaline lagoons of the southern Texas coast.

The chaetognath, *Sagitta tenuis* (Figure 11.2), is a copepod predator that is sporadically abundant. This chaetognath, or "arrow-worm," as it is sometimes called, uses its long fins to glide through the water. Its large hooks flanking the mouth are used to capture copepods and other small crustaceans. Its size permits it to subdue even small fish larvae.

Among the most exotic animals in the Gulf are the sergestid shrimps *Lucifer faxoni* (Figure 11.3) and *Acetes americanus louisianensis.* These small shrimps have their eyes mounted on long stalks—the ultimate in peripheral vision. Like many other plankters, their presence is sporadic. *Acetes* is an estuarine species that is most abundant in low-salinity bays. *Lucifer* is an oceanic species that moves into the bays during the summer. *Acetes* has minute claws on the last three pairs of legs on the first body section;

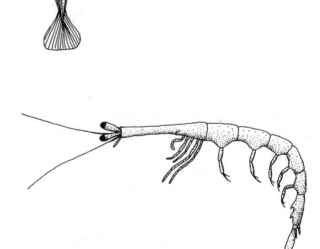

**FIGURE 11.3.** The sergestid shrimp, *Lucifer faxoni.* (x4.7)

*Lucifer* has only a rudimentary claw on the last pair of these legs.

## Sea Nettles, Sea Wasps, and Sea Walnuts

Medusae, or typical "jellyfish," are usually shaped like a bell or saucer, with tentacles and/or oral arms trailing behind them. They propel themselves through the water with pulsating contractions of the bell, which function much like the kick of a swimmer doing the breaststroke. The slender tentacles usually extend from the rim of the bell. The oral arms, which are typically longer and broader than the tentacles, are attached near the mouth under the bell. Both the oral arms and the tentacles contain nematocysts, with which the medusa immobilizes its prey. The margin of the bell is the site of the compound sensory structures, the rhopalia, that control the orientation and beat of the medusa. These structures are spaced in multiples of four at regular intervals around the bell. The medusa is only one stage in the life of these animals; in many species it alternates with a sessile stage called a polyp, which resembles a small sea anemone. The polyp, which is called a scyphistoma, produces larvae through a budding process called strobilization. These larvae, the ephyrae, develop into the medusae. Each medusa produces either sperm or eggs and sheds them into the seawater. After fertilization in the water, the zygote develops into another larva called a planula, which settles to the bottom and develops into a polyp. Thus the cycle is completed.

The most conspicuous medusa in the Gulf coastal waters is the cabbagehead, *Stomolophus meleagris* (Figure 11.4). This large oceanic medusa comes into the bays during the summer and frequently washes ashore in large numbers. These carcasses provide food for numerous shore dwellers, such as the stone crab, *Menippe adina*, and the ghost crab, *Ocypode quadrata*. *Stomolophus* is a harmless filter-feeder whose nematocysts

are too weak to endanger man. It eats primarily copepods and the larvae of crabs and shrimp. Other animals, such as the spider crab, *Libinia dubia*, and the harvestfish, *Peprilus alepidotus*, hitch a ride or gain sanctuary in the bell. *Stomolophus* is easily recognized by its lack of tentacles and its short oral arms that are fused into a tight bundle. It is a favored food of the leatherback turtle in some locales.

Another jellyfish, somewhat less common than the cabbagehead, is the moon jellyfish, *Aurelia aurita* (Figure 11.5). This medusa is also a plankton-feeder. Although it may have a diameter that exceeds that of *Stomolophus*, it is much less bulky. *Aurelia* can be recognized by its shallow bell that is fringed with numerous very short tentacles and its four short, unfused oral arms. The four lobes of its stomach are often visible through the bell. Small spider crabs are sometimes found on *Aurelia* and may burrow into the bell and feed on the tissues. These crabs probably crawl onto the bell when *Aurelia* brushes against the bottom or against submerged vegetation. Very large swarms of *Aurelia* are often observed offshore in midsummer or late autumn.

The sea nettle, *Chrysaora quinquecirrha* (Figure 11.6), occurs sporadically in the Gulf coastal waters. Its bell is about the same size as that of *Aurelia*, but it has fewer (24 to 40) and longer tentacles and longer oral arms. It is usually pale yellow or pink and sometimes has radiating stripes on the bell. *Chrysaora* spends the summer and early fall as a medusa and the winter and spring as a polyp. The colorless or pale pink polyps are often found attached to the undersides of oyster shells. The young medusae are produced in late spring or early surnmer and grow rapidly on a diet that consists primarily of the ctenophore, *Mnemiopsis mccradyi*. They, in turn, are eaten by adult spade-

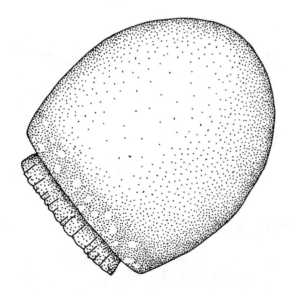

**FIGURE 11.4.** The cabbagehead medusa, *Stomolophus meleagris*. (x0.3)

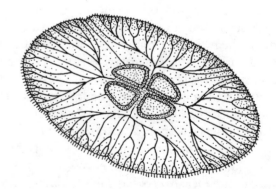

**FIGURE 11.5.** The moon jellyfish, *Aurelia aurita*. (x0.3)

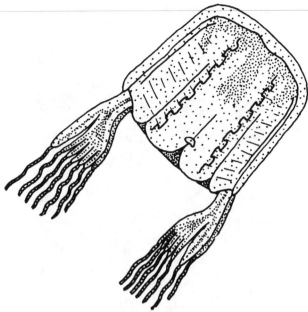

**FIGURE 11.7.** The sea wasp, *Chiropsalmus quadrumanus.* (x0.5)

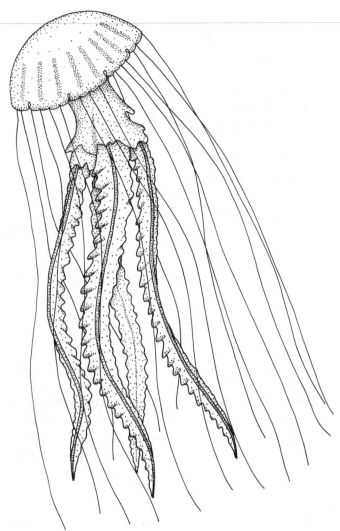

**FIGURE 11.6.** The sea nettle, *Chrysaora quinquecirrha.* (x0.3)

fish, *Chaetodipterus faber.* As is the case with other medusae, *Chrysaora* is often found with spider crabs or young blue crabs riding on its bell. As its name suggests, the sea nettle's nematocysts can deliver painful stings; thus, contact with this medusa should be avoided. Sea-nettle stings are commonly experienced by divers taking advantage of warm summer temperatures by diving without wetsuits near offshore oil platforms. Individual reactions vary, but the pain generally persists as an irritating itching sensation for 15 minutes to several hours. The pain from nematocyst stings can often be relieved by applying meat tenderizer to the moistened wound.

The sea wasp, *Chiropsalmus quadrumanus* (Figure 11.7), is another medusa with a painful sting. *Chiropsalmus* prefers water with a high salinity;

hence, it is not common in northwestern Gulf Coast bays. However, during periods of prolonged drought, it may be found in large numbers. It prefers to stay near the bottom and so is most often observed in shrimp trawls. Its diet seems to consist mainly of sergestid shrimp, shrimp larvae, and crab larvae. *Chiropsalmus* is a cubomedusa, suggesting that the bell is somewhat cube shaped. It has four clusters of filamentous tentacles, each of which is attached to a single base located at one of the corners of the bell.

The lion's mane jellyfish, *Cyanea capillata versicolor* (Figure 11.8), is occasionally encountered during the winter months. In the Gulf of Mexico, this species is about the same size as *Aurelia* but may reach a diameter of more than 2 meters in the Arctic Ocean. It has eight clusters of tentacles around the underside of the bell. The number of tentacles in each cluster increases as the medusa grows older. Like the sea nettle, *Cyanea* eats primarily ctenophores. The gulf butterfish, *Peprilus burti,* has been observed eating *Cyanea.*

The hydromedusa, *Nemopsis bachei* (Figure 11.9), is a small, transparent jellyfish often abundant in the bays in winter and spring. It is only about 1 cm in diameter and is thus easily overlooked. *Nemopsis* is more bell shaped than most local common medusae, except perhaps the cabbagehead, *Stomolophus.* Its

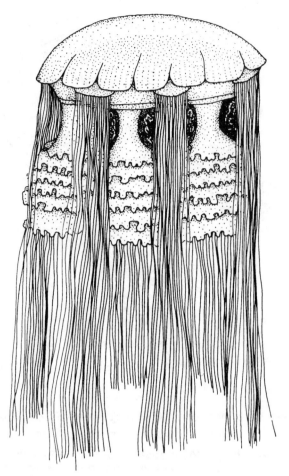

**FIGURE 11.8.** The lion's mane jellyfish, *Cyanea capillata versicolor*. (x0.3)

four radial canals are clearly visible, extending from its central digestive cavity to clusters of 16 to 18 tentacles on the edge of the bell. A cluster of oral tentacles can be seen inside the bell suspended from the junction of the radial canals. The radial canals usually seem swollen near their junction due to the gonads, which extend about two-thirds of the length of these canals. The larvae produced by these medusae develop into sessile hydroids which, in turn, produce the next generation of medusae.

Ctenophores are similar to medusae in that they are jellylike in appearance and are plankton-feeders. They differ in that they lack the nematocysts that characterize the medusae. They are seasonal in their abundance, being most common in the summer in low-salinity bays. They may be very abundant at one end of a bay and almost absent at the other end. The most common species on the northwestern Gulf Coast is the phosphorus jelly, *Mnemiopsis mccradyi* (Figure 11.10). It is a fairly large animal but is often overlooked because of its transparency. It is easily recognized by the two lobes that make up most of its bulk. Between these lobes are two retractable tentacles used in capturing prey. Like other ctenophores, *Mnemiopsis* has eight rows of cilia used to propel it through the water. Hence, it is a very slow swimmer. The cilia are coordinated by an aboral sense organ that responds primarily to gravity. *Mnemiopsis* is a voracious predator on zooplankton. A single ctenophore may eat as many as 500 *Acartia* per hour. Unfortunately, *Mnemiopsis* also eats shrimp, crab, and oyster larvae, and on several occasions it has been accused of seriously reducing the crop of

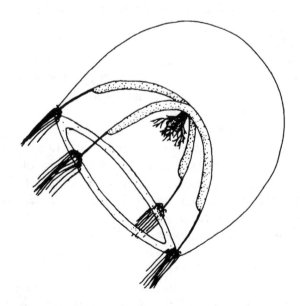

**FIGURE 11.9.** The hydromedusa, *Nemopsis bachei*. (x6)

**FIGURE 11.10.** The phosphorus jelly, *Mnemiopsis mccradyi*. (x1)

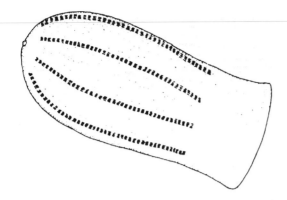

**FIGURE 11.11.** The sea walnut, *Beroë ovata.* (x1)

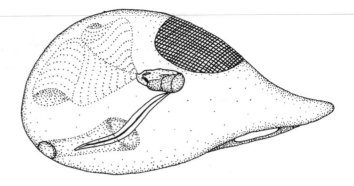

**FIGURE 11.13.** The larvacean, *Oikopleura* sp., in its gelatinous house. Note the filtering screens, the food-gathering net, and the escape hatch in the bottom of the house. (x18)

oyster larvae. It is not, however, without voracious enemies of its own, including the medusae, *Chrysaora* and *Cyanea,* and the gulf butterfish.

Another ctenophore that can often be found in the bays is the sea walnut, *Beroë ovata* (Figure 11.11). It is about the same size as *Mnemiopsis* but is somewhat more flattened and lacks lobes and tentacles.

Ctenophores are luminescent organisms; light is produced in the walls of canals under the rows of cilia. Thus, they seem to glow faintly in the dark, especially if disturbed. *Beroë* is usually the more common ctenophore during the winter, and *Mnemiopsis* is the more common species during the summer.

Mysids are small, shrimplike crustaceans that swim just above the bottom in the bays and along the sandy beaches. *Mysidopsis almyra* (Figure 11.12) is one of the more common species of this area. Unlike the true shrimps, it has a beadlike equilibrium organ called a statocyst on each side of the tail fan, and its abdominal appendages or pleopods are much reduced. It uses its legs to stir up the water and to fil-

ter out any small plants, animals, or detritus that pass by.

The larvacean *Oikopleura* spp. is certainly one of the most interesting planktonic organisms (Figure 11.13). It is quite small (3 to 4 mm long) but unmistakable in form. Its body consists of a kidney-shaped head that is perpendicularly attached to a long tail. Even more remarkable than the animal itself is the "house" that it constructs as a feeding aid. This house is equipped with two screens, which admit only very small food particles, and a finer mesh inside that collects these particles. The beating of *Oikopleura*'s tail forces water through the house, at which time the food is removed. Eventually the screens become clogged with particles too large to pass through, and the house is abandoned and a new one is built. Nearly all species of *Oikopleura* are protandric, maturing as males first and then as females. Larvaceans resemble the larvae of sea squirts, to which they are related. Hence, the name "larvacean." The different species of *Oikopleura* are not easily distinguishable without the aid of a high-resolution microscope.

## Nekton

A few invertebrates that live in Gulf bay waters are able to swim faster than one knot. Therefore, they cannot be considered plankton. These animals are included with the fishes as nekton. The most conspicuous nektonic invertebrates are the squids. Two species are commonly found here: *Loligo pealei* (Figure 11.14) and *Lolliguncula brevis.* The latter species is smaller, reaching a maximum length of 23 cm, and has rounded fins. *Loligo*

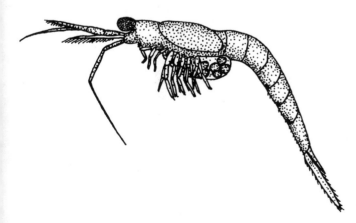

**FIGURE 11.12.** The mysid shrimp, *Mysidopsis almyra.* (x8)

**FIGURE 11.14.** The squid, *Loligo pealei.* (x1)

*pealei* is longer (to one meter) and more slender and has triangular fins. *Lolliguncula* is readily distinguished by its relatively large fins, which are 70 to 80 percent as wide as the mantle is long, compared to those of *Loligo*, which are only 45 to 55 percent as wide as the mantle length. *Loligo* is usually an offshore species, whereas *Lolliguncula* is more common in the bays. Both squids are widely distributed along the Atlantic coast of North and South America. *Loligo* is found from Nova Scotia to Venezuela and *Lolliguncula* from Chesapeake Bay to Brazil.

Squids have highly developed vision, which they put to good use in locating their prey. Locomotion is accomplished by a form of "jet" propulsion. A large, water-filled cavity inside the squid is connected to the outside through a stubby siphon located under the squid's head. As the water is squeezed out of the cavity through the narrow opening in the siphon by the contracting of the squid's body wall, it produces a rapid jet of water that pushes the squid in the opposite direction. Because the cavity must be refilled periodically, the squid usually moves in short spurts. In contrast to the octopus, which has eight arms, squids have ten arms that they use for the capture of small fish and crustaceans. Two of the arms of the male squid are modified as copulatory structures. They pass small packets of sperm, called spermatophores, to the female and implant them in her mantle cavity. The squid's body is covered with chromatophores containing melanin, which enable the squid to change its color. This pigment can also be secreted into the water from the "ink" gland, concealing the squid's retreat.

# CHAPTER TWELVE

# Sea Turtles

Five species of sea turtles are known in the Gulf of Mexico. They are the loggerhead, *Caretta caretta*; green turtle, *Chelonia mydas*; Kemp's ridley turtle, *Lepidochelys kempi*; hawksbill, *Eretmochelys imbricata*; and leatherback, *Dermochelys coriacea*. The first four species belong to the family Chelonidae, while the leatherback, which lacks the hardened carapace of other species, is the sole member of the family Dermochelidae. Each of these species is distributed worldwide with the exception of Kemp's ridley, which is confined to the Gulf of Mexico and the northern Atlantic.

Altogether, there are seven species of sea turtles in the world; the others are the flatback turtle, *Chelonia depressa*, found only in Australian waters, and the Olive ridley turtle, *Lepidochelys olivacea*, which is found in the Pacific, the Indian Ocean, and the South Atlantic, but only rarely in the Caribbean.

Turtle experts vary in their opinions about the status of another form that is closely related to the green turtle. This is the black turtle, *Chelonia m. agassizi*, which occurs in the eastern and central Pacific.

Presently, the loggerhead is the most common species in the Gulf region. Under the U.S. Endangered Species Act of 1983, its status throughout the world is classified as "threatened," while the Kemp's ridley, the leatherback, and the hawksbill throughout the world are each classified as "endangered" species. The green turtle is listed as "threatened" throughout its range with the exception of the breeding-colony populations of the Florida coast and Pacific coast of Mexico, which are classified as "endangered." The classification of "endangered" indicates a species currently in danger of extinction; that of "threatened" indicates a species likely to become endangered in the near future. Thus, at the outset of this discussion of these unique and ancient animals, it must be noted that laws promulgated under the Endangered Species Act, along with international agreements and many state laws, prohibit the unauthorized taking or harassment of sea turtles, dead or alive, the taking of their eggs, or the disturbance of their nests.

In the last decade, research on sea turtles has burgeoned. More and more of the lifestyles of these enigmatic creatures is being understood with the advent of techniques that permit the genetic relationships among turtles in distant locales to be unraveled and migration patterns to be revealed. There have been more concentrated research efforts on the best conservation measures and continued accumulation of information through careful ecological studies. While annual censuses of nesting turtles have served as indicators of population status, the results of long-term, more detailed studies that track individuals in colonies indicate increased opportunities to assess population trends. Analysis of stranded sea-turtle remains has improved understanding of diet, exposure to parasites, pathogens and environmental contaminants, migration and habitat-usage patterns, and mortality associated with fishing and other human water-related activities. But there are still significant knowledge gaps that are understandable with such long-lived creatures that spend 99 percent of their life in the sea. The physiology and pathology of sea turtles remain research areas critical to evaluating the effects of both natural and anthropogenic factors on survival. Because sea turtles grow slowly as they mature, the estimation of size at maturity from growth models remains problematic. In many cases, a probabilistic function relating age to size is the best description.

The five species of sea turtles that occur in U.S. waters vary in their ecology and life-history characteristics. While female sea turtles of all species have been recorded to nest on Gulf shores, only the loggerhead and green turtles nest in significant numbers, and mostly on Florida's east coast. The Florida rookeries are important globally for the loggerhead, but the largest nesting population of green turtles in the western central Atlantic is at Tortuguero, Costa Rica, protected within the Tortuguero Conservation Area since the 1950s. Kemp's ridley nesting is being reestablished in Texas through conservation programs; however, its primary nesting area is near Rancho Nuevo in Tamaulipas, Mexico, which is also protected. In the western Atlantic, the hawksbill and leatherback primarily nest at sites in the Caribbean, with isolated nesting on Florida beaches. Nesting sites and feeding areas are separate in adults, remarkedly so in green turtles and leatherbacks, for whom the greatest adult migrations have been recorded. Feeding areas also differ between adults and subadults and juveniles for whom the term "developmental habitat" is often used.

Turtle eggs incubate in unguarded nests excavated on beaches. The young turtles hatch at night, scramble from the nest site to the water, and swim away. Loggerheads, green turtles, and Kemp's ridley young enter a pelagic phase, which lasts a few or many years, depending on the species. Loggerheads and green turtles hatched on Florida beaches enter the North Atlantic gyre, which circulates across the Atlantic to the Azores, southward to the Cape Verde Islands off Africa and then westward to the Caribbean. Kemp's ridley young from Rancho Nuevo are transported northward in the Mexican Current into the eddying currents of the Gulf of Mexico, where some are swept into the Loop Current, then into the Florida Current and up the Atlantic Seaboard. Some of these Kemp's ridleys enter the Atlantic gyre. As juveniles, loggerheads, greens, and Kemp's ridleys leave the pelagic realm, and take up life in benthic habitats along the Gulf Coast or along the U. S. Eastern Seaboard. Immature Kemp's ridleys, loggerheads, and green turtles frequent New York waters around Long Island in the summer and migrate south when temperatures fall in

October. Chesapeake Bay is another summer feeding ground for loggerheads and Kemp's ridleys. Leatherbacks spend their entire life at sea. Where the young spend the first four years of their life is still a mystery, although large juveniles occur along the U.S. East Coast. Adult and subadult leatherbacks occur in waters offshore of New York in the summer and are common visitors to New England waters. Hawksbills have the shortest (in some areas a nonexistent) pelagic phase and are associated with *Sargassum* rafts in the Caribbean; they are the most tropical species, and juvenile hawksbills are found in the same Caribbean feeding areas as adults where there is a range of depth around reefs. Hawksbills are the rarest visitors to Gulf shores and are seen mostly along the southeast Atlantic coast and Texas coastal bend.

Man's impact on each of these species arises from different activities and varies geographically. Loggerheads appear at greatest risk from drowning or injury by shrimp trawling and destruction of nesting areas by beach development. While much commercial exploitation of green turtles for eggs and meat has ended, indigenous harvesting for subsistence poses a real threat to the viability of nesting colonies along with poaching. The commercial ranching of hawksbills to meet the demand for tortoiseshell may mitigate impacts on some wild populations and help to conserve them. Finally, Kemp's ridley, the rarest sea turtle, while suffering in the past from egg harvesting and adult slaughter on nesting beaches, now appears at risk mostly from shrimp trawling in the Gulf of Mexico.

Concern for the fate of sea turtles in U.S. waters expressed in the Endangered Species Act Amendments of 1988 mandated the establishment of the Committee on Sea Turtle Conservation by the National Academy of Sciences. This committee, which convened in 1989, was charged with reviewing the available data and recommending conservation measures. Because of the very high natural mortality rates suffered by hatchlings, the committee concluded that reducing the death rates of juveniles and older turtles was central to conservation efforts. Further, they determined that the greatest cause of human-induced mortality of juveniles, subadults, and adults in U.S. waters was due to incidental capture by fishing gear, primarily shrimp trawls. Other sources of mortality identified were dredging, collisions with boats, removal of oil rigs by blasting, and ingestion of plastics and debris, with the latter being of particular concern.

Recognition of the effects of shrimp trawling on turtles as early as 1978 led to the development of as many as six types of Turtle Excluder Devices, or TEDs, by the end of 1989 under sponsorship of the U.S. National Marine Fisheries Service. However, objections to the use of TEDs by the shrimp fisheries throughout this period remained strong due to perceptions of reduced fishing efficiency. Therefore, the establishment of requirements for the use of TEDs was challenged by the shrimp fisheries. The conclusions of the Sea Turtle Conservation Committee supported enactment of provisions of the 1988 amendments requiring the use of TEDs beginning in 1989 in offshore waters and in 1990 in inshore waters. Towing time restrictions, in lieu of the use of TEDs, were applied to small trawlers operating in inshore waters. The effectiveness of TED designs, regulations regarding their usage, and the relative impact of U.S. shrimp trawling on turtle populations is a continuing controversy. Protection for sea turtles at risk from shrimp-fishing operations in other countries that export shrimp to the United States has also been mandated by the U.S. government, which includes use of TEDs as a protection measure. Nations that do not meet U.S. protection levels, as reflected in verifiable turtle by-catch and mortality rates, face an embargo on importation of their shrimp products into the United States.

The relationship between turtle strandings and the shrimp-fishing effort has been used as a measure of the impact of trawling on turtles and as an indicator of the effectiveness of TED regulations in reducing turtle mortalities along the U.S Atlantic and Gulf coasts. Decreases in strandings have been observed in relation to fishing moratoria and increases in strandings to fishing onsets. While declines in turtle strandings as a function of fishing effort expended during pre-TED years compared to TED-required years have not been clear in data analyzed for the Texas coast offshore shrimp fishery up to 1993, below-average strandings during TED-use periods by shrimp trawlers in Georgia waters during this time period have been demonstrated. These findings illustrate the complexity of unraveling specifics of the shrimp trawl-turtle mortality relationship. For example, while turtles can survive submergence in trawls for thirty minutes, the probability of survival declines with increased trawling times. Also, while turtles may be released from trawls apparently unharmed, repeated capture of individuals may ultimately inflict injury or death. The intensity of fishing in an area, shrimp abundance, and changing abundances of turtle populations in areas are additional complicating factors.

Recent studies have suggested that the use of TEDs has reduced the mortality of turtles in the Gulf of Mexico by 84 percent in offshore waters and by 27 percent in inshore waters. While the percent of turtles killed after capture has not changed much with the use of TEDs, the action of TEDs to prevent capture has been of primary importance in conservation efforts.

Other fisheries also inflict mortality on turtle populuations. The summer flounder *(Paralichthys dentatus)* trawl fishery that operates in the winter in the coastal waters of North Carolina catches turtles incidentally. Catch rates are related to the turtles' migratory habits along the Eastern Seaboard—moving north to summer feeding grounds and south in the fall, seeking warm waters in which to overwinter. These captures are mostly of loggerheads and Kemp's ridleys, along with a few green turtles and hawksbills. Regular, annual fall and winter turtle strandings in southern Virginia and near Cape Hatteras, North Carolina, have been related to the onset of this fishery. Sea turtles, mostly loggerheads and leatherbacks, are commonly entangled or hooked by the U.S. swordfish longline fishery operating off the Eastern Seaboard in the northwestern Atlantic. Estimates for the 1990s suggest that as many as 2,000 sea turtles annually may be captured, though luckily most are released alive.

Recognition of the impact of channel dredging by hopper dredges has led to agreements between the U.S. National Marine Fisheries Service and the U.S. Army Corps of Engineers to limit dredge operations to periods when turtles are not abundant. The extent of dredging impacts on sea turtles can be appreciated considering the many miles of intracoastal waterways and the some 45 ship channels along the Atlantic and Gulf coasts that must be maintained by dredging. Jetties and channel entrances are used by juvenile and subadult Kemp's ridleys along the upper Texas coast and the Louisiana coast, while green turtles occur in these areas along the lower Texas coast. Along the Atlantic Seaboard, loggerheads and green turtles are most at risk to dredging operations. Research aimed at finding ways to reduce this souce of mortality include studies of turtle feeding and overwintering habits.

The ingestion of or entanglement in marine debris by sea turtles remains a recognized threat to their survival, although scientists have not been able to assess its relative importance in recovery and management plans mandated by the Endangered Species Act. Scientists now think that the convergence patterns of ocean currents that create "fronts," rips, and driftlines, resulting in accumulations of biota, are important to the survival of young and old turtles. However, these processes also concentrate nondegradable debris from human activities—plastic beads, bags, bottles, buckets, cups, fishing lines, sheeting, and packing material-as well as tar balls that turtles ingest, probably to their detriment.

Recent studies indicate that several tons of plastic litter enter the world oceans every year, most of which is derived from merchant shipping. In recent years, the concentration of plastic pellets alone has been estimated at 3,500 per kilometer in the Sargasso Sea, while that along the United States from Cape Cod to Cape Canaveral, considered an area of high concentration, was 8,318 pellets per kilometer. The International Convention for the Prevention of Pollution from Ships of 1973, amended by The Protocol 1978 (MARPOL), consists of five annexes. That pertaining to oil pollution came into force in October 1983, while that pertaining to dumping of garbage by ships became active in December 1988. However, gains are still to be made in adherence and enforcement, and existing debris may persist for some time in the marine enviroment.

The Sea Turtle Stranding and Salvage Network (STSSN) database maintained by the National Marine Fisheries Service has proved useful to research on the question of the impact of marine debris on turtles. This database was begun in 1980. Data analyzed from 1980 through 1992, on 22,547 turtles found stranded on the U.S. Atlantic and Gulf of Mexico coasts, Puerto Rico and U.S. Virgin Islands, revealed that 12 percent of necropsied turtles had ingested plastic, ballons, fishing hooks or monofilament line. Most of the turtles that ingested plastic or ballons were loggerheads, primarily in the Gulf of Mexico. Most of the turtles that ingested fishing hooks or monofilament line occurred in the southeastern Atlantic and were loggerheads and green turtles. Most of the turtles entangled in fishing traplines or rope were leatherbacks, while most turtles entangled in nonfishing-gear debris were hawksbills.

## Loggerhead Turtles, *Caretta caretta*

The loggerhead receives its common name from the relatively large size of its head in comparison to its body (Figure 12.1). Dorsally, it is reddish-brown in color; its underside is yellow, with tinges of its dorsal coloration. As noted above, this is the most common species of sea turtle in U.S. waters. Although the flesh of loggerheads was not much esteemed here, gathering eggs for bakery products was once a thriving industry at St. Augustine, Florida. Loggerheads are favored food in locales of the Mediterrean, Africa, and South America.

Adults average 90 cm in carapace length and 135 kg in weight, although very large individuals weighing more than twice that have been recorded. The age of loggerheads at sexual maturity, estimated from mark-release-recapture studies and from skeletochronology measures, range from 12 to 30 years, although most indicate 20 to 24 years. The upper age limit is thought to be more correct, because the age of maturity of loggerheads in Australia has been estimated to be greater than 30 years. Size at maturity corresponding to these estimates is 74 to 92 cm in carapace length. The size of subadults commonly accepted is 20 to 60 cm in carapace length.

**FIGURE 12.1.** The loggerhead turtle, *Caretta caretta*, mature female. Note large size of head in relation to body. (x0.10)

In contrast to the other species of sea turtles, the loggerhead nests primarily in subtropical waters. In U.S. waters, nesting has been recorded from Virginia to Texas, although most occurs on the Atlantic shores of the southeastern United States. Loggerhead turtles also nest on beaches in southern Brazil, South Africa, Japan, and in the temperate region of Australia. The timing of nesting varies geographically, extending from May through August in Florida, and from November to January at Tongaland, South Africa.

Four loggerhead nesting subpopulations have recently been identified in the western North Atlantic based on analysis of mitochondrial DNA, which is maternally inherited. These are the Northern Nesting Subpopulation (ranging from North Carolina to northeastern Florida at about 29° north latitude), the South Florida Nesting Subpopulation (extending from 29° north latitude in northeastern Florida to Sarasota on Florida's west coast), the Florida Panhandle Nesting Subpopulation (at Elgin Air Force Base and on beaches near Panama City), and the Yucatán Nesting Subpopulation (along the eastern shore of the Yucatán Peninsula, in Quintana Roo). Researchers attribute the broader geographic affiliation of nesting females in the Northern Nesting Subpopulation to more recent colonization of this warm temperate zone, made possible after the retreat of the glaciers, and not to present gene flow among rookeries. While analysis of DNA inherited from both parents is necessary to identify truly separate stocks, the distinctness of the females nesting at these sites is significant to conservation efforts.

Regular surveys of beaches within these areas in recent years (1989–1995) indicate that the South Florida Nesting Subpopulation, with an average of 64,000 nests per year, is the largest loggerhead nesting group in the Atlantic and the second largest in the world. A decade ago, around 20,000 nests per year were recorded in this area. The Northern Nesting Subpopulation amounts to about 6,200 nests per year. Around 450 nests per year occur in the Florida Panhandle region and 1,500 to 2,300 in the Yucatán. Altogether, these subpopulations account for about 40 percent of the worldwide nesting activity of loggerheads.

Loggerhead females that nest along the southeastern United States range from 70 to 115 cm in carapace length, averaging around 95 cm. Nesting females come ashore at night, preferring beaches with background vegetation, no artificial lighting, and little human activity. On steep beaches, such as those south of Daytona, Florida, females crawl up the beach 50 to 75 m to nest. Farther north, on more gently sloping beaches, the females make longer crawls to reach suitable nesting sites. In South Carolina, females may crawl farther than 150 m, and in some places, due to coastal erosion thinning the sand to only 25 cm or so over ancient marsh remains, females are forced to excavate more than one location before actually nesting. Individual females nest every two weeks on the average within a season, usually within 4 to 6 km of previous locations. However, disturbances on nesting beaches have caused some females to go as far as 22 km along shore before re-nesting. Such travel distances are often preceded by so-called "false crawls," where the female returns to the water without nesting because she is disturbed or fails to find suitable nesting habitat. On Hutchison Island, Florida, false crawls may equal 40 percent or more of the number of successful nesting crawls. Typically, individual females return to breed every two to three years, although the return rate is not high.

Usually 110 to 125 eggs are laid per nest, although the number can vary slightly with locality. In addition, the size of the clutch deposited by a female in her last nest may be 10 to 20 eggs fewer than the initial clutch, according to observations made on Georgia beaches. The average size of the eggs is almost 40 mm in diameter; the mean length of hatchlings is 45 mm in carapace length (Figure 12.2). The sex of hatchlings is not genetically determined but is a function of incubation temperature. This phenomenon, considered surprising in a vertebrate, was discovered in freshwater turtles in the early 1970s and investigated in sea turtles a few years later. It is characteristic of all sea-turtle species. The critical incubation temperature occurs during the middle third of the development period. In loggerhead embryos, the threshold is between 29°C and 30°C. At 28°C, all hatchlings are male; at 30°C, females predominate by about 10 percent; at 32°C, all hatchlings are females. The molecular mechanism is not known, but some investigators feel it's likely that an enzyme or hormone that is temperature-sensitive controls the expression of sex-specific DNA sequences. However, not all outcomes of hatches can be predicted from knowledge of the temperature regime, suggesting that still other factors or environmental interactions are involved. The

**FIGURE 12.2.** A loggerhead hatchling, illustrating typical body proportions of cheloniid hatchlings. (x1)

minute effects of the environment on turtle nests have even been traced to the type of sand in which the nests are made. Coarse-grained sand has poor thermal conductivity, resulting in lower nest temperatures compared to sites on the same beach with finer texture. While the typical nesting area of loggerheads is considered to be a wide, moderate- to high-wave-energy beach, careful observations on Florida mangrove islands has revealed relatively high nesting densities of loggerheads. These atypical and cooler nesting areas may be significant to the population in producing a preponderance of male turtles, as most nests on the hotter beaches of Florida produce females.

Nest depredation by raccoons and feral pigs in the southeastern United States has been a serious threat to nesting success on some beaches. In order to protect the eggs, conservationists often excavate the natural nests and re-bury them in protected areas. This activity saves nests that would be in peril from drowning at high tides, too. Since first described as rare in 1989, depredation of loggerhead nests by armadillos at Hobe Sound National Wildlife Refuge in southeastern Florida has increased, amounting to 14 percent of the nests there in 1996. In northwestern Florida, programs to eradicate raccoons and feral hogs from pristine, protected loggerhead-nesting beaches have decreased the number of depredated nests by 90 percent.

Study of the factors affecting loggerhead hatchling movements under laboratory conditions indicates that hatchlings can detect and orient to magnetic fields and that their directional preference is related to the direction of light exposure. Further examination under controlled conditions in the field has indicated that the magnetic orientation established by hatchlings on the beach is maintained by them once they reach the water. While these findings elucidate the mechanisms that allow the hatchlings to orient to the sea, they also underline the importance of eliminating light pollution from nesting areas when hatchlings are emerging. This magnetic compass senses the angle of the lines of magnetism encircling the earth, which vary by latitude, and is thus an inclination compass, not a polar compass.

The first several years of a loggerhead hatchling from Atlantic beaches are passed in the pelagic realms of the Atlantic, and during this time, the young turtles may cross the ocean more than once. Hatchlings from Gulf of Mexico beaches may join this sojourn in the Atlantic via the Loop and Florida currents, or may stay in the Gulf. The habitat of the young was not understood for many years, although anecdotal evidence pointed toward a pelagic existence. In September 1979, Hurricane David blew hundreds of loggerhead hatchlings ashore on Florida beaches in masses of *Sargassum*; stomach contents of some hatchlings contained bits of the weed, and invertebrates. At another time, hatchlings that had been washed ashore were noticed to be lightly encrusted with bryzoans and worm tubes common to the *Sargassum* community, also suggesting an association. In addition, some observations of the offshore movements of hatchlings suggested that when they reached clumps of *Sargassum* a kilometer or more offshore, they would take refuge in it. Much evidence now has been accummulated indicating that young loggerheads circulate in the North Atlantic gyre, formerly mostly inferred from geographical patterns in size distributions of loggerheads. For example, immature loggerheads around 20 cm in carapace length were known to occur in the Azores, a size not seen in U.S. waters. One pen-reared loggerhead, released as a yearling in Florida and recovered seven years later at the island of Madeira, off the west coast of Africa, was further evidence of the linkage. With the advent of genetic techniques, recent analysis of mitochondrial DNA sequences of more than 100 juvenile loggerheads found in pelagic habitats around the Azore Islands and Madeira Island in the eastern Atlantic indicated that they all were born either in the southeastern United States or the Yucatán. The size of loggerheads occurring in the Azores ranges mostly from 20 to 50 cm. Loggerheads remain "pelagic immatures" until reaching 40 to 60 cm in carapace length, when they take up a coastal existence and become benthic feeders.

Immature loggerheads are common in New England waters as well as in Canadian waters of the Gulf of Maine. Immature loggerheads, averaging 50 cm, are usually the most common turtles in the waters around Long Island, New York, during the summer. Subadult female loggerheads 50 to 90 cm in carapace length are regular visitors to Chesapeake Bay, where they occur from May to November. However, June is the peak month, as evidenced from strandings and pound-net captures. This immigration has been interpreted as part of a general northward spring movement of loggerheads occurring inside the 60 m depth contour from south of Cape Hatteras into the mid-Atlantic as the water warms. Loggerheads stranded along the Eastern Seaboard of the United States between Virginia and Massachusetts in 1995 were traced to three rookeries in the southeastern United States and Mexico.

The northward movement of loggerheads along the Eastern Seaboard into Chesapeake Bay has been corroborated by the presence of *Balanus trigonus* on about 10 percent of the immatures, since this barnacle doesn't commonly occur north of Cape Hatteras. However, the low numbers of immature males that seem to occur in the Chesapeake Bay suggest that the sexes may differ in their movement patterns. Also, analysis of the isotopes $^{18}O$ and $^{13}C$ in shells of the barnacles *Chelonibia testudinata* encrusting subadults in Chesapeake Bay indicated that the barnacles had grown in warm and cold water and in bay and ocean environments, confirming turtle use of many environments.

On the eastern coast of Florida, immature loggerheads greater than 50 cm in carapace length may remain in some coastal lagoons for as long as fifteen months, providing evidence that the inshore waters of the southeastern United States, such as Indian River Lagoon, serve as important subadult habitats. In southern Florida and the eastern Gulf of Mexico, loggerheads 70 to 90 cm are most common. Most all of the loggerheads stranded on the Texas coast are subadults, ranging in size from 50 to 80 cm in carapace length, as are most of the loggerheads that are observed swimming around oil platforms, rock reefs, and jetties in that region.

Adult loggerheads appear to make seasonal migrations that are less structured than those of the green turtle. Females tagged on nesting beaches of the southeastern states have been recaptured in the Gulf of Mexico, although more have been recaptured along the Eastern Seaboard in the months following nesting. These recaptures have occurred as far north as New Jersey. Also, tagging of loggerheads on the western coast of Florida has indicated some movement to the Yucatán Peninsula of Mexico, the Bahamas, and the Dominican Republic. Loggerheads along the Cuban shelf were identified from Florida and Mexico tagging locales.

Loggerheads are commonly quite encrusted with organisms, unlike other species of sea turtles. This biota grows on the front margin and latter third of the carapace; the bare portion is due to the loggerheads' habit of resting in the water with their front flippers over the carapace. Carapace epibionts that have been found on nesting female loggerheads along the southeastern United States represent 48 species belonging to six phyla. Of these, 17 species were found on at least 20 percent of the animals, while 31 species were rarer in occurrence. The commoner species included the slipper shell, *Crepidula plana*; the oyster, *Ostrea equestris*; the tube worm, *Sabellaris vulgaris*; the barnacles, *Balanus amphitrite, Chelonibia testudinaria,* and *Lepas anatifera*; the tanaeid, *Zeuxo robustus*; seven species of amphipods, *Caprella andreae, Ampithöe ramondi, Elasmopus rapax, Erichthonius brasiliensis, Hyale sp., Podocerus cheloniae,* and *Stenothosa minuta*; and finally, the sea squirt, *Mogula manhattensis.* Interestingly, the fauna appeared to constitute two communities—one tropical, one temperate—suggesting that females that nested in Florida migrated from the Caribbean, whereas those that nested in South Carolina and Georgia remained in coastal waters or migrated to the Sargasso Sea.

In offshore waters, the loggerhead eats jellyfish such as *Aurelia*, the Portuguese man-o-war *Physalia*, pteropods, and encrusting organisms like the stalked barnacle *Lepas.* Recently, studies have revealed the presence of a row of four sharp, raised scales on the leading edge of each front flipper of loggerhead hatchlings from the Mediterranean. The little turtles use these scales to saw chunks off food being held in the mouth which is too large to swallow. This is accomplished by alternately turning the head to each side, extending the flipper on that side, and then bringing it down rapidly to shear away the food. And, secondarily, they eat the pieces of food that stick to the scales. Not all hatchlings, though, seem

to have these "pseudo-claws," suggesting that some geographic variation in morphology exists.

In inshore waters, loggerheads eat a variety of invertebrates such as crabs, conchs, clams, sponges, sea urchins, and lobsters. Their jaws are well adapted for crushing shelled prey, because the jaw plates are wide and their jaw musculature is strong—so much so that they are capable of crushing the sturdy queen conch *Strombus gigas.* Immatures occurring in the lower Chesapeake Bay appear to prefer to eat the horseshoe crab *Limulus polyphemus,* a trait also displayed by some immatures and adults observed in Mosquito Lagoon, Florida. An observation from 1914 on one loggerhead noted an exclusive dinner of hermit crabs *(Pagurus pollicaris)* and moon snails *(Neverita duplicata).* Those captured in shrimp trawls sometimes appear to have dined on the discarded by-catch. Off Texas, loggerheads consume a variety of crabs and even sea pens.

Man's disposal of waste at sea poses a serious threat to sea turtle survival. Accounts have reported oil clots and plastic fragments in guts of immature loggerheads in the Azores, and of plastic debris in bloody excreta from subadults in the Mediterranean. From 1980 to 1992, examination of stranded turtles along the Gulf Coast indicated that loggerheads were the species most likely to have ingested plastic or balloons.

Sharks appear to be important predators on adult loggerheads, because many nesting females have scars or are missing parts of flippers or their carapace. One account cites the remains of loggerheads in the stomach contents of several tiger sharks caught near Key West. Hatchling loggerheads fall prey to predatory fish such as the dolphinfish, *Coryphaena hippura,* and the amberjack, *Seriola dumerili,* which frequent weed wrack and other flotsam. In simulated attacks, loggerhead hatchlings become immobile, unlike green-turtle hatchlings that will attempt to swim away.

Immature loggerheads are the most frequently captured turtle by shrimp trawls, although the rate of capture per trawling hour is about 20 times greater in the Southeast Atlantic compared to the Gulf of Mexico. Numbers of captures are about three times higher in the South Atlantic than in the Gulf of Mexico, while the number of deaths due to shrimp trawls is about twice that of the Gulf of Mexico. In the Gulf of Mexico, about half of the captures occur from shrimping operations in the central Gulf region, extending from the Florida Panhandle to Louisiana. Forty percent of the deaths occur in the central Gulf region, with the remainder about equally divided between the Florida west coast and Keys, and the Texas coast.

As described above, to stem this mortality, the National Marine Fisheries Service has worked for several years to develop turtle excluder devices (TEDs), which were orginally termed trawling-efficiency devices because their function was to exclude unwanted portions of the catch. Turtles caught in shrimp nets damage them, crush portions of the catch, and lower fishing efficiency. TEDs are constructed so that an encountered turtle is swept up and out of the net. Observations indicate that TEDs can be 97 pecent effective in reducing the incidental catch of sea turtles. Underwater observations made during the development of TEDs indicated that during daylight hours, loggerheads try to outswim an approaching trawl rather than swerving out of its way. Soon the turtle becomes fatigued and is overtaken by the net, and as it struggles to free itself, it becomes entangled further. If the trawl is towed for a long time, as is the case in some areas, the turtle eventually drowns, having depleted its oxygen reserves in struggling. More signficantly, perhaps, much shrimp fishing occurs at night, and it is probable that the turtles do not see the net coming. Under present law, fishermen must return loggerheads that they catch to the water, resuscitating them first if they are comatose.

Most of the turtles that are stranded along the Texas coast are subadult loggerheads. Strandings occur between March and December, with most occuring in the summer except during the period of the Texas shrimp-fishing closure, when strandings decline. Off the southeastern United States, most loggerheads stranded are also subadults that are 50 to 80 cm in carapace length. Recent results obtained from numerical models designed to investigate the population dynamics of loggerheads have indicated that reducing the mortality of large juveniles is the most important action that can be taken to promote recovery of loggerhead populations. In the Southeast Atlantic, the single most important source of mortality is thought to be drowning in shrimp trawls.

Loggerheads have also been caught incidentally by the Japanese longline fishery that formerly fished within the U.S. Fishery Conservation Zone in the Gulf of Mexico from January to March, and along the Atlantic Seaboard during August and September. The turtles were usually hooked in the mouth, indicating that they were trying to eat the bait set for tuna. The pelagic stage of loggerheads (5–64 cm) is also impacted by longline fisheries operating in the eastern Atlantic.

Turtle strandings, while often related to fishing operations, are also due to natural causes. Loggerheads found stranded live in Chesapeake Bay were found to be suffering from encephalitis, and investigators were able to link behavioral symptoms observed in stranded turtles in previous years to this cause. In Florida, emaciated loggerheads, which were likely stranding candidates, were found to have bowels filled with shell debris. Also, strandings due cold shock occur around Long Island and southward along the Atlantic Coast when summer foragers fail to migrate south early enough to avoid cold temperatures.

## Green Turtles, *Chelonia mydas*

When full-grown, the green turtle ranks as a medium to large sea turtle, attaining a carapace length of around one meter and weighing 136 kg or more. The Florida Department of Environmental Protection classifies juveniles as 5 to 59 cm, subadults as 60 to 89 cm, and adults as greater than or equal to 90 cm in carapace length. The green turtle has a small head for its body size, compared to other turtles, and a graceful, ovate carapace shape (Figure 12.3). The color of the carapace varies individually from medium to dark brown and is mottled with light tan; the ventral shell, known as the plastron, is yellow. The name of "green turtle" stems from the color of fat under its shell. Its other common names include "the edible turtle" and "the soup turtle," which give a hint of a major cause of its decline. Its scientific name, *Chelonia mydas,* stems from the Greek words for tortoise, *chelone,* and wetness, *mydos.*

The green turtle was once very abundant in the western Caribbean and, in fact, was also known historically as the Texas turtle because of the fishery for it in the Corpus Christi area that was in existence up to the 1890s. The demise of this fishery is thought to have been due to overexploitation. Elsewhere in U.S. waters of the Gulf of Mexico, green-turtle fisheries existed at Cedar Key in western Florida, in the Florida Keys, and in the Dry Tortugas.

**FIGURE 12.3.** The green turtle, *Chelonia mydas*, mature female. Note small head in relation to body size. (x0.07)

The green turtle has been highly esteemed culinarily for centuries, being written of as early as the first century A.D. It was introduced in England during the eighteenth century but was a rare enough item in 1753 that how to dress it was not well-known. However, by 1879, about 15,000 turtles were being shipped live to England every year, where they were in great demand as a luxury food. The flesh from the carapace was known as calipash; that from the plastron, calipee. Traditional recipes included a West Indian soup made with sherry, hot peppers, ginger, cloves, and nutmeg; devotees considered it to be properly made when, after eating it, the diner was obliged to rest with his mouth open, cooling his palate with sips of madeira or port. Another preparation was called boucaneered turtle and was made by baking the plastron with the meat and fat attached. As it cooked, the meat was pricked so that the juices combined with seasonings of lemon juice, cayenne, cloves, and beaten eggs to form a savory gravy. This was supposedly a method of cooking derived from buccaneers, to whom, as to the British Royal Navy, turtles were an important food resource, taken on as live shipboard provisions at specially scheduled stops. Green turtles nesting in Bermuda during the 1600s, despite turtle-conservation legislation adopted there in 1620, were exploit-

ed to extinction; today, only immatures frequent those shores. Perhaps the green turtle even sustained the explorers of the New World. An account of Christopher Columbus's last voyage to the New World in 1503 remarked of the great abundance of (green) turtles in what became the Cayman Islands. Exploitation of this large rookery began in the 1650s and ended virtually 100 years later, with the colony close to extinction. During its heyday in the 1680s, up to 13,000 turtles a year were harvested from nesting beaches there and from feeding areas off Cuba.

In the United States, green turtles were shipped live from Key West to the Fulton Fish Market in New York, and from there to other states. Key West was the focal point of landings, which by 1950 consisted of catches made primarily in the West Indies and on the eastern coasts of Nicaragua and Costa Rica. By that time, the Florida harvest of green turtles had dwindled due to overfishing. Catches in Nicaragua and Costa Rica amounted to about 750 females a year, captured ashore during their nesting season. These turtles sold at market for about 80 cents per pound. Turtles were also captured with gill nets that were fished by schooners or sloops. The fishing season extended from March through September. During May, June, and July females carrying both immature and mature eggs were landed and were much enhanced in value, because immature eggs, which sold by the pound, were deemed a great delicacy. Females yielded six to thirty pounds of eggs depending on their size and reproductive state. A measure of the size of the trade at Key West in 1948 is seen from the import of some 790,000 pounds of live sea turtles, all species combined, valued then at $57,000. The turtles were held in pens, called "turtle crawls" (which can still be viewed today), until they were shipped to market or slaughtered at Key West for canning as soup or meat. Little of the meat was sold fresh. As early as the 1880s, the Key West cannery exported some 200,000 pounds of green-turtle soup annually, most of it to England and Cuba.

Perhaps the reason why the flesh of the green turtle is so favored is related to its vegetarian diet, a habit not shared by other turtle species. Yearlings and older turtles feed on *Thallassia testudinaria*, commonly known as turtle grass, as well as red, green, and brown algae and other marine grasses. The particular combination of these items in the diet varies geographically and is related to the relative availability of sea grasses and algae, and the local herbivore community. Green turtles in the Torres Strait, for example, eat algae and turtle grass, whereas those in western Samoa feed on drifting lines of a sea grass that washes out from the lagoons. Although green turtles in captivity will eat fish and crabs, and will grow rapidly on such a high-protein diet, these are not naturally selected foods.

In the Caribbean, turtle grass is abundantly available and is a primary food item. Green turtles there repeatedly graze the same patches, which can be 10 to 100 m in size, although the patch boundaries tend to shift slowly. This repeated cropping, which occurs every four to ten days, results in harvests of new growth which are 6 to 11 percent higher in nitrogen and 100 percent lower in lignin than old blade parts, and therefore are more nutritious. This is because lignin chemically combines with the cellulose of the grass, making it indigestible. Like cows, green turtles must break down cellulose, a complex carbohydrate that forms the cell walls of plants, in order to derive energy from it. This breakdown is accomplished by microflora that live in a specialized portion of the upper end of the large intestine. The microflora that digest sea grass, however, are different from those that digest the noncellulose carbohydates of algae. Thus, in order to maintain the highest digestive efficiency, turtles that eat algae and sea grass don't eat them at the same time, or they make short-term switches. Morphological adaptations of green turtles to their herbivorous habit include a serrated cutting edge on their jaws that helps to shear off vegetation, and a long intestine in relation to their size (9.5 times the carapace length), which furthers food absorption and fiber elimination. This volume can be appreciated by knowing that green turtles ingest 3 to 4 gm dry weight of turtle grass per kilogram of live weight per day; thus, a 135-kg turtle would ingest just over a pound of turtle grass (dry weight) per day. A remarkable divergence in gut morphology was discovered in 1997 between Hawaiian and Australian and Florida green turtles. Hawaiian and Australian green turtles have a crop (at the end of the esophagus before the stomach) that stores food, whereas no Florida turtles appear to have this structure.

The effect of green turtles on the production of turtle grass has been described as positive and negative. Regrazing causes a plant stress response that produces narrow, often flaccid blades that translate into lower production per unit area. On the other hand, the turtles apparently recycle the grass faster than the normal detrital cycle that occurs as the grass grows and dies naturally. The so-called "carrying capacity," or support capability, of one hectare of turtle grass in the Caribbean is nearly 140 adult females, leading experts to estimate that the number of turtles that existed there before the onslaught of European colonization was immense.

Green turtles in the Caribbean alternate feeding and resting periods. Shortly after dawn, they casually swim to their feeding patches and usually begin feeding about two hours after sunrise. Although they feed on and off throughout the day, peak times are from 8 to 10 A.M. and 2 to 5 P.M. In between, they take a siesta, returning to a resting place. Although individuals don't return to their own particular resting spots, the areas used for resting are particular places, usually the deepest in the area. Observations on juveniles have indicated that feeding and resting areas may be a half kilometer apart. Observations gathered on young green turtles that frequent the lower Texas coast suggest that those less than 40 cm in carapace length prefer to graze on algae along the jetties, while larger individuals feed on sea grasses in bay habitats.

Age at maturity in western Atlantic green turtles has been estimated variously from 12 to 30 years: 18 to 27 years (27 likely, Florida), 25 to 30 years (Florida), 27 years (Bermuda), 12 to 26 years (Costa Rica), 17 to 35 years (Ascension Island), 27 to 33 years (Virgin Islands), 24 to 36 years (Suriname), and 19 to 24 years (western central Atlantic). In Australia, the age of maturity has been estimated to be 30 years, while in Hawaii, studies on immature green turtles have suggested that green turtles there mature at ages 9 to 60. However, growth rate and diet are linked. Green turtles raised in captivity that are fed a high-protein diet mature in 8 to 10 years; the slower growth rate of wild turtles has been attributed to their diet of turtle grass, which is comparatively low in protein and high in fiber. The great time to maturity of some of the Hawaiian populations is thought to be related to the higher proportion of algae in their diet, which is nutritionally poorer than turtle grass. Growth rates estimated for immature green turtles decline with size. Average estimates for western Atlantic wild green turtles are 6.5, 6.6, 4.8, 4.2, 2.6, and 1.7 cm per year for turtles 20 to 30, 30 to 40, 40 to 50, 50 to 60, 60 to 70, and 70 to 80 cm in carapace length, respectively.

Green turtles are known to nest in several localities around the world. Rookeries historically occurred in the Florida Keys and Dry Tortugas, but today most nesting in the United States occurs on selected beaches along the Atlantic Coast of Florida from June to September. On Florida beaches, numbers of green-turtle nests counted have varied from 60 to 2,500 per year and seem to follow a biennial pattern of "lows" and "highs." Nesting along the southwestern Florida coast (29 nests from 5 counties) and in the Florida Panhandle (three counties) was first documented in 1994. A linkage between the sparse Gulf rookeries and larger Florida east coast rookeries was made with the recapture in 1994 of a nesting female on the east coast, which had been tagged nesting on the west coast in 1992 (then she had been misidentified as a loggerhead). From 1980 to 1994, diligent observations of sea turtle nesting on North Carolina beaches have indicated a small (up to 9 nests per year), but seemingly persistent, nesting of green sea turtles there. Formerly, green sea turtles were thought to nest regularly only as far north as Amelia Island, in northwestern Florida near the Georgia border. Close to Gulf shores, green turtles frequent the Cuban shelf and nest on the south coast of Cuba. Turtles tagged in Cuba have been captured in Florida and in the Caribbean, and turtles tagged in Florida and elsewhere have been in Cuba. Green turtles also occasionally nest on the Texas coast.

In the western Atlantic region, studies have been undertaken on green turtles in their major nesting areas. These include beaches in Guianas-Guyana, Surinam, and French Guiana; near Tortuguero, Costa Rica; Aves Island in the Leeward Islands; and Ascension Island, a volcanic product of the mid-Atlantic rift some 2,250 km (1,400 miles) off the bulge of Brazil. The number of nesting females in the Caribbean between 1971 and 1981 was estimated to be 23,000, within a possible range of 8,000 to 76,000. Numbers nesting since then have declined. The timing of nesting differs among areas. The nesting season extends from June to October at Tortuguero, from mid-July to mid-October at Aves Island, from March to August in Guyana, from February to July at Surinam, and from December to May at Ascension Island.

Analysis of mitochrondrial DNA of nesting females from Hutchinson Island, Florida; Quintana Roo, Mexico; Tortuguero, Costa Rica; Aves Island, Venezuela; Matapica, Surinam; Atol das Rocas, Brazil; Ascension Island, United Kingdom; and Pailoa, Guinea-Bissau indicated that females nesting in all areas were distinct genetically with the exception of those from Surinam and Aves Island, and Guinea-Bisseau and Ascension Island, respectively. Further genetic studies have demonstrated that at Tortuguero, not only do females return to their natal beaches to nest, but that females nesting close together spatially were more related to one another than to others nesting further away. This small-scale phenomenom was not found in females nesting in Melbourne, Florida, and may be the result of beach disturbances or lower kinship in Florida nesters. While natal homing of nesting females has been established, only recently have studies begun to look at whether males also exhibit fidelity to natal areas. Examination of genetic diversity among males at breeding and feeding grounds in four regions of Australia has indicated differences among males in most regions that are largely comparable to those of females.

The nesting at Ascension Island affords an example of the spectacular migrations made by female green turtles between their particular feeding localities and particular nesting locations to which they faithfully return. The females that nest on Ascension Island apparently swim at least from the bulge of Brazil, where females tagged on Ascension Island have been subsequently recaptured. The 2,200-km trip across open ocean from the coast of Brazil to Ascension Island and back has been estimated to take six months total. This is based on measured swimming speeds of some females, which can be up to 36.8 km per day, thus alloting two months for swimming each way, sandwiching in a two-month period of nesting. During this time, females apparently don't feed, as no known feeding grounds exist at Ascension Island and opportunities to feed during the long swim are thought to be nil. Scientists postulate that the link between feeding grounds along the coast of Brazil and the nesting areas on Ascension Island was made before spreading of the seafloor during the early Tertiary geological epoch.

The females that nest at Ascension Island make the journey every three years, based on returns of tagged females to the island. How the females navigate not only to the island, but to their original tagging site on the island, is an unanswered question. How females that nest on the beach at Tortuguero, Costa Rica, every two to three years find their way there from places throughout the Caribbean where they feed, based on recaptures from Cuba, the Yucatán, Honduras, near Jamaica, and Colombia, as well as Brazil, is also not known. However, the difference in minimum return frequency of females between these areas is thought to be related to the arduousness of the journey, because the females nesting at Tortuguero have smaller distances to swim from their feeding grounds.

Results of tagging studies on nesting females at Aves Island begun in the mid-1970s indicates the international scope of green-turtle biology in the western Atlantic. Females that nested on Aves Island were recaptured on feeding grounds in the Dominican Republic, Nicaragua, Guyana, Nevis, St. Lucia, Venezuela, Cuba, Guadeloupe, Martinique, Puerto Rico, Brazil, Carriacou, Columbia, Grenada, Haiti, Mexico, and St. Kitts. Further, this work showed the great extent that feeding grounds are shared by females that nest in Tortuguero, Costa Rica, and Ascension Island.

Celestial navigation is not thought to be of major importancer. Navigation by following chemical clues has been hypothesized based on the presence of well-developed olfactory organs and the ability of green turtles to perform tasks based on scent cues. This theory is supported by observations that females appear to "smell" the sand when they emerge from the surf, as if determining that they have arrived where they intended. Other studies have found that chemical imprinting of green turtles can occur during their incubation as embryos and during a subsequent period as hatchlings, causing them to orient to the chemical environment in which they were raised. But what chemical clues might be followed in their natural environment, as well as those that might be operative in their natal environment, are unknown. Use of a magnetic compass is thought to be highly probable, based on the very similar, virtually straight-line migration patterns of some females monitored by satellite from nesting grounds on Ascension Island to feeding grounds.

Recent morphological comparisons of green turtles from Hawaii and Florida have revealed some intriguing differences. Turtles from Hawaii have 74 percent larger hind flippers and 48 percent larger front flippers than turtles of the same body size from Florida. Researchers speculate that the larger flippers may be related to the greater distances Hawaiian turtles swim between feeding and nesting areas, and perhaps, too, to the rougher coastal environment of oceanic islands, because even hatchlings display these differences.

Observations on captive green turtles from the Caribbean indicate that mating may occur during several short intervals that can be as small as two to three minutes, or continuously over a protracted time period as long as five days. However, it is the total time spent in mating, which occurs at the beginning of the breeding season, that is important, because this is correlated with whether or not a female nests. On the average, the total mating time of nesting females was observed to be just over 25 hours, whereas that of non-nesting females was only about an hour and a half. After mating, most females nested within a month's time, although this time span, too, seems related to the total amount of time spent mating. Females that mated for short times were observed to take up to two months before nesting. Mating takes place in wild populations off the nesting beaches. There is a difference of opinion among scientists whether it is those matings that fertilize the eggs laid that season, or the matings from the previous nesting period. Although females seem capable of storing sperm, opinion now seems to favor the in-season mating hypothesis. In mating, the male maintains a grasp on the female's carapace using a specially hooked nail on his front flipper, holding her beneath his plastron.

Female green turtles come ashore at night to lay their eggs, avoiding the hot beach temperatures during the day that would cause them thermal stress or death. First, the female strands herself on the beach and crawls from the surf up the beach past the high-tide mark, where she selects the nest site, clearing it of debris. Unlike other species of sea turtles except the leatherback, the female first excavates a "body pit" with her front flippers, which is about as deep as her body, and piles up the excavated sand with her hind flippers. She lays in this depression as she digs the hole with her hind flippers. The deeper she digs, the more she leans up on her front flippers, while her hind flippers dig, lifting the sand out and throwing it behind her. It takes her about 20 minutes to dig the hole, which, when finished, is shaped like a flask and is about 45 cm deep. Then the female deposits her eggs in the nest, extending her flippers backward in the laying process. When she is finished, she covers the eggs with sand using her hind flippers, firms the surface with her body, and sweeps sand with her front flippers to camouflage the nest location. The eggs are laid and covered in such a way that the sand is not packed around the eggs or sifted between them. The nesting process takes about two hours. The female then finds her way back to the water by its brightness. She maintains a straight course to the water by balancing the amount of light striking each eye. Females with one eye experimentally blindfolded continuously circle to the side of the illuminated eye, indicating a phototaxis is operative.

The average-size female of 100 cm in carapace length that nests at Tortuguero, Costa Rica, in the Caribbean, will deposit around 110 eggs at each nesting. "Clutch size" varies with female size, which, in turn, varies among localities. Thus, in the Galapagos Islands, the average size of nesting females is around 80 cm and the average clutch size is 80 eggs, whereas at the upper end of the size range, females nesting on Europa Island in the Mozambique Channel, Indian Ocean, average 110 cm in length and lay an average of 150 eggs at each nesting. Nesting females on Florida beaches average around 100 cm in carapace length, but clutch size is slightly larger on the average—around 135 eggs. Most females come ashore four to six times to nest during a nesting season, at intervals of 10 to 15 days.

Green-turtle eggs average around 45 mm in diameter. The eggs incubate in the nest for about two months, a period that can be shorter or longer according to local conditions; e.g., rain will extend the time, as will low temperature. The average temperature of the nest during development affects the time to hatching of the eggs by the same relation as noted for loggerheads. During incubation, repiratory gases from the embryo are exchanged across shell membranes and the parchmentlike eggshell with the air in the nest. As the eggs develop, the partial pressure of oxygen at the center of the nest declines, with the rate of decline increasing as hatching nears due to the increased consumption of oxygen by the developing embryos, and the amount of oxygen in the sand that diffuses into the nest. The partial pressure of carbon dioxide at the nest center increases in an opposite fashion during egg development. Studies have determined that an envelope of sand measuring a half meter in thickness is required for adequate gas exchange in green-turtle nests dug in the fine-grained beach sand of Tortuguero. If gas-exchange rates in nests are artificially lowered from natural levels, incubation time increases, as does egg mortality. Thus, the physics of gas exchange and embryo size and development have prompted scientists to speculate about the evolution of clutch size in sea turtles and other reptiles, such as dinosaurs, which put their eggs in nests.

The temperature of the nest during the middle third of the development time affects the sex ratio of the clutch, as in other sea turtles. Temperatures below 28°C result in clutches that are 90 to 100 percent male, while those at or above 30.5°C result in clutches that are 94 to 100 percent females; between 28.5°C and 30.2°C, fewer females and more males develop. These temperature "thresholds," however, appear to vary geographically, and in some cases intersex hatchlings result. At Tortuguero, Costa Rica, the percentage of hatchlings that are female has been related to the nest site. At one spot, nests nearest the beach produced 72 percent females, those at the upper edge under dense vegetation produced only 7 percent females, and nests between these zones on the open beach produced 87 percent females. Thus, at some locales, like Tortuguero, many more female hatchlings than male hatchlings are produced by virtue of where most of the females choose to nest.

The total time spent in mating by a female seems to be positively correlated with the percentage of her eggs that hatch over a twofold range. However, other factors affect the number of hatchlings that emerge. In most cases, hatching success varies between 50 and 75 percent. Size at hatching varies somewhat by locality. At Ascension Island, hatchlings range from 49 to 55 mm in carapace length; at Tortuguero, from 46 to 56 mm; and on Florida beaches, from 49 to 56 mm. Green-turtle hatchlings, unlike others in the family Chelonidae, are strongly countershaded in coloration, being black on their backs and white on their undersides. This coloration has been suggested to be an adaptation for a pelagic lifestyle, because it is a color pattern commonly exhibited by oceanic travelers.

After emerging from the nest, the hatchlings make their way to the water and, like the young of other species, exhibit a swimming frenzy that takes them through the surf and away from the beach. Studies have found that green-turtle hatchlings may swim continuously, covering distances up to 6.5 km before resting either on weed wrack or by floating at the surface, which they do with their flippers tucked to their sides. They swim about 20 cm below the surface at an average rate of about 1.5 km per hour. At 5- to 10-second intervals, they surface to breathe, treading water with all four flippers.

Until recently, a great mystery existed about where the hatchlings go after entering the water up to the time they appear as juveniles in shallow waters, where they eat benthic plants. This mystery period was tagged "the lost year." Now, evidence indicates that the young take up a pelagic mode of existence, seeking refuge in and obtaining food from floating communities of *Sargassum* weed. Estimates of the time spent in this phase by western Atlantic green turtles ranges from seven months to three years. In the Caribbean, green-turtle hatchlings have been observed resting on clumps of weed and swimming in the vicinity of weed lines that were 40 km off the Panamanian coast and some 160 km from the nearest nesting beach, leading scientists to speculate that the young drift along passively in the water currents that make up the Caribbean gyre or that flow to South America. Thus, the swimming frenzy of the hatchlings is thought to bring them to longshore currents that carry them into the pelagic realm. After having passed the gauntlet of predators on the beach, however, different dangers await in the water—the barracuda, *Sphyraena barracuda,* and the dolphin-fish, *Coryphaena hippurus,* both of whom are known to prey on hatchlings. Other predators at sea include frigate birds, which the little turtles avoid by power diving.

Tag returns of pen-reared green turtles released as yearlings off east-coast Florida beaches have confirmed the oceanic dispersal and long-term survival of little turtles. One yearling released in July was recaptured the following February in the Azores. Others released at various times turned up in Colombia, Honduras, Belize, and Mexico, while several recoveries occurred along the Caribbean island chain from the Bahamas to the West Indies. During their oceanic phase, young green turtles are carnivorous. That their diet may consist of jellyfish is suggested by good growth rates of captive green turtles fed the jellyfish *Cassiopea xamachana,* and by the oceanic distribution and abudance of coelenterates.

The Eastern Seaboard of the United States and the Gulf Coast offer developmental habitats for green turtles. Researchers observed in 1993 that in east-central Florida, the largely winter seasonal capture pattern of juvenile and subadult greens (20 to 70 cm in carapace length) changed to a year-round pattern. Dramatic increases in the number of these turtles captured passively near St. Lucie nuclear power plant that continued the following two years sug-gested that young green sea turtles were extending their temporal use of nearshore habitats and increasing in numbers in this area. Off the Gulf Coast, immature green turtles are also common in the warm, shallow, protected tidal bays of the Bahamas and in developmental habitats in Bermuda, where they find abundant food. The linkage of these sites to other areas has been demonstrated. Turtles tagged in the Bahamas have been recovered throughout the Caribbean Basin, and genetic analysis of 50 green turtles in Bermuda indicated that all but three were from Atlantic rookeries. Along the lower Texas coast, young greens graze along the jetties and feed on sea grasses in bay habitats. The jetties of the Brazos–Santiago Pass provide year-round foraging habitat and protection from predators for these post-pelagic green turtles.

Green turtles are said to outswim shrimp trawls and therefore are seldom caught. They are, however, the third most frequently caught turtle in shrimp nets fished along the United States. Although they are caught twice as frequently per unit of trawling effort in the southeastern Atlantic shrimp fishery as they are in the Gulf of Mexico shrimp fishery, the greater amount of shrimp fishing in the Gulf of Mexico results in probably similar number of captures and deaths in each geographic area. Most captures occur in the central part of the Gulf of Mexico, from the Florida Panhandle to Louisiana.

Fibropapillomatosis is a disease of green turtles, often designated GTFP, that creates internal tumors or wartlike external tumors (fibropapillomas) in afflicted animals. Researchers have found that is it caused by an infectious subcellular agent, and they strongly suspect a herpesvirus to be the agent. To date, the only treatment for the disease is surgical removal of the tumors, and in many cases, the tumors regrow within a few months. Biologists hope to develop a vaccine to combat the disease. Only in some instances have infected turtles spontaneously recovered. The tumors grow around the eyes, causing impaired vision or blindness, in the oral cavities, inhibiting feeding or normal breathing, and on the skin and scales, affecting swimming. Internal tumors can affect the lungs and functioning of other organs. Starting as small lesions, the tumors can rapidly grow to 30 cm or more in size. Diseased turtles are anemic, perhaps immunosuppressed and stressed, and often parasitized by leeches or tapeworms, suggesting some pathological linkage with spirochid trematodes. While the disease has been recognized for more than 50 years, it is since the middle 1980s that it has become prevalent in Hawaii and Florida. In the Caribbean, the disease appears to have onset about five years later. About 60 percent infection rates have been reported in different areas, including some Florida waters. Fibropapillomas may count substantially as the cause of death in some strandings.

Green turtles are the only sea turtles that bask on shore as well as in the water and were thought to be the only sea turtles that basked. Recently, however, loggerheads and olive ridleys have been reported to bask at sea. Terrestrial basking by green turtles has been observed in Australia, the northwestern Hawaiian Islands, Socorro Island off Chile, the Galapagos Islands, Namibia, and Ascension Island, the only Atlantic location. In Australia, basking by internesting females and some adult males has been observed, while turtles of all sizes have been observed basking in Hawaii. In the Galapagos, most baskers are females and subadults. On Ascension Island, internesting females bask.

Many reasons have been advanced for terrestrial basking. It is thought to be a method of energy conservation by nesting females. Basking females have low oxygen-consumption levels, despite increased body temperature, allowing energy to be saved for the demands of nesting when foraging opportunities are also decreased. Other basking benefits may be avoidance of courting males by females, avoidance of cool water temperatures or sharks, body warming, accelerated egg maturation, synthesis of vitamin D, or acceleration of digestion. Terrestrial basking may also be a behavioral response to sickness or exhaustion. Basking by captive green turtles seems to be more common among those that are sick, and scientists have speculated that it may be a method of achieving a behavioral fever, which in other ectotherms is known to enhance the immune- system response. In Hawaii, green turtles afflicted with fibropapillomatosis are common, as is basking behavior, suggesting a linkage between the two. Basking females on nesting beaches in the Galapagos often seem exhausted—appearing soundly asleep or quite groggy if disturbed. This behavior may be related, investigating scientists suggest, to the 2,000 km or more that nesting females must swim from mainland South America. Studies of the thermoregulatory behavior of basking on land by healthy green turtles in Hawaii suggests that they keep from overheating by choosing the windy, cooler

side of islands, and by flipping sand over their carapace and flippers to reduce surface heating while permitting deep body warming. Apparently, turtles may actively beach themselves or strand themselves against an outgoing tide.

Establishment of cleaning stations by green turtles in the Hawaiian Islands has been more and more documented by divers. Turtles arriving at these specific sites, often marked by a coral formation, assume a posture that invites certain fish species to nibble off algae and barnacles encrusting the turtles.

Counts of turtles stranded along the southeastern Atlantic Coast of the United States that had ingested plastic or balloons from 1980 to 1992 indicated that green turtles were most commonly affected. Study of the results of ingestion of plastic by green turtles has indicated that gut blockage is not as much a concern as is interference in the normal functioning of the gut. Research animals fed plastic in conjunction with a normal diet exhibited bloating of the intestines to such an extent that the animals floated. The bloating was due to a disturbance of the microbial action of the gut flora, so important to an herbivore like the green turtle for proper food breakdown. Also, investigators noted that turtles so incapacitated would be at risk to boat collisions and capture in nets.

## Kemp's Ridley Turtles, *Lepidochelys kempii*

This is the smallest species of sea turtle. It attains maturity at a carapace length of 56 to 76 cm and usually weighs less than 45 kg. The Florida Department of Environmental Protection classifies juveniles as 5 to 44 cm, subadults as 45 to 59 cm , and adults as greater than or equal to 60 cm in carapace length. Others have termed juveniles as less than 20 cm, subadults as 20 to 60 cm and adults as greater than 60 cm. An additional approach is perhaps less confusing in terming benthic immatures as 20 to 60 cm and adults as greater than 60 cm. Estimates of probable age at maturity range from 7 to 15 years. The carapace is almost as wide as it is long, and this circular form is distinctive (Figure 12.4). In adults, the carapace is light olive-green in color, and the plastron is yellow. The carapace of immatures is gray, and the plastron is yellowish-white and is raised into two longitudinal ridges that subside with maturity. Juveniles differ even more in coloration,

**FIGURE 12.4.** Kemp's ridley turtle, *Lepidochelys kempi*, mature female. Circular shape of carapace is distinctive of species. (x0.15)

The first published record of nesting of this species was on Padre Island, Texas. Thus, it seems logical that the first conservation attempts to resite this species occurred on Padre Island. During 1964, 1965, and 1966, conservationists attempted to transplant eggs from Rancho Nuevo in Mexico but failed. In 1967, the group flew back 2,000 eggs, of which half hatched. The difference in the success of these efforts was related to a critical feature of turtle-egg development not appreciated until recently. Unlike chicken eggs, the developing embryo is not encased in albumin and thus lacks the twisted strands of albumin that help support the embryo. Turtle embryos sit instead on the top of the albumin. About 36 hours after the egg is laid, two membranes begin to enclose the embryo, which apparently support it for about two to three weeks, keeping it near the shell surface until other developmental structures arise. This development is marked by an expanding disc of whiteness on the outside of the shell—unfertilized eggs remain uniformly beige. Moving a turtle egg during this critical period ruptures its support structure, causing the embryo to die. The carapace of the hatchling becomes apparent after approximately 19 days of development.

Whether the two to three female ridleys that nested on Padre Island between 1974 and 1976 were a result of these initial efforts is not known, although one of the females that came ashore in 1974 nested one-half mile south of the 1967 hatchling-release location. Beginning in 1978, in cooperation with the Mexican Departmento de Pesca, which started a turtle protection program in 1966, a head-start program was undertaken by the U.S. National Marine Fisheries Service at Galveston. In this program, which ended after 1988, thousands of hatchlings were raised at Padre Island from almost 22,500 eggs collected at Rancho Nuevo, and various studies were undertaken to understand their biological requirements. Despite these efforts, hatchlings proved difficult to maintain in tanks due to their aggressive behavior and susceptibility to disease. Those that survived (about 12,000) were tagged and released, mostly off Mustang Island and north Padre Island, as head-started 9- 11-month-old turtles, having previously been released as hatchlings into the surf and recovered from the beach of Padre Island National Seashore to stimulate natal- beach imprinting. In 1996, six ridley nests were found on the Texas coast, the most ever recorded annually since 1979,

being black dorsally and white ventrally, while hatchlings are completely gray-black. This uniform coloration of hatchlings is peculiar to the Kemp's ridley and its congener, the olive ridley, among sea turtles. In addition, this genus has the smallest eyes.

The Kemp's ridley was formerly abundant and widely distributed. Off Florida, Cedar Key was an important area of fishing for ridleys. Its primary nesting beaches were unknown until 1961, when an aerial film made by a Mexican engineer in 1947 showing thousands of nesting ridleys amazed scientists at a colloquium. At the time of the filming, an estimated 40,000 females nested on the beaches near Rancho Nuevo in the state of Tamaulipas, Mexico. Due to excessive exploitation of nesting females and eggs, by 1964 the number of nesting females had dwindled to 2,000. Estimates placed the number of nesting females at 1,200 in 1974, and the figures continuously declined through 1985 to about 500 females. However, the number of Kemp's-ridley nests found in Mexico has increased almost every year since then. Despite this, the number of nesting females lags far behind the 40,000 that nested in one day in 1947, and the Kemp's ridley is still considered to be the most endangered species of sea turtles.

and two of the nesting females were identified from the head-start program. One had been released off Mustang Island in June 1984 and the other probably off the same area in April 1986. In 1997, 9 nests were found, and in 1998, 13 nests were found. Three of the 1998 nesting females were from the head-start program—and aged 11, 12, and 14. These results illustrate the long-term nature of turtle research and associated risks—these females did not attain sexual maturity and return to nest for more than 10 years. To enhance the survival of Kemp's-ridley offspring from the nesting females found on Padre Island, eggs from these nests have been hatched under supervision, a program ongoing since 1980.

Kemp's ridleys are known for the mass nesting of the females referred to as *arribadas* in Spanish. During these "arrivals," females emerge to nest during the daytime when the wind is blowing strongly. This nesting behavior has caused much speculation, and some experts suggest that the mass nesting is a ploy to overwhelm predators like coyotes, thus ensuring the survival of some nesting females and nests, as well as a portion of the hatchlings, which synchronously emerge, too. The nesting of females during windy conditions has been interpreted as a behavior that ensures the secrecy of nesting sites, because the wind very quickly obliterates the females' light tracks. Recently, studies of convective cooling of turtle shapes have indicated that turtles the small size of ridleys can survive the heat of daytime nesting by coming ashore on windy days.

Females nest primarliy on the beaches of Tamaulipas, although some nest regularly in Veracruz and now in South Texas. Occasional nests have been recorded in Florida and Georgia, but these have been considered as outside the typical nesting range. Individual females nest either annually or biennially. Most nesting occurs between April and July, with May and June being peak months. Most females nest twice during a season, two to three weeks apart. The average size of nesting females is 65 cm in carapace length, within a range of 60 to 75 cm. Clutch size varies from 54 to 185 eggs, with 110 eggs representing the average number laid. The eggs range in size from 35 to 45 mm. Hatchlings emerge in 50 to 70 days, depending on conditions, and range from 38 to 46 mm in carapace length. Studies on incubation conditions have revealed that 30°C is the critical temperature at which equal numbers of male and female hatchlings develop. Thus, male hatchlings predominate in early-season nests, while female hatchlings predominate in late-season nests.

As noted above, Kemp's ridley young from Rancho Nuevo are transported northward in the Mexican Current into the eddying currents of the Gulf of Mexico, where they remain while others are swept into the Loop Current, then the Florida Current, and up the Atlantic Seaboard. Some of these Kemp's ridleys enter the Atlantic gyre. This species is an inferred trans–Atlantic traveler, because it breeds primarily in Mexico, and ridleys are often sighted off England, France, and the Netherlands. Adults occur essentially in the Gulf of Mexico, along the shore in depths less than 50 m.

Kemp's ridley's young undergo a pelagic existence until they reach about 20 cm in carapace length. As they mature, Kemp's ridleys become benthic feeders and move into relatively shallow waters along the Atlantic and Gulf coasts, where individuals may forage along considerable lengths of coastline. Kemp's ridleys around 27 to 28 cm frequent New York waters around Long Island and Cape Cod Bay in the summer. They also appear to be regular visitors in the Gulf of Maine, where strandings seem to be the result of injuries, not adverse environmental conditions. As they become older, they appear to utilize more southern feeding habitats. Subadults 30 to 50 cm are common in the lower Chesapeake Bay between May and November and are most numerous in June. Recent estimates suggest population numbers of 200 to 1,100 Kemp's ridleys there. Spring strandings in this area appear to be related to the northward spring migration of the turtles and peak interaction with the black drum gill net fishery in May and June. Fall strandings occur with the migration of turtles south when temperatures fall in October and are associated with the flounder fishery off southeastern Virginia and northern North Carolina. In the Gulf of Mexico, it appears that the coastal waters of Louisiana are an important juvenile habitat; in former times, the Kemp's ridley was known as the Louisiana turtle. The Texas coast is also an important foraging and migrational habitat. Head-started turtles released from Galveston or Padre Island have been recaptured several weeks to more than a year later in feeding localities in the northeastern Florida Panhandle at sizes of 25 to 29 cm.

Knowledge of the diet of posthatchling small turtles is based on two turtles 10 cm in size that stranded on the Texas coast. They were found to have eaten *Sargassum* and mollusks typically associated with *Sargassum*, as well as unidentifiable crabs. In later life, as it takes up its benthic existence, Kemp's ridley is primarily a crab eater. Along the Texas coast, gut analysis of many stranded turtles has revealed several prey species, including the true crabs, *Arenaeus cribrarius*, *Callinectes sapidus*, *C. similus*, *Portunus gibbessii*, *Ovalipes floridanus*, *Hepatus epheliticus*, *Persephona mediterranea*, *P. crinita*, *Menippe adina*, *Libinia sp.*, and *Calappa sp.*; the hermit crabs, *Isocheles wurdemanni*, *Pagurus pollicaris*, and *P. longicarpus*; and mollusks, including *Neverita duplicata*. Shrimp-fishing discards are also consumed, as evidenced by the presence of both shrimp or fish and the scavenger snail *Nassarius* in stomach contents. The diet of Kemp's ridley in other regions reflects the locally abundant crab and benthic fauna. Along the coast of New York, *Libinia emarginatus*, *Cancer irroratus*, and *Ovalipes ocellatus* have been recorded as prey. In Chesapeake Bay, the most common prey of immature ridleys is the blue crab, *Callinectes sapidus*, which is also the most common crab in the bay. Subadults along the Georgia coast eat both crabs and mollusks, typically *Callinectes sapidus*, and the moon snail, *Neverita duplicata*, in varying proportions, depending on the area. In Florida, Kemp's ridleys eat shallow-water crabs like *Hepatus ephelitium* and are known to get into crab pots, causing fishermen to hate them. It is also known to eat the box crab, *Calappa flammea*.

This species is the second most commonly caught turtle in shrimp trawls in both the Gulf of Mexico and the South Atlantic. Although the number of captures per unit of fishing effort is about four to five times lower in the Gulf of Mexico compared to the southeastern Atlantic, the greater frequency of trawling in the Gulf results in a greater number of captures there. In the Gulf of Mexico, most of the captures occur in the central Gulf region from the Florida Panhandle to Louisiana, and in the western Gulf off Texas. However, because nets are usually towed for longer times in the western Gulf, mortalities off Texas are thought to be double those in the central Gulf region.

Observed strandings of Kemp's ridley turtles between 1976 and 1979 along the Texas coast consisted of six recent hatchlings (45 to 76 mm) from July to September, and seven subadults (14 to 52 cm) and two adults (62 and 66 cm) from October to November. With the establishment of the Sea Turtle Stranding and Salvage Network in 1980, strandings along the Gulf Coast have been monitored and coverage of beaches has improved over the years. Seasonal strandings data available during 1991–1999 indicated that Texas strandings were most numerous between March and August, except for the summer period of the Texas shrimp-fishing closure, when strandings were low. Sizes of Kemp's ridleys stranded on Texas beaches in 1994 ranged from 20 to 69 cm, with 10 percent being adults larger than 60 cm. Numbers of Kemp's ridleys found stranded on Texas beaches between 1994 and 1998 ranged from 254 to 132, respectively.

## Leatherback Turtles, *Dermochelys coriacea*

Many of the superlatives that one could supply in a discussion of sea turtles would apply to the leatherback turtle or luth, so called because of its leathery skin. Its specific name "coriacea" stems from the Latin word for leather, "corium," while the genus incorporates the Greek *derma* of the same meaning. The leatherback is the largest sea turtle, growing to a carapace length of 190 cm and a weight of 600 kg. It has seven longitudinal ridges or keels on its back, which are thought to be hydrodynamic adaptations (Figure 12.5). Underneath is a thick insulation of oily, cartilaginous tissue. Adults are black dorsally, with white flecks that vary in abundance from individual to individual; the underside is white, with black blotching. The skin is rubbery to the touch but is delicate and easily abraded by rough sand or surfaces. Hatchling leatherbacks are strikingly colored, with white along their dorsal ridges and flipper margins, and are covered with small scales that are shed after one or two months of age (Figure 12.6). The front flippers are quite large in relation to the body length, compared to other species. As one might surmise from these characteristics of countershading coloration, delicate skin, and large flippers, leatherbacks lead a pelagic existence and make the longest-known journeys of sea turtles.

The leatherback is distributed in all three oceans and occurs regularly in near-boreal waters, from Alaska to Chile and from Labrador to the Cape of Good Hope. In the Gulf of Mexico, they occur most commonly off the west coast of Florida but have been observed in December near the Texas coast at Port Aransas in association with large numbers of cabbagehead medusae. They are well-known on the Eastern Seaboard, from the eastern coast of Florida northward. Small numbers of

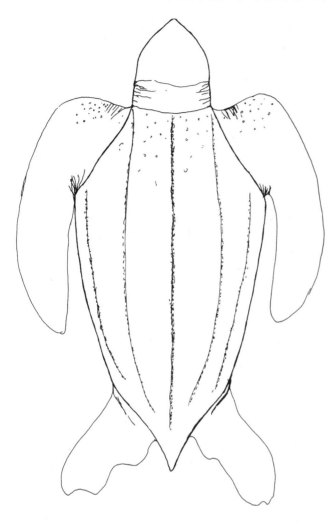

**FIGURE 12.5.** The leatherback turtle, *Dermochelys coriacea*, mature female. The streamlined shape and large front flippers reflect its pelagic lifestyle. (x0.06)

**FIGURE 12.6.** A leatherback hatchling. The striking dorsal coloration disappears with maturity. (x0.75)

immatures have been recorded in the Chesapeake Bay between May and December. Leatherbacks occur regularly enough in New England waters that the locale has been suggested to be a critical leatherback habitat. Until recently, sightings of leatherbacks in northern waters were thought to represent unusual events; but examination of records has revealed a systematic summer occurrence in northern waters that is thought to indicate regular migrations to feed on the abundant giant arctic jellyfish, *Cyanea capillata arctica*, which can attain a diameter of more than two meters. However, more males than females seem to occur in those waters. Data on incidental captures of leatherbacks—usually due to entanglement—by the Japanese longline fishery operating in the Gulf of Mexico between 1978 and 1981 led to the suggestion that the central Gulf of Mexico might be a major habitat of leatherbacks in the western Atlantic.

The leatherback has been described as a temperate turtle with a tropical nesting habit. In the western Atlantic, the major leatherback rookeries exist in Surinam and French Guiana. The numbers of nesting females in these areas, which comprise a single nesting population, were placed at 15,000 in 1996 and characterized as stable. Other nesting locales of lesser magnitude include Costa Rica, Trinidad, Puerto Rico, the U.S. Virgin Islands, and Panama. On the U.S coastline, some leatherbacks have been documented nesting on beaches from Texas to Georgia, but only consistently on Florida beaches. This sparse nesting occurs in southeastern Florida, while sporadic occurremces have been recorded in northwestern Florida. Nesting by ten leatherbacks on the central Atlantic Coast of Florida in 1996 in the Archie Carr National Wildlife Refuge and adjacent beach areas was the greatest observed in a decade, and one female was a repeat from 1994. In other oceans, nesting occurs on the east coast of Malaya, Tongaland, South Africa, Indonesia, and Sri Lanka, although most of these major rookeries have seriously declined.

The largest-known rookery was on the southern coast of Pacific Mexico, on beaches of the states of Michoacán, Guerrero, and Oaxaca, which only became internationally known in the early 1980s. On these beaches, an estimated 75,000 females nested but were heavily slaughtered for their meat in Oaxaca. By comparison, at that time an estimated 15,000 females nested in French Guiana. In the 1995–1996 nesting season, only 1,100 nesting females were estimated from the first census of leatherback nesting colonies on the Mexican Pacific Coast. The census used aerial surveys and ground patrols to cover 4,186 km of coastline and found only four beaches supporting nest densities greater than 50 per km. The largest eastern Pacific nesting aggregation of leatherbacks is now in Las Baulas National Park in Costa Rica; in the 1994–1995 season, about 1,200 females nested along the 5 km of beach area.

The leatherback provides a sad chronology of population estimates. In 1952, it was thought to nest nowhere in any number, and the world population in 1961 was thought to be as small as 1,000 pairs. The discovery of the Mexican colony resulted in a triple-fold increase in the estimated world population of breeding females from 29,000 to 40,000 in 1971, and to 115,000 in 1982. In 1995, the number was estimated to be as low as 20,000 to 30,000.

Possibly because of their great bulk, the females nest on beaches that are relatively steep and that border deep water. Leatherback nesting tracks are easily distinguished from other turtle tracks by their size, which can range in width from 1.5 to 2 m. At most locales, leatherback females excavate a large body pit prior to nest construction. Because of the large size of the females, leatherback nests are usually deeper than those of other species and the disturbed area is larger, ranging from 2.5 to 5 m in diameter. The average clutch size varies but in most locales ranges from 80 to 90 eggs. At the end of each nesting, some very small eggs are usually laid. These small eggs, which can be 30 to 60 percent of the diameter of normal eggs, are a characteristic feature of leatherback nesting. Normal eggs average 65 mm in diameter. Within a breeding season, a female may nest six or seven times at ten-day intervals. Analysis of genotype frequencies of offspring in leatherback clutches at St. Croix, U.S. Virgin Islands, suggests that offspring in a single clutch have the same father, although clutches laid by the same female at other times during the nesting season are fertilized by other males. On the average, females nest periodically every two to three years. Female leatherbacks do not consistently return to the same beach to lay their eggs and are considered to be the least "philopatric" of sea turtles. Even within a nesting season, females are known to shift from Suriname to French Guiana. Recent genetic studies of nesting leatherbacks from Florida and sites in the Carribean indicate that leatherback females return less faithfully to their natal beaches to nest than do female green turtles or female hawksbills in this region.

The average incubation time of eggs varies from 56 days in Malaysia to 65 days in Suriname. Hatchlings vary from 55 to 64 cm in carapace length. As in other sea turtles, incubation temperature affects the sex ratio of the clutch. Incubation temperatures less than 29°C produce all males; those above 30°C result in nearly 100 percent females. Leatherback nests seem particularly vulnerable to tidal inundation, which has been observed to affect 40 percent of nests in some areas. The migratory paths taken by the hatchlings are uncharted. However, related to their oceanic lifestyle is the observation that hatchling leatherbacks can only swim forward, and they do so by synchronously beating their front flippers.

Recoveries of female leatherbacks tagged when nesting in the Guianas indicate that after nesting they travel in all directions. Subsequent recoveries occurred southeast of Freeport, Texas, and at Beaufort, North Carolina, about three years after tagging, and off New Jersey, the Yucatán, the Gulf of Venezuela, and Ghana after approximately one year. One female tagged in Suriname was recovered eleven months later in Ghana, having covered 5,900 km. Migrational aspects of nesting female arrivals at St. Croix in the Virgin Islands have been inferred by examining encrustation patterns of northern barnacle species and growth patterns of the stalked barnacle, *Conchoderma virgatum*. These studies suggested that the females came from temperate waters, nested within a few days of their arrival, and individually arrived at various times during the March-to-July nesting season.

The development of satellite telemetry has permitted the longest distance and greatest depth tracking of leatherback turtles. Transmitters attached to two nesting females in Trinidad monitored their movements for a year afterward and indicated that both females traveled more than 11,000 km in this time. One female swam to the Bay of Biscay, off France, then south in November to within 200 km of Mauritania by March, then back northward close to the Canary Islands. The other female piloted up into the middle of the North Atlantic to between 40 and 50 degrees north latitude, and remained there until November, when it headed directly to Africa, getting as far as a few hundred km of Mauritania until the transmitter died. At the outset of their journeys in the South Atlantic, both of these turtles made dives deeper than the 750 m recording capacity of the transmitter.

Traveling companions of leatherbacks include the shark-sucker, *Echeneis naucrates*, and the remora *Remora remora*. In one case, 1,000 little shark-suckers were observed swimming around a large leatherback off Sarasota, Florida.

Information on the diet of the leatherback indicates it feeds most frequently on gelatinous foods, especially scyphomedusae and tunicates, although fish, and even hatchling olive ridleys, have been found in the stomach contents of leatherbacks on the Pacific Coast of Mexico. The leatherback's jaws are sharp-edged, and the central part of the upper jaw is deeply notched, appearing beaklike (Figure 12.7). These morphological features are thought to be adaptations for handling soft-bodied prey as are the spines, 5 to 8 cm in length, that line the interior of the mouth and esophagus. These feeding habits appear to predispose the leatherback to ingest plastic bags and similar items that masquerade as food, causing the concern of conservationists.

All sea turtles possess salt glands, which are an important part of the excretory system. The salt glands are located in the head and are highly modified tear glands that eliminate excess salt from the body. In contrast to those of other sea turtles, the salt glands of the leatherback appear to flow continuously. These continuous "tears" appear to be in response to the leatherback's higher salt intake as a result of its salty jellyfish diet.

Leatherbacks off the U.S. Atlantic Coast and in the Gulf of Mexico have been recorded feeding on the cabbagehead medusa, *Stomolophus meleagris*. Many species of jellyfish were found in gut contents of leatherbacks examined from waters around southern England and the North Sea. Leatherbacks have been observed off the coast of France feeding on the seasonally abundant jellyfish *Rhizostoma pulmo*. In the Mediterranean, deep-water salps have been found in stomach contents, indicating, too, that the leatherback can forage deeply. Off St. Croix, dive depths of internesting leatherbacks ranged from 32 to 84 m, suggesting that they were feeding on siphophores, salps, and medusae within the deep-scattering depth. In this regard, a leatherback with a 1.2-m carapace length, and thus perhaps immature, took a line baited with an octopus being fished at 50 m in Australian waters.

Recent investigations of the diving physiology of leatherbacks, one of the deepest-diving species (records exist for more than 1,000 m), have indicated that as a leatherback dives, its heartbeat slows on the average by 35 percent to around 17 beats per minute during the descent, speeding up to normal as the animal ascends to the surface. Because the leatherback is a continuous diver, spending only a short time on the surface between dives, this adaptation represents a considerable saving in oxygen reserves. This phenomenon is known as diving brachycardia and is exhibited by some other diving vertebrate species. Typical heartbeats of leatherbacks at the sea surface are 26 beats per minute; nesting females have elevated heartbeats about 40 beats per minute.

Leatherback turtles are unique among sea turtles in their skeletal growth in that their cartilage is vascularized, gaining them a description as a mammal-like reptile. This condition is considered to permit rapid growth to a large size. However, little information exists on the growth rate of these animals. Some information suggests that maturity may be attained between the ages of three to six. In captivity, a hatchling fed on jellyfish gained 64 pounds in a year and 10 months. How an animal as large as a leatherback can derive sufficient nutrition from a diet of jellyfish is an interesting puzzle. Recent estimates relating typical leatherback metabolic rates and jellyfish energy content (1 kg jellyfish = 52 kcal) indicate that small leatherbacks would need to consume the equivalent of their weight per day in jellyfish and that large leatherbacks (e.g., 340 kg) would need to consume

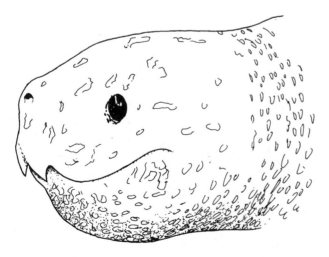

**FIGURE 12.7.** A portrait of a female leatherback turtle showing the distinctive cusps on the upper jaw. (x0.2)

some 60 kg of jellyfish per day! Scientists speculate that leatherbacks often frequent oceanic fronts, because such prey would be accumulated in these areas by hydrographic dynamics. Other large pelagics such as swordfish, tuna, and whales are known to frequent these fronts and, in fact, leatherbacks are often incidentally caught on longlines set in such areas to harvest swordfish. These hydrographic conditions prevail off the southeastern coast of the United States due to the flow of the Gulf Stream and in the eastern Gulf of Mexico to a lesser extent due to the Loop Current. Counts of leatherbacks from aerial surveys made along the North Carolina coast suggested that the abundance of leatherbacks and cabbagehead jellyfish (*Stomolophus meleagris*) were correlated seasonally in some years.

Although the leatherback is an ectotherm (like all reptiles), it can keep its body temperature 18°C above the ambient water temperature when the water is cold. This phenomenon was discovered from deep-body temperature measurements made on a large male leatherback (158 cm carapace length; 417 kg in weight) that was captured after it had become entangled in a fishing net off Nova Scotia. While this heat differential was thought to be generated by muscular activity, and partially maintained by the insulating fat layer under the skin, dissection of a female leatherback that died at the New England Aquarium in 1972 soon after its capture indicated the presence of bundles of veins and arteries that function as countercurrent heat exchangers. These bundles occur near the base of the flippers and help to retain the heat generated by the muscles when the animal is in cold water. This was the first discovery of such a heat exchange mechanism in a reptile. The black coloration of the carapace is thought to be thermally important, too, in the absorption of solar radiation.

While the leatherback has not been hunted in most regions for its flesh, in some regions the fat under its carapace has been rendered into an oil that is used for caulking boats, and for medicinal applications. In the Florida Keys, leatherbacks were once used as shark bait. Leatherback eggs are avidly collected in many regions of the world, resulting in near 100 percent destruction of broods in some areas.

## Hawksbill Turtles, *Eretmochelys imbricata*

The hawksbill turtle is uncommon in the northern Gulf of Mexico (Figure 12.8). At one time,

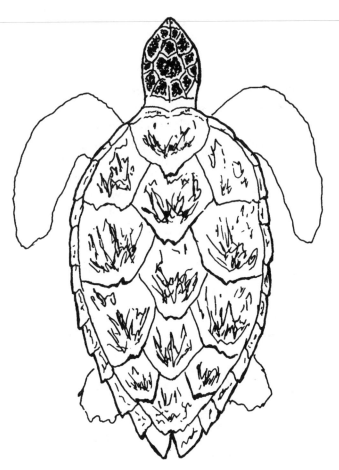

**FIGURE 12.8.** The hawksbill turtle, *Eretmochelys imbricata*, mature female. The thick, overlapping scutes of the carapace of adults give this turtle its descriptive name of imbricata. (x0.1)

females were frequent nesters in Florida, but between 1979 and 1992, only zero to 2 nests have been recorded annually. This species is circumtropical in distribution and is considered to be the most tropical of all sea-turtle species. The small hawksbill turtles that are regularly stranded, usually in the fall, on the Texas coast mostly near Corpus Christi, fall into two size groups—posthatchling (less than 10 cm) and juveniles (20 to 29 cm) in length. Luckily, most of these little turtles are found alive and some are able to be rehabilitated. The posthatchlings are thought to come from nesting beaches in Mexico based on their size and current drift times. Very small numbers of juveniles have also been recorded regularly in Texas; sightings or strandings of adults have been sporadic in the Gulf. Adults average about 100 cm in carapace length and weigh 45 to 90 kg. Its specific name, *imbricata*, refers to the overlapping of the scutes of its carapace, which are the source of tortoiseshell, and the cause of its overexploitation.

In the western Atlantic, nesting occurs throughout the Caribbean on small, isolated beaches, where females come ashore singly at night. Some scientists believe that the present scattered nesting by females is a result of heavy exploitation and that hawksbills are naturally group nesters. Nesting females in the Caribbean range from 63 to 91 cm. The average size egg laid by females nesting in the Caribbean area varies from 36 to 42 mm in diameter. Clutch size is strongly correlated with the size of the female. At Tortuguero, Costa Rica, the average size of females is about 83 cm in carapace length, and they lay about 160 eggs per nest. Hatchlings emerge after an incubation of about two months duration, and they range in size from 40 to 46 mm in carapace length. Females in the Caribbean may nest every two to three years and within a season two or three times, every two to three weeks. This frequency, combined with the average number of eggs in each clutch, makes the female hawksbill close to the most reproductively active of all sea turtles.

Once hatchling hawksbills leave their nesting beaches, they enter a pelagic phase typically associated with *Sargassum* rafts in the Caribbean, on which they feed. They apparently do not typically enter the Atlantic Sargasso Sea, as loggerheads hatching from U.S. Atlantic beaches do. Scattered sightings of pelagic-stage hawksbills associated with *Sargassum* along the U.S. Eastern Seaboard have been made. Hawksbills become benthic reef-feeders at the size of 15 to 25 cm. Juveniles forage in shallower waters than adults, which may dive as deep as 100 m. In areas of depth diversity, juveniles and adults are found in close proximity. Migration patterns in the Caribbean are not clear from tagging studies, but most turtles seem to make primarily local movements or small migrations. The pigmentation patterns of hawksbill hatchlings differ from one island to another, suggesting that little intermixing of breeding population occurs.

The hawksbill occurs on coral reefs and rocky bottoms, where its slender jaws are capable of extracting prey from crevices (Figure 12.9). It appears to be an opportunistic feeder, although sponges, particularly Demospongiae, are a favored food in Caribbean and Hawaiian locales. This diet is unusual, because not many vertebrates—only some fish species and the hawksbill—are capable of digesting the glass spicules

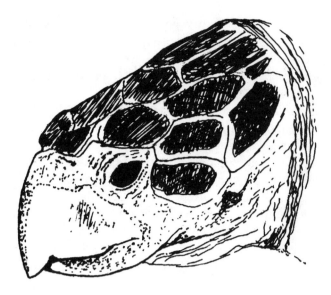

**FIGURE 12.9.** A portrait of a female hawksbill turtle showing the beaked, birdlike jaws of the species. (x0.3)

that serve as the skeleton of these sponges. This trait is considered to be adaptive for reducing food competition with other species. Tunicates and zooanthids have also been recorded as major diet components of some Carribean hawksbills.

Hawksbills appear to grow fast when young and slower when older. Well-fed hatchlings in captivity grew to about 20 cm in a year and 35 cm in two years. Estimates based on recaptured wild animals vary from 3 to 4 cm per year for small juveniles (27 to 61 cm in length) to 1 to 2 cm per year for larger juveniles (40 to 90 cm). Adult growth, based on nesting females, is negligible. The age at which hawksbills become mature is not known, although 30 to 50 years has been postulated.

The hawksbill is most famous as the source of tortoiseshell. Although the carapaces of other species have interesting patterns, too, only the shell of the hawksbill is thick enough for most uses. The amount of shell obtained from an individual turtle averages about 3 kg, although this varies according to the age and size of the turtle. World trade in hawksbill shell has been severely restricted, with more and more nations ratifying and enforcing harvesting restrictions imposed by the Convention on International Trade of Endangered Species of Wild Fauna and Flora (CITES), which originiated in 1975. Amendments adopted in 1977 prohibited commercial trade in wild, caught sea-turtle products by signers, although enforcement lagged conservation intentions in many areas. Estimates of the extent of the annual harvest of this species worldwide, in the first few years after CITES, averaged 200,000 to 500,000 turtles. Turtles are still harvested despite laws that protect them, leading to greatly reduced populations in most areas of the world. Ranching of hawksbills in some areas has been thought to be a practice that may reduce wild-population mortality levels. Hawksbill eggs are commonly eaten; however, hawksbill flesh is considered poisonous in some areas.

At present, no world-population estimates are available. Of all the sea turtles, more is yet is to be learned of this species' ecology and population dynamics. Recent studies of hawksbill nesting on the Yucatán Peninsula in the states of Yucatán, Campeche, and Quintana Roo have found nesting levels to be increasing in the last few years, with up to 3,000 nests having been recorded.

# A Note on Biological Terminology

All recognized species of organisms have a two-part scientific name. The first part is the name of the genus to which the species belongs, and it is always capitalized. The second part is the name of the species, and it is not capitalized. Although two species may have the same genus name or the same species name, no two species have both names in common. Species names are selected by the first person to publish a description of the organism, and they often refer to some physical property of the species (e.g., *Crepidula plana, Stylochus zebra, Chthamalus fragilis*), to the species' habitat (e.g., *Anemonia sargassensis, Glaucus atlanticus, Corophium louisianum*), or to some individual who is being honored (e.g., *Polydora websteri, Albunea gibbesii, Panopeus herbstii*). In formal usage, the name of the person who described the species and the date that the description was published follow the species name—e.g., *Littorina irrorata* Say, 1822. If the species is later moved to a different genus, the describer's name is enclosed in parentheses—e.g., *Odostomia impressa* (Say, 1822). Frequently, one will see a species name followed by L. or Linn. These abbreviations refer to Linnaeus, an eighteenth-century Swedish botanist who instigated the binomial nomenclature system and organized the known plant and animal kingdoms in his book, *Systema Naturae*.

Most of the more conspicuous species have common names (e.g., blue crab, white shrimp) as well as scientific names. Unfortunately, these common names are of local origin, and a wide-ranging species may have several such names in various areas of its range. For example, *Sesarma cinereum* is known as the marsh crab, the wharf crab, the friendly crab, and the square-backed crab in different parts of the world. Hence, common names are most useful in a local context and may not be helpful in communicating an organism's identity to someone living on a distant shore. One notable exception is the bird fauna for which one set of common names has become standard, at least among English-speaking peoples, through extensive communication and common use of one set of guidebooks.

Abbreviations are commonly used when referring to organisms by their scientific names. When a name is used repeatedly, or when two or more species in the same genus are mentioned, the first letter of the genus name may be used as an abbreviation after the first reference—e.g., *Balanus eburneus* and *B. improvisus*. Sometimes an organism is found whose genus is known but that has not been identified further. Then the genus name is given, followed by the abbreviation sp., e.g., *Balanus* sp. If two or more species in the same genus are involved, this notation becomes *Balanus* spp.

Animal families, which are groups of related genera, have names that end in the suffix *-idae*. If no other common name exists, an abbreviation of the family name, formed by dropping the *-ae*, may be used. For example, a crab in the family Portunidae may be called a portunid crab.

# Phylogenetic List

Phylum Porifera
  Class Calcispongia
    Family Heterocoelidae
      *Scypha barbadensis* (Schuffner, 1877)
  Class Demospongiae
    Family Haliclonidae
      *Haliclona loosanoffi* Hartman, 1958
      *Haliclona permollis* (Bowerbank, 1866)
      *Haliclona rubens* (Pallas, 1766)
      *Haliclona viridis* (Duchassaing & Michelotti, 1864)
    Family Halichondriidae
      *Halichondria bowerbanki* Burton, 1930
    Family Clionidae
      *Cliona celata* Grant, 1826
      *Cliona truitti* Old, 1941

Phylum Cnidaria
  Class Hydrozoa
    Order Siphonophora
      Family Physaliidae
        *Physalia physalis* (Linnaeus, 1758)
    Order Chondrophora
      Family Velellidae
        *Velella velella* (Linnaeus, 1758)
      Family Porpitidae
        *Porpita porpita* (Linnaeus, 1758)
    Order Athecata
      Family Tubulariidae
        *Tubularia crocea* (Agassiz, 1862)

      Family Corynidae
        *Syncoryne eximia* (Allman, 1859)
      Family Hydractinidae
        *Hydractinia echinata* Fleming, 1828
        *Podocoryne selena* Mills, 1976
      Family Bougainvillidae
        *Bougainvillia inaegualis* Fraser, 1944
        *Nemopsis bachei* Agassiz, 1849
    Order Thecata
      Family Campanularidae
        *Clytia cylindrica* L. Agassiz, 1862
        *Gonothyraea gracilis* (Sars, 1851)
        *Obelia dichotoma* (Linnaeus, 1758)
      Family Plumularidae
        *Aglaophenia latecarinata* Allman, 1877
        *Plumularia diaphana* (Heller, 1868)
  Class Scyphozoa
    Order Semaeostomeae
      Family Ulmaridae
        *Aurelia aurita* (Linnaeus, 1758)
      Family Pelagidae
        *Chrysaora quinquecirrha* (Desor, 1848)
      Family Cyanidae
        *Cyanea capillata* (Linnaeus, 1758)
    Order Rhizostomeae
      Family Stomolophidae
        *Stomolophus meleagris* Agassiz, 1862
    Order Cubomedusae
      Family Chirodropidae
        *Chiropsalmus quadrumanus* (Muller, 1859)

Class Anthozoa
  Order Gorgonacea
    Family Gorgoniidae
      *Leptogorgia setacea* (Pallas, 1766)
      *Leptogorgia virgulata* (Lamarck, 1815)
  Order Pennatulacea
    Family Renillidae
      *Renilla mülleri* Kölliker, 1872
  Order Actiniaria
    Family Actinidae
      *Anemonia sargassensis* Hargitt, 1908
      *Bunodosoma cavernata* (Bosc, 1802)
      *Bunodactis texaensis* Carlgren & Hedgpeth, 1952
    Family Actinostolidae
      *Paranthus rapiformis* (Lesueur, 1817)
    Family Hormathiidae
      *Calliactis tricolor* (Lesueur, 1817)
    Family Aiptasiomorphidae
      *Aiptasiomorpha texaensis* Carlgren & Hedgpeth, 1952
  Order Madreporaria
    Family Astrangidae
      *Astrangia poculata* (Ellis and Solander, 1786)
Phylum Ctenophora
  Class Tentaculata
    Order Lobata
      Family Mnemiidae
        *Mnemiopsis mccradyi* Mayer, 1900
  Class Nuda
    Order Beroida
      Family Beroidae
        *Beroë ovata* Chamisso & Eysenhardt, 1821

Phylum Platyhelminthes
  Class Turbellaria
    Order Polycladida
      Family Stylochidae
        *Stylochus ellipticus* (Girard, 1850)
        *Stylochus frontalis* Verrill, 1893
        *Stylochus zebra* (Verrill, 1882)
      Family Planoceridae
        *Gnesioceros sargassicola* (Graff, 1892)

Phylum Rhynchocoela
  Class Anopla
    Order Heteronemertea
      Family Lineidae
        *Cerebratulus lacteus* Verrill, 1892
        *Micrura leidyi* (Verrill, 1892)

Phylum Annelida
  Class Polychaeta
    Order Phyllodocida
      Family Phyllodocidae
        *Eteone heteropoda* Hartman, 1951
        *Phyllodoce mucosa* Oersted, 1843
      Family Polynoidae
        *Harmothoë aculeata* Andrews, 1891
        *Lepidonotus sublevis* Verrill, 1873
      Family Glyceridae
        *Glycera americana* Leidy, 1855
      Family Nephtyidae
        *Aglaophamus verrilli* McIntosh, 1885
      Family Syllidae
        *Haplosyllis spongicola* (Grube, 1855)
        *Trypanosyllis gemmipara* Johnson, 1901
      Family Nereidae
        *Ceratonereis irritabilis* (Webster, 1879)
        *Laeonereis culveri* (Webster, 1879)
        *Neanthes succinea* (Frey & Leuckart, 1847)
        *Platynereis dumerilii* (Andouin & Milne-Edwards, 1833)
    Order Capitellida
      Family Capitellidae
        *Capitella capitata floridana* Hartman, 1959
        *Mediomastus californiensis* Hartman, 1944
      Family Arenicolidae
        *Arenicola cristata* Stimpson, 1856
      Family Maldanidae
        *Clymenella torquata* (Leidy, 1855)
        *Clymenella zonalis* (Verrill, 1874)
    Order Spionida
      Family Spionidae
        *Paraprionospio pinnata* (Ehlers, 1901)
        *Polydora ligni* Webster, 1879
        *Polydora websteri* Hartman, 1943
        *Spiophanes bombyx* (Claparéde, 1870)
      Family Paraonidae
        *Aricidea fragilis* Webster, 1879
      Family Chaetopteridae
        *Chaetopterus variopedatus* (Renier, 1804)
        *Spiochaetopterus costarum*
    Order Eunicida
      Family Onuphidae
        *Diopatra cuprea* (Bosc, 1802)
        *Onuphis eremita oculata* Hartman, 1951
      Family Lumbrinereidae
        *Lumbrineris tenuis* (Verrill, 1873)
    Order Magelonida
      Family Magelonidae
        *Magelona phyllisae* Jones, 1963

Order Ariciida
  Family Orbiniidae
    *Scoloplos capensis* Day, 1963
    *Scoloplos rubra* (Webster, 1879)
Order Oweniida
  Family Oweniidae
    *Owenia fusiformis* delle Chiaje, 1841
Order Sabellida
  Family Sabellidae
    *Hypsicomus elegans* (Webster, 1884)
  Family Serpulidae
    *Eupomatus protulicola* (Benedict, 1887)
    *Hydroides dianthus* Verrill, 1873
    *Spirobranchus giganteus* (Pallas, 1766)

Phylum Mollusca
  Class Gastropoda
    Order Rhipidoglossa
      Family Neritidae
        *Nerita fulgurans* Gmelin, 1791
        *Neritina virginea* (Linnaeus, 1758)
    Order Ctenobranchia
      Family Littorinidae
        *Littorina irrorata* Say, 1822
        *Nodilittorina lineolata* (d'Orbigny, 1840)
      Family Potamididae
        *Cerithidea pliculosa* (Menke, 1829)
      Family Cerithiidae
        *Bittiolum varium* (Pfeiffer, 1840)
      Family Epitoniidae
        *Epitonium tollini* Bartsch, 1938
      Family Janthinidae
        *Janthina janthina* (Linnaeus, 1758)
        *Janthina pallida* (Thompson, 1841)
        *Janthina prolongata* Blainville, 1822
      Family Calyptracidae
        *Crepidula fornicata* (Linnaeus, 1758)
        *Crepidula plana* Say, 1822
      Family Ovulidae
        *Simnialena uniplicata* (Sowerby, 1848)
      Family Naticidae
        *Naticarius canrena* (Linnaeus, 1758)
        *Neverita duplicata* (Say, 1822)
        *Sinum perspectivum* Say, 1831
        *Tectonatica pusilla* (Say, 1822)
      Family Cassididae
        *Phalium granulatum* (Born, 1780)
      Family Personidae
        *Distorsio clathrata* (Lamarck, 1816)

Family Terebridae
  *Hastula salleana* Deshayes, 1859
  *Terebra dislocata* Say, 1822
  *Terebra protexta* (Conrad, 1846)
Family Buccinidae
  *Cantharus cancellaria* (Conrad, 1846)
  *Pollia tincta* Conrad, 1846
Family Nassariidae
  *Nassarius acutus* (Say, 1822)
  *Nassarius vibex* (Say, 1822)
Family Fasciolariidae
  *Fasciolaria lilium lilium* G. Fischer, 1807
  *Pleuroploca gigantea* (Kiener, 1840)
Family Melongenidae
  *Busycon pulleyi* Hollister, 1958
  *Busycotypus plagosus* (Conrad, 1862)
Family Columbellidae
  *Anachis semiplicata* Stearns, 1873
Family Muricidae
  *Hexaplex fulvescens* (Sowerby II, 1834)
  *Stramonita haemastoma canaliculata* (Gray, 1839)
  *Stramonita haemastoma floridana* (Conrad, 1837)
Family Olividae
  *Oliva sayana* Ravenel, 1834
  *Olivella minuta* (Link, 1807)
Order Dendronotoidea
  Family Scyllaeidae
    *Scyllaea pelagica* Linnaeus, 1758
Order Eolidoidea
  Family Glaucidae
    *Glaucus atlanticus* Forster, 1777
Order Steganobranchia
  Family Bullidae
    *Bulla striata* Bruguiére, 1792
  Family Aplysiidae
    *Aplysia brasiliana* Rang, 1828
Order Actophila
  Family Ellobiidae
    *Melampus bidentatus* Say, 1822
Order Hygrophila
  Family Siphonariidae
    *Siphonaria pectinata* (Linnaeus, 1758)
Class Bivalvia
  Order Arcoidea
    Family Arcidae
      *Anadara brasiliana* (Lamarck, 1819)
      *Anadara ovalis* (Bruguiére, 1789)

*Arca imbricata* Bruguiére, 1789
*Noetia ponderosa* (Say, 1822)
Order Mytiloidea
  Family Mytilidae
    *Brachidontes exustus* (Linnaeus, 1758)
    *Geukensia demissa granosissima* (Sowerby, 1914)
    *Ischadium recurvum* (Rafinesque, 1820)
    *Lithophaga aristata* (Dillwyn, 1817)
    *Lithophaga bisulcata* (d'Orbigny, 1845)
  Family Pinnidae
    *Atrina seminuda* (Lamarck, 1819)
    *Atrina serrata* (Sowerby, 1825)
Order Pterioidea
  Family Pteridae
    *Pteria colymbus* (Roding, 1798)
  Family Isognomonidae
    *Isognomon bicolor* (C. B. Adams, 1845)
  Family Pectinidae
    *Argopecten irradians amplicostatus* (Dall, 1898)
  Family Ostreidae
    *Crassostrea virginica* Gmelin, 1792
    *Ostrea equestris* Say, 1834
Order Veneroidea
  Family Lucinidae
    *Lucina pectinata* (Gmelin, 1791)
Order Hippuritoidea
  Family Chamidae
    *Chama macerophylla* Gmelin, 1791
  Family Cardiidae
    *Laevicardium robustum* (Lightfoot, 1786)
  Family Mactridae
    *Mulinia lateralis* (Say, 1822)
    *Rangia cuneata* (Gray, 1831)
  Family Tellinidae
    *Macoma constricta* (Bruguiére, 1792)
    *Macoma mitchelli* Dall, 1895
    *Tellina altemata* Say, 1822
    *Tellina lineata* Turton, 1819
    *Tellina versicolor* DeKay, 1843
  Family Donacidae
    *Donax texasiana* Philippi, 1847
    *Donax variabilis roemeri* Philippi, 1849
  Family Solecurtidae
    *Tagelus plebeius* (Solander, 1786)
  Family Scrobiculariidae
    *Abra aequalis* (Say, 1822)
  Family Veneridae
    *Chione cancellata* (Linnaeus, 1767)
    *Chione grus* (Holmes, 1858)

*Dosinia discus* (Reeve, 1850)
*Mercenaria campechiensis texana* (Dall, 1902)
Order Myoidea
  Family Myidae
    *Paramya subovata* (Conrad, 1845)
  Family Pholadidae
    *Cyropleura costata (Linnaeus, 1758)*
    *Diplothyra smithii* Tryon, 1862
  Family Teredinidae
    *Bankia gouldi* (Bartsch, 1908)
    *Teredo bartschi* Clapp, 1923
Class Scaphopoda
  Family Dentaliidae
    *Dentalium texasianum* Philippi, 1849
Class Cephalopoda
  Order Teuthoidea
    Family Loliginidae
      *Loligo pealei* Lesueur, 1821
      *Lolliguncula brevis* (Blainville, 1823)
    Family Spirulidae
      *Spirula spirula* Linnaeus, 1758
  Order Octopoda
    Family Octopodidae
      *Octopus vulgaris* Linnaeus, 1758

Phylum Arthropoda
  Class Pantopoda
    Family Tanystylidae
      *Tanystylum orbiculare* Wilson, 1878
    Family Endeidae
      *Endeis spinosa* (Montagu, 1808)
  Class Merostomata
    Order Xiphosurida
      Family Limulidae
        *Limulus polyphemus* (Linnaeus, 1758)
  Class Crustacea
    Subclass Copepoda
      Family Acartiidae
        *Acartia tonsa* Dana, 1849
    Subclass Cirripedia
      Family Lepadidae
        *Lepas anatifera* Linnaeus, 1767
        *Lepas anserifera* Linnaeus, 1767
        *Lepas pectinata* Spengler, 1793
        *Octolasmis lowei* (Darwin, 1851)
      Family Chthamalidae
        *Chthamalus fragilis* Darwin, 1854
      Family Balanidae
        *Balanus amphitrite amphitrite* Darwin, 1854
        *Balanus venustus niveus* Darwin, 1854

*Balanus reticulatus* Utinomi, 1967
*Balanus tintinnabulum* (Linnaeus, 1767)
*Balanus eburneus* Gould, 1841
*Balanus improvisus* Darwin, 1854
*Chelonibia patula* (Ranzani, 1818)
*Chelonibia testudinaria* Linnaeus, 1758
Subclass Malacostraca
Order Stomatopoda
Family Squillidae
*Squilla empusa* Say, 1818
Order Cumacea
Family Diastylidae
*Oxyurostylis salinoi*
Order Tanaidacea
Family Paratanaidae
*Leptochelia dubia* (Krøyer, 1842)
Order Isopoda
Family Limnoridae
*Limnoria tripunctata* Menzies, 1951
Family Sphaeromidae
*Dynamene perforata* Moore, 1902
*Sphaeroma quadridentatum* Say, 1818
Family Ligididae
*Ligia exotica* (Roux, 1828)
Family Bopyridae
*Bopyrissa wolffi* Markham, 1978
Order Amphipoda
Family Ampeliscidae
*Ampelisca abdita* Mills, 1964
Family Bateidae
*Batea cartharinensis* Müller, 1865
Family Corophiidae
*Corophium acherusicum* Costa, 1857
*Corophium louisianum* Shoemaker, 1934
*Erichthonius brasiliensis* (Dana, 1853)
Family Gammaridae
*Gammarus mucronatus* Say, 1818
Family Ischyroceridae
*Jassa falcata* (Montagu, 1808)
Family Leucothoidae
*Leucothoë spinicarpa* (Abildgaard, 1789)
Family Oedicerotidae
*Synchelidium americanum* Bousfield, 1973
Family Talitridae
*Orchestia grillus* Bosc, 1802
Order Caprellidea
Family Caprellidae
*Caprella equilibra* Say, 1818
Order Mysidacea
Family Mysidae
*Mysidopsis almyra* Bowman, 1964

Order Decapoda
Family Penaeidae
*Parapenaeus longirostris* (Lucas, 1849)
*Penaeus aztecus* Ives, 1891
*Penaeus duorarum* Burkenroad, 1939
*Penaeus setiferus* (Linnaeus, 1767)
*Sicyonia dorsalis* Kingsley, 1878
*Trachypeneus constrictus* Stimpson, 1871
*Trachypeneus similis* (Smith)
*Xiphopeneus krøyeri* Heller, 1862
Family Sergestidae
*Acetes americanus louisianensis* Burkenroad, 1934
*Lucifer faxoni* Borradaile, 1915
Family Pasiphaeidae
*Leptochela serratorbita* Bate, 1888
Family Palaemonidae
*Palaemonetes pugio* Holthuis, 1949
*Palaemonetes vulgaris* (Say, 1818)
Family Alpheidae
*Alpheus estuarensis* Christoffersen, 1984
*Synalpheus fritzmeulleri* Coutiere, 1909
Family Ogyrididae
*Ogyrides limicola* Williams, 1955
Family Hippolytidae
*Lysmata wurdemanni* Gibbes, 1850
*Hippolyte pleuracantha* (Stimpson, 1871)
*Latreutes fucorum* (Fabricius, 1798)
*Latreutes parvulus* (Stimpson, 1866)
*Tozeuma carolinense* Kingsley, 1878
Family Scyllaridae
*Scyllarides nodifer* (Stimpson, 1866)
Family Callianassidae
*Callianassa louisianensis* Schmitt (1935, 12)
Family Diogenidae
*Clibanarius vittatus* (Bosc, 1802)
*Dardanus fucosus* Biffar & Provenzano, 1972
*Isocheles wurdemanni* Stimpson, 1862
*Paguristes puncticeps* Benedict, 1901
*Petrochirus diogenes* (Linnaeus, 1758)
Family Paguridae
*Pagurus annulipes* (Stimpson, 1862)
*Pagurus bonairensis* Schmitt, 1936
*Pagurus impressus* (Benedict, 1892)
*Pagurus longicarpus* Say, 1817
*Pagurus pollicaris* Say, 1817
Family Porcellanidae
*Euceramus praelongus* Stimpson, 1860
*Petrolisthes armatus* (Gibbes, 1850)
*Porcellana sayana* (Leach, 1820)

Family Hippidae
*Emerita portoricensis* Schmitt, 1935
Family Albuneidae
*Albunea paretii* Guérin, 1853
*Lepidopa websteri* Benedict, 1903
Family Raninidae
*Raninoides louisianensis* Rathbun, 1933
Family Calappidae
*Calappa sulcata* Rathbun, 1898
*Hepatus epheliticus* (Linnaeus, 1763)
Family Leucosiidae
*Persephona aquilonaris* Rathbun, 1933
Family Dromiidae
*Dromidia antillensis* Stimpson, 1858
Family Majidae
*Libinia dubia* Milne-Edwards, 1834
*Libinia emarginata* Leach, 1815
*Stenorynchus seticornis* (Herbst, 1788)
Family Portunidae
*Arenaeus cribrarius* (Lamarck, 1818)
*Callinectes marginatus* Milne-Edwards, 1861
*Callinectes ornatus* Ordway, 1863
*Callinectes sapidus* Rathbun, 1896
*Cronius ruber* (Lamarck, 1818)
*Ovalipes quadulpensis* (Saussure, 1858)
*Portunus gibbesii* (Stimpson, 1859)
*Portunus sayi* (Gibbes, 1850)
*Portunus spinimanus* (Latreille, 1819)
Family Xanthidae
*Eurypanopeus depressus* (Smith, 1869)
*Hexapanopeus paulensis* Rathbun, 1930
*Menippe mercenaria* (Say, 1818)
*Menippe adina* Williams and Felder, 1986
*Neopanope texana texana* (Stimpson, 1859)
*Panopeus simpsoni* Rathbun, 1900
*Panopeus obesus* Smith, 1880
*Panopeus turgidus* Rathbun, 1930
*Pilumnus dasypodus* Kingsley, 1879
*Pilumnus pannosus* Rathbun, 1897
*Pseudomedaeus agassizi* (A. Milne-Edwards, 1880)
*Rithropanopeus harrisii* (Gould, 1841)
Family Pinnotheridae
*Pinnotheres maculatus* Say, 1818
*Pinnotheres ostreum* Say, 1817
*Pinnixa chaetopterana* Stimpson, 1860
*Pinnixa lunzi* Glassell, 1937
Family Grapsidae
*Pachygrapsus transversus* (Gibbes, 1850)
*Sesarma cinereum* (Bosc, 1801 or 1802)
*Sesarma reticulatum* (Say, 1817)

Family Gecarcinidae
*Cardisoma guanhumi* Latreille, 1825
*Gecarcinus lateralis* (Freminville, 1835)
Family Ocypodidae
*Ocypode quadrata* (Fabricius, 1787)
*Uca longisignalis* Salmon & Atsaides, 1968
*Uca minax* (Le Conte, 1955)
*Uca panaceae* Salmon, 1974
*Uca rapax* (Smith, 1870)
*Uca subcylindrica* (Stimpson, 1859)
*Uca vocator*

Phylum Sipuncula
*Phascolion strombi* (Montagu, 1804)

Phylum Echiura
Family Thalassemidae
*Thalassema hartmani* Fisher, 1947

Phylum Phoronida
*Phoronis architecta* Andrews, 1890

Phylum Brachiopoda
Family Lingulidae
*Glottidia pyramidata* (Stimpson, 1860)

Phylum Bryozoa
Class Gymnolaemata
Order Cheilostomata
Family Aeteidae
*Aetea anguina* (Linnaeus, 1758)
Family Membraniporidae
*Membranipora commensale* (Kirkpatrick & Metzelaar, 1922)
*Membranipora savartii* (Audouin, 1826)
*Membranipora tenuis* Desor, 1848
Family Bugulidae
*Bugula neritina* (Linnaeus, 1758)
*Bugula rylandi* Maturo, 1966
Family Schizoporellidae
*Schizoporella errata* (Waters, 1878)
Family Smittinidae
*Parasmittina trispinosa* (Johnson)
Family Savignyellidae
*Savignyella lafonti* (Audouin)

Phylum Echinodermata
Class Asteroidea
Order Platyasterida
Family Luidiidae
*Luidia alternata* (Say, 1825)

*Luidia clathrata* (Say, 1825)
Order Paxillosida
   Family Astropectinidae
     *Astropecten duplicatus* Gray, 1840
Class Ophiuroidea
   Order Ophiurida
     Family Amphiuridae
       *Hemipholis elongata* (Say, 1825)
       *Micropholis atra* (Stimpson, 1852)
       *Ophiactis savignyi* (Müller & Troschel, 1842)
       *Orphiophragmus moorei* Thomas, 1965
     Family Ophiothrichidae
       *Ophiothrix angulata* (Say, 1825)
Class Echinoidea
   Order Diadematoida
     Family Diadematidae
       *Diadema antillarum* Philippi, 1845
   Order Arbacoida
     Family Arbaciidae
       *Arbacia punctulata* (Lamarck, 1816)
   Order Echinoida
     Family Echinometridae
       *Echinometra lucunter* (Linnaeus, 1758)
   Order Clypeasteroida
     Family Mellitidae
       *Mellita quinquiesperforata* (Leske, 1778)
Class Holothuroidea
   Order Dendrochirotida
     Family Cucumariidae
       *Thyone mexicana* Deichmann, 1946

Phylum Chaetognatha
   *Sagitta tenuis* Conant, 1896

Phylum Chordata
   Class Ascidiacea
     Order Pleurogona
       Family Molgulidae
         *Molgula manhattensis* (DeKay, 1843)
   Class Larvacea
     Family Oikopleuridae
       *Oikopleura sp.*
   Class Cephalochordata
     *Branchiostoma caribaeum* Sundevall, 1853

Subphylum Vertebrata
   Class Reptilia
     Order Testudinata
       Family Dermochelidae
         *Dermochelys coriacea* (Linnaeus, 1758)
       Family Cheloniidae
         *Chelonia mydas* (Linnaeus, 1758)
         *Eretmochelys coriacea* (Linnaeus, 1766)
         *Caretta caretta* (Linnaeus, 1758)
         *Lepidochelys kempi* (Garman, 1880)

# Glossary

**abalone.** A limpet-like gastropod whose large foot is considered a delicacy in California and Japan.

**adductor muscle.** The large muscle of a clam or scallop that closes the shell upon contraction.

**amphipod.** A small crustacean with a laterally compressed body and usually having enlarged hind legs for jumping. Beach fleas, *Orchestia, Gammarus.*

**anisomyarian.** Adductor muscles of clams or scallops that are not equal in size.

**antenna (pl. antennae).** A sensory appendage found on the head, e.g., the "feeler" of a lobster or insect.

**antennal scale.** Bladelike projection from the base of the antenna of certain crustaceans, e.g. *Squilla.*

**antennule.** One of the more anterior pair of antennae in crustaceans possessing two pairs of antennae.

**autotomize.** To self-amputate a part of the body, such as a leg or tail, usually to facilitate escape.

**avicularium.** A small defensive heterozooid in some bryozoans.

**benthic.** Living on or in the sediments of aquatic habitats, as opposed to *pelagic.*

**berried.** Carrying eggs on the outside of the body like a large mass of minute berries. *See also* gravid.

**bryozoan.** A moss animal; a member of the phylum Bryozoa.

**budding.** A method of asexual reproduction in which a new individual arises as an outgrowth of its parent.

**byssus (or byssal threads).** The tuft of fibers produced by the foot of mussels, ark clams, and a few other bivalves to anchor themselves to the substrate.

**carapace.** The top portion of a crustacean's external skeleton, e.g. the broad, flat "shell" of a blue crab; or the top part of a turtle's shell.

**carina.** A ridge, or keel, commonly found on the exoskeletons of certain arthropods.

**carpus.** The third segment from the tip of a shrimp or crab leg, often forming an elbow.

**carrion.** The dead body or carcass of an animal, such as a fish or crab, that is washed up on the beach.

**cercaria.** (pl. **cercariae**) The free-swimming larval stage of a fluke. *See also* trematode.

**chela.** (pl. **chelae**) A claw found on the first pair of legs of some crustaceans.

**cheliped.** A leg that bears a claw, as in the blue crab or lobster.

**chemoreception.** The reception of chemical stimuli, such as those produced by food or pollutants in the water; corresponds to senses of taste and smell.

**chitin.** A protein that is used to form the shells of crustaceans.

**chromatophore.** A pigment-containing cell, especially one with branching processes which enable the pigment to be dispersed or concentrated.

**cilia.** (sing. **cilium**) Minute, hairlike structures whose beating aids in locomotion, feeding, and/or transport of wastes.

**ciliary mucous feeder.** Organism that traps suspended food in mucus and transports the mixture to its mouth on cilia.

cirrus (pl. cirri). A flexible projection from the body of an animal, usually contributing to a sense of touch.

commensal. A relationship between organisms of different species that live together in a close association.

conchiolin. A protein used to form a matrix in which calcite and aragonite are embedded to form the shell of a snail or clam.

copepod. A minute crustacean with very long antennae; a dominant animal in the zooplankton.

cosmopolitan. Having a worldwide distribution.

coxal plate. A flattened extension of the basal segment of an amphipod leg that gives the bearer the appearance of being armor plated.

crustacean. A group of aquatic animals characterized by jointed legs and a hard shell which is shed periodically, e.g., shrimp, crabs, crayfish, isopods, and amphipods.

ctenodont. A comblike tooth structure found in the hinge teeth of some bivalves.

ctenolium. A comb-line structure of small teeth found near the anterior margin of the right valve in young Pectinidae (scallops).

ctenophore. A nonstinging "jellyfish" characterized by eight rows of cilia that propel it through the water.

cuticle. A noncellular membrane that covers the epidermis of many invertebrates.

cypris. A free-swimming larval form of barnacles.

dactylozooid. A protective individual in a hydroid colony.

deposit feeder. An animal that derives nourishment by swallowing mud or sand and digesting whatever food particles may be present.

diatom. A unicellular plant possessing a siliceous shell.

ectoparasite. A parasite that lives on the exterior surface of its host.

epipodite. A branch from the basal segment of a crustacean leg that often functions as a gill.

epithelium. A tissue lining the surfaces of gland ducts and cavities.

epitoky. A reproductive phenomenon occurring in certain polychaete worms in which the anterior asexual portion (the atoke) differs from the posterior portion (the epitoke) of the worm.

errant. Wandering, as in certain active worms which continually crawl through the sand or mud. Prone to traveling.

estuary. An area at the intersection of a river and the sea, usually a bay, where seawater and freshwater are mixed, producing brackish water.

euryhaline. Tolerant of a wide range of salinities. A property of most estuarine animals.

evisceration. Discharge of the internal organs in sea cucumbers.

filter-feeder. An animal that derives nourishment by screening small organisms or other food particles from the water.

flotsam. Wreckage of a ship or its cargo, especially when cast up on the shore. Usually refers to any form of driftwood or other nonliving object adrift.

fouling organism. A sessile organism living where it is unwanted, e.g., barnacles on a ship's hull.

freshet. A short, heavy rainstorm that causes a large amount of fresh water to enter the marine environment.

gastrozooid. A feeding individual in a hydroid colony.

gemmule. An environmentally resistant asexual reproductive body found in freshwater and some marine sponges.

gonopore. An opening through which sperm or eggs leave an animal's body.

gonozooid. A reproductive individual in a hydroid colony.

gorgonian. A soft coral, e.g., a sea whip or sea fan, of the order Gorgonacea.

gravid. Bearing eggs, e.g., the "sponge crab" stage of a blue crab. See also berried.

groin. A short breakwater usually constructed in rows perpendicular to the beach to impede longshore currents that would erode the beach.

halophyte. A plant that is tolerant of a high salt concentration in the soil.

hermaphroditic. Monoecious; having both male and female sex organs.

holoplankton. Organisms that spend their entire life cycles suspended in the water.

hydroid. The polypoid or anemonelike form of a member of the class Hydrozoa.

hydrotheca. Chitinous protective case around a feeding zooid on a hydrozoan colony.

hypersaline. Having a salt content higher than that of normal seawater ( > 35.0 parts per thousand).

integument. The surface covering of an animal's body.

interstitial. Living in the spaces between mud or sand particles. See also pore space.

introvert. Necklike region in many sipunculids which can be inverted into the trunk of the body.

**isomyarian.** Adductor muscles in clams that are equal in size.

**isopod.** A small, flattened crustacean belonging to the order Isopoda.

**jetsam.** Anything jettisoned from a ship in distress and subsequently washed ashore.

**larva** (pl. **larvae**). An embryo that differs markedly in appearance from its parents and becomes self-sustaining before assuming the physical characteristics of its parents.

**littoral.** Intertidal; pertaining to the shore zone between the high and low tide levels.

**littorine.** A snail of the genus *Littorina. See also* periwinkle.

**lophophore.** Spiraled crown of tentacles used for food capture in bryozoans, brachiopods ,and phoronids.

**lunule.** A notch or hole in a sand dollar test.

**malacologist.** A biologist who specializes in the study of mollusks.

**mantle.** A fold of tissue in the mollusks and a few other animals that is nearest the shell and is responsible for depositing the layers of shell.

**mantle cavity.** A space formed between the mantle and the body of mollusks usually containing the gills.

**maxilliped.** A crustacean thoracic appendage usually used in handling food.

**medusa (pl.medusae).** The "jellyfish" stage in the life cycles of certain hydrozoans and their kin. Usually appears as a gelatinuous bell with trailing tentacles. *See also* hydroid, polyp.

**megalops.** A free-swimming larval stage of crabs that follows the zoea stage.

**meroplankton.** Organisms that spend a portion of their life cycles suspended in the water, e.g., the larvae of crabs.

**MLLW.** Mean lower low water: water level during the lower of two daily low tides occurring in areas with semi-diurnal tides.

**molt.** To shed one's outer covering (feathers, skin, or shell) during growth. The outer covering that has been shed.

**morphology.** The form or structure of an animal or plant.

**mysid.** A small, shrimplike crustacean belonging to the order Mysidacea.

**mysis.** A larval stage in the life cycle of shrimp.

**nauplius.** The first larval stage of certain crustaceans, such as shrimp.

**nekton.** Pelagic animals capable of swimming faster than one knot (one nautical mile/hour).

**nematocyst.** A capsule containing an evertible dart used for food capture and defense in medusae, sea anemones, and their kin.

**nematophore.** Nematocyst-bearing defensive structure on certain hydrozoan colonies.

**nudibranch.** A type of snail that lacks a shell and often has fingerlike or lobelike projections on its back.

**odontophore.** A cartilagelike structure that supports the radula of a snail.

**operculum.** A lid or plug used to close an opening, as in many snails (shell) and some polychaete worms (tube).

**opisthobranch.** A snail belonging to the subclass Opisthobranchia.

**osculum.** Large, excurrent pore in a sponge.

**osmoconformer.** An organism that adjusts to changes in the salinity of its environment by changing the salinity of its body fluid accordingly.

**parapodium** (pl. **parapodia**). A segmental appendage on a polychaete worm. May be leglike or variously modified as a gill, pump, etc.

**pedicle.** Stalk used to anchor a brachiopod in sand or to a hard substrate.

**pelagic.** Living suspended in the water, as opposed to benthic (on the bottom).

**penis** (pl. **penes**). A male copulatory organ.

**pereiopod.** A crustacean thoracic leg; a walking leg of crabs, shrimp, isopods, and their kin.

**periostracum.** The horny layer that coats the exterior surface of the shells of most mollusks.

**perisarc.** A thin, chitinous layer covering a hydroid colony.

**periwinkle.** A snail of the genus *Littorina. See also* littorine.

**permeable.** Capable of being penetrated by water and certain ions. An animal with a permeable integument will dry out easily in an arid environment.

**phytoplankton.** Plant plankton; generally microscopic plants adrift in the sea.

**plankter.** An individual member of the plankton.

**planula.** A free-swimming larva of certain hydroids and their kin.

**pleopod.** An abdominal appendage of a crustacean, which may be used for swimming, respiration, or attach the body of mollusks usually containing the gills.

**podium** (pl. **podia**) A small foot, usually terminating in a sucker, found on sea stars, sea urchins, sand dollars, and their kin.

**polyp.** The sessile or anemonelike stage in the life cycles of certain cnidaria. Usually appears as an attached stalk with a crown of tentacles. *See also* medusa.

**pore space.** The space between particles of sand or mud. It provides a habitat for a variety of microscopic organisms. *See also* interstitial.

**postlarva.** The last larval stage in the life cycle of shrimp.

**probosci.s** Usually a tubelike extension of the mouth of a snail or worm that can either be shot out to grab passing prey or extended into narrow crevices to obtain food.

**propodium.** The anterior portion of the foot of certain snails, such as the moon snail.

**prosobranch.** A snail belonging to the subclass Prosobranchia.

**prostomium.** Anterior segment in an annelid worm, usually modified as a head.

**protandry.** In individual organisms bearing both male and female gonads, the male reproductive system matures and atrophies, before the maturation of the female system.

**protozoea.** A larval stage in the life history of certain crustaceans that follows the nauplius larva and precedes the zoea larva.

**pseudofeces.** A mixture of mucus and particles rejected by certain filter-feeders before ingestion, as in the oyster.

**pulmonate.** A snail that lacks gills and must exchange gases across the wall of the mantle cavity. Usually terrestrial or freshwater species.

**radiole.** A pinnate, tentaclelike projection from the head of certain filter-feeding polychaete worms, such as fanworms.

**radula.** A ribbonlike band bearing many rows of teeth found in the mouth of many mollusks.

**raptorial leg.** A leg adapted for seizing and tearing prey.

**rhopalium** (pl. **rhopalia**). A structure containing various sense organs found on the margin of a medusa's bell.

**rostrum.** A spearlike projection from the carapace of certain crustaceans, such as shrimp and crayfish, that extends forward between the eyes.

**scyphistoma.** A polyplike stage in the life history of certain medusae which develops into free-swimming ephyra larvae by strobilization. *See also* strobilization.

**sessile.** Sedentary; permanently attached to a rock, shell, or other firm substrate.

**seta** (pl. **setae**). A stiff bristle or hairlike structure found on the bodies of certain worms and crustaceans; usually tactile.

**shoal.** A shallow place, such as a sand bar, in a body of water.

**siphon.** A tube used to channel the flow of water in many mollusks and sea squirts.

**spat.** Newly settled oysters.

**spermatophore.** A packet containing spermatozoa which is transferred to the female in certain mollusks and crustaceans.

**spicule.** Calcareous or siliceous skeletal component in some sponges and gorgonians.

**statocyst.** An equilibrium organ consisting of an inorganic weight, the statolith, which is balanced on numerous sensory hairs.

**stenohaline.** Tolerant of only a very narrow range of salinities. A property of most truly marine animals.

**stolon.** A rootlike outgrowth from the base of certain cnidarians that produces new individuals by budding.

**strobilization.** A form of asexual reproduction in the phylum Cnidaria in which ephyra larvae are budded off of a polyp. *See also* scyphistoma.

**subchelate.** Forming a grasping appendage by folding the terminal segment of a leg back over the sub-terminal segment.

**substrate.** The base or foundation on which an animal lives or moves, e.g., the ground or a plant stalk.

**tactile.** Pertaining to a sense of touch.

**telson.** The last body segment of most crustaceans, often part of the tail fan or modified for digging or protecting eggs.

**test.** The skeleton of a sea urchin or sand dollar.

**thixotropy.** The property of becoming fluid when agitated, as in wet sand or mud.

**trematode.** A fluke or parasitic flatworm.

**trilobite.** An extinct marine arthropod that inhabited Paleozoic seas and had a three-lobed carapace.

**trochophor.** A larval stage found in the mollusks and a few other animal groups that is characterized by two large lobes containing cilia whose beating simulates the action of an egg-beater and propels the trochophore, bringing it in contact with food particles.

**tube foot.** *See* podium.

**umbilicus.** A depression in the shells of certain snails, such as the moon snail, formed at the center of the shell coils.

**varix** (pl. **varices**). A prominent ridge in a whorl of the shell of certain snails (e.g., *Cerithidea*) which represents a previous position of the lip of the shell.

**water table.** The water level in beach sand or soil characterized by a layer of moist sand or mud.

**whelk.** A common name applied to certain snails, e.g., *Busycon*.

**zoea** (pl. **zoeae**). A larval stage in the life cycle of certain crustaceans, such as shrimp.

**zooid.** An individual member in a colony of animals, such as a hydroid colony or a bryozoan colony.

**zooplankton.** Animal plankton; usually small animals adrift in the sea that are unable to swim against a one-knot current.

# Bibliography

## GENERAL READING

Abbott, R. T. 1954. *American Seashells*. New York: Van Nostrand.

Amos, W. H. 1966. *The Life of the Seashore*. New York: McGraw–Hill.

Andrews, J. 1977. *Shells and Shores of Texas*. Austin: Univ. of Texas Press.

Andrews, J. 1971. *Sea Shells of the Texas Coast*. Austin: Univ. of Texas Press.

Arnold, A. F. 1968. *The Sea–beach at Ebb–tide*. New York: Dover.

Briggs, J. C. 1974. *Marine Zoogeography*. New York: McGraw–Hill.

Eltringham, S. K. 1971. *Life in Mud and Sand*. New York: Crane, Russak & Co.

Evans, I. 0. (Ed.), 1962. *Sea and Seashore*. New York: Warne.

Green, J. 1968. *The Biology of Estuarine Animals*. London: Sidgwick & Jackson.

Hardy, A. C. 1956. *The Open Sea*. Boston: Houghton Mifflin.

Jagersten, G. 1964. *Life in the Sea*. New York: Basic Books.

Le Danois, E. 1957. *Marine Life of Coastal Waters*. Harrap.

Marshall, N. B. 1971. *Ocean Life*. New York: MacMillan.

Miner, R. W. 1950. *Field Book of Seashore Life*. New York: G.P. Putnam's Sons.

Newell, R. C. 1970. *Biology of Intertidal Animals*. New York: American Elsevier.

Reed, C. T. 1941. *Marine Life in Texas Waters*. Houston: Anson Jones Press.

Rudloe, J. 1968. *The Sea Brings Forth*. New York: Alfred A. Knopf.

Rudloe, J. 1971. *The Erotic Ocean*. New York: World Publ. Co.

Russell, F. S., and C. M. Yonge. 1963. *The Seas: Our Knowledge of Life in the Sea and How it is Gained*. New York: Warne.

Teal, J. M., and M. Teal. 1969. *Life and Death of the Salt Marsh*. Boston: Little, Brown & Co.

Wilson, D. P. 1952. *Life of the Shore and Shallow Sea*. New York: McBride.

Wimpenny, R. S. 1966. *The Plankton of the Sea*. New York: American Elsevier.

Yonge, C. M. 1963. *The Sea Shore*. New York: Atheneum.

Zim, H. S., and L. Ingle. 1955. *Seashores*. New York: Golden Press.

## PORIFERA

Cobb, W. R. 1969. "Penetration of calcium carbonate substrates by the boring sponge, *Cliona*," *Amer. Zool.* 9:783–790.

de Laubenfels, M. W. 1953. "Sponges from the Gulf of Mexico," *Bull. Mar. Sci.* 2:511–557.

Elvin, D. W. 1976. "Seasonal growth and reproduction of an intertidal sponge, *Huticlona permollis* (Bowerbank)." *Biol. Bull.* 151: 108–125.

Fell, P. E. 1976. "The reproduction of *Haliclona loosanoffi* and its apparent relationship to water temperature," *Biol. Bull.* 150:200–210.

Hopkins, S. H. 1956. "Notes on the boring sponges in the Gulf Coast estuaries and their relation to salinity," *Bull. Mar. Sci.* 6:44–58.

Storr, J. F. 1976. "Ecological factors controlling sponge distribution in the Gulf of Mexico and the resulting zonation." In Harrison, F. W. and R. R. Cowden (eds.), *Aspects of Sponge Biology*. New York: Academic Press.

Teerling, J. 1975. "A survey of sponges from the northwestern Gulf of Mexico." Ph.D. Diss., Univ. Southwestern Louisiana. x + 187 p.

Wells, H. W., M. J. Wells, and I. E. Gray, 1960. "Marine sponges of North Carolina." *J. Elisha Mitchell Sci. Soc.* 76:200–245.

## CNIDARIA

Ballard, W. W. 1942. "The mechanism for synchronous spawning in *Hydractinia* and *Pennaria.*" *Biol. Bull.* 82:329–339.

Bayer, F. M. 1961. Studies on the fauna of Curaçao and other Caribbean Islands: No. 55. The shallow–water Octocorallia of the West Indian Region. Vol. 12. Natuurwet. Stud. Suriname No. 23 1961: 1–373.

Burke, W. D. 1976. "Biology and distribution of the macrocoelenterates of Mississippi Sound and adjacent waters." *Gulf Res. Repts.* 5: 17–28.

Cargo, D. G., and L. P. Schultz, 1966. "Notes on the biology of the sea nettle, *Chrysaora quinquecirrha,* in Chesapeake Bay," *Chesapeake Sci.* 7:95–100.

Cargo, D. G., and L. P. Schultz. 1967. "Further observations on the biology of the sea nettle and jellyfishes in Chesapeake Bay." *Chesapeake Sci.* 8:209–220.

Carlgren, O., and J. W. Hedgpeth. 1952. "Actinaria, Zoantharia and Ceriantharia from the shallow water in the northwestern Gulf of Mexico," *Publ. Inst. Mar. Sci. Texas* 2:143–172.

Cones, H. N., Jr. 1968. "Strobilation of *Chrysaora quinquecirrha* polyps in the laboratory," *Vir. J. Sci.* 20:16–18.

Cones, H. N., Jr., and D. S. Haven. 1969. "Distribution of *Chrysaora quinquecirrha* in the York River," *Chesapeake Sci.* 10:75–84.

Cowles, P. R. 1920. "The transplanting of sea anemones by hermit crabs," Proc. Natn. Acad. Sci. U.S. 6:40–42.

Cutress, C., and D. M. Ross. 1969. "The sea anemone *Calliactis tricolor* (LeSueur) and its association with the hermit crab *Dardanus venosus* (H. Milne–Edwards)," *J. Zool.* 158:225–241.

Cutress, C., D. M. Ross, and L. Sutton. 1970. "The association of *Calliactis tricolor* with its pagurid, calappid, and majid partners in the Caribbean," *Can. J. Zool.* 48:371–376.

Deevey, E. S. 1950. "Hydroids from Louisiana and Texas, with remarks on the Pleistocene biogeography of the western Gulf of Mexico." *Ecology* 31:334–367.

Defenbaugh, R. E., and S. H. Hopkins. 1973. "The occurrence and distribution of the hydroids of the Galveston Bay, Texas area," *Texas A & M Univ. Sea Grant Publ.* TAMU–SG–73–210.

Edwards, C. 1966. "*Velella velella* (L.): the distribution of its dimorphic forms in the Atlantic Ocean and the Mediterranean, with comments on its nature and affinities." In Barnes, H. (Ed.). *Some contemporary studies in marine science,* pp. 283–296. Allen & Unwin Ltd.

Field, L. R. 1949. "Sea anemones and corals of Beaufort, North Carolina," *Duke Univ. Mar. Sta. Bull.* 5:1–39.

Fraser, J. H. 1969. "Experimental feeding of some medusae and chaetognatha," *J. Fish. Res. Bd. Canada* 26:1743–1762.

Guest, W. C. 1959. "The occurrence of the jellyfish *Chiropsalmus quadrumanus* in Matagorda Bay, Texas," *Bull. Mar. Sci.* 9:79–83.

Gutsell, J. S. 1928. "The spider crab, *Libinia dubia,* and the jellyfish, *Stomolophus meleagris,* found associated at Beaufort, N.C.," *Ecology* 9:358–359.

Jachowski, R. 1963. "Observations on the moon jelly, *Aurelia aurita,* and the spider crab, *Libinia dubia.*" *Chesapeake Sci.* 4:195.

Kornicker, L. S., and J. T. Conover. 1960. "Effect of high storm tide levels on beach burial of jellyfish (Scyphozoa) and other organisms," *Int. Rev. Hydrobiol.* 45:203–214.

Kramp, P. L. 1961. "Synopsis of the medusae of the world," *J. Mar. Biol. Assoc. U.K.* 40:1–469.

Kramp, P. L. 1965. "The hydromedusae of the Atlantic Ocean and adjacent water," *Dana Rept.* 49:159.

Lane, C. E., and E. Dodge. 1958. "The toxicity of *Physalia* nematocysts," *Biol. Bull.* 115:219–226.

Leversee, G. J. 1976. "Flow and feeding in fan–shaped colonies of the gorgonian coral, *Leptogorgia.*" *Biol. Bull.* 151:344–356.

Littleford, R. A., and R. V. Truitt. 1937. "Variation of *Dactylometra quinquecirrha,*" *Science* 86:426–427.

Marsical, R. N. 1972. "The nature of the adhesion to shells of the symbiotic sea anemone *Calliactis tricolor* (LeSueur)," *J. Exp. Mar. Biol. Ecol.* 8:217–224.

McNamara, P. 1955. "Sea nettles observed to feed on sea walnuts in laboratory," *Maryland Tidewater News* 12:3.

Merrill, A. S. 1968. "Shell deformity of mollusks attributable to the hydroid, *Hydractinia echinata,*" *U.S. Fish Wildl. Serv. Fish. Bull.* 66:273–279.

Mills, C. E. 1976. "*Podocoryne selena,* a new species of hydroid from the Gulf of Mexico, and a comparison with *Hydractinia echinata,*" *Biol. Bull.* 151:214–224.

Peters, E. C., S. C. Cairns, M. E. Q. Pilson, J. W. Wells, W. C. Jaap, J. C. Lang, C. E. (Cummings) Vasleski, and L. St. Pierre Gollahon. 1988. "Nomenclature and biology of *Astrangia poculata*" (=A. danae, = A.astreiformis) (Cnidaria: Anthozoa). Proc. Biol. Soc. Washington 101:234–250.

Phillips, P. J., W. D. Burke, and E. L. Keener. 1969. "Observations on the trophic significance of jellyfishes in Mississippi Sound with quantitative data on the associative behavior of small fishes with medusae," *Trans. Amer. Fish. Soc.* 98:703–712.

Singer, J. 1968. "Man against jellyfish," *Sea Frontiers* 14:87–93.

Thompson, T. E., and I. Bennett. 1969. "*Physalia* nematocysts: utilized by mollusks for defense," *Science* 166:1532–1533.

Wilson, D. P. 1947. "The Portuguese man–of–war, *Physalia physalis* L., in British and adjacent seas," *J. Mar. Biol. Assoc. U.K.* 27:139–172.

Woodcock, A. H. 1956. "Dimorphism in the Portuguese man–of–war," *Nature*. Lond. 178:253–255.

## CTENOPHORA

Bishop, J. W. 1967. "Feeding rates of the ctenophore, *Mnemiopsis leidyi*," *Chesapeake Sci.* 8:259–264.

Cronin, L. E., J. D. Daiber, and E. M. Hulbert. 1962. "Quantitative seasonal aspects of zooplankton in the Delaware River Estuary," *Chesapeake Sci.* 3:63–93.

Mayer, A. G. 1912. "Ctenophores of the Atlantic Coast of North America," *Carnegie Inst. Wash. Publ.* 162:1–58.

Nelson, T. C. 1925. "On the occurrence and food habits of ctenophores in New Jersey coastal waters," *Biol. Bull.* 48:92–111.

## PLATYHELMINTHES

Hopkins, S. H. 1949. "Preliminary survey of the literature on *Stylochus* and other flatworms associated with oysters," Texas A&M Res. Found. Proj. 9:1–16.

Hyman, L. H. 1940. "The polyclad flatworms of the Atlantic Coast of the United States and Canada," *Proc. U.S. Natn. Mus.* 89:449–495.

Pearse, A. S. 1949. "Observations on flatworms and nemerteans collected at Beaufort, N.C.," *Proc. U.S. Natn. Mus.* 100:25–37.

Pearse, A. S., and G. W. Wharton. 1938. "The oyster 'leech' *Stylochus inimicus* Palombi, associated with oysters on the coasts of Florida," *Ecol. Monogr.* 8:605–655.

## POLYCHAETA

Barnes, R. D. 1965. "Tube–building and feeding in chaetopterid polychaetes." *Biol. Bull.* 129:217–233.

Bishop, J. 1974. "Observations on the swarming of a nereid polychaete, *Neanthes succinea*, from the northern Gulf of Mexico," *Proc. La. Acad. Sci.* 37:60–63.

Blake, J. A., and J. W. Evans. 1973. "*Polydora* and related genera as borers in mollusk shells and other calcareous substrates (Polychaeta: Spionidae)," *Veliger* 15:235–249.

Brown, S. C., J. B. Bdzil, and H. L. Frisch. 1972. "Responses of *Chaetopterus variopedatus* to osmotic stress, with a discussion of the mechanism of isoosmotic volume–regulation," *Biol. Bull.* 143:278–295.

Dales, R. P. 1957. "The feeling mechanism and structure of the gut of *Owenia fusiformis*." *J. Mar. Biol. Assoc. U.K.* 36:81–89.

Daly, J. M. 1973. "Behavioral and secretory activity during tube construction by *Platynereis dumerilii*. Aud. & M. Edw. (Polychaeta: Nereidae)." *J. Mar. Biol. Assoc. U.K.* 53:521–529.

Dauer, P. M., C. A. Murphy, and R. M. Ewing. 1981. "Feeding behavior and general biology of several spionid polychaetes from the Chesapeake Bay," *J. Exp. Mar. Biol. Ecol.* 54:21–38.

Dean, D. 1978. "The swimming of bloodworms (*Glycera* spp.) at night, with comments on other species." *Mar. Biol.* 48:99–104.

Evans, S. M. 1973. "A study of fighting reactions in some nereid polychaetes." *Anim. Behav.* 21:138–146.

Fauchald, K. 1977. "The polychaete worms: definitions and keys to the orders, families and genera." Natural History Museum of Los Angeles County, Science Series. 28:1–190.

Grassle, J. F., and J. P. Grassle. 1974. "Opportunistic life histories and genetic systems in marine benthic polychaetes." *J. Mar. Res.* 32:253–284.

Gray, I. E. 1961. "Changes in abundance of the commensal crabs of *Chaetopterus*," *Biol. Bull.* 120:353–359.

Haigler, S. A. 1969. "Boring mechanism of *Polydora websteri* inhabiting *Crassostrea virginica*," *Amer. Zool.* 9:821–828.

Hartman, O. 1951. "The littoral marine annelids of the Gulf of Mexico," *Publ. Inst. Mar. Sci.* 2:7–124.

Hopkins, S. H. 1958. "The planktonic larvae of *Polydora websteri* Hartman (Annelida: Polychaeta) and their settling on oysters," *Bull. Mar. Sci.* 8:268–277.

Hubbard, G. F. 1977. "A quantitative analysis of benthic polychaetous annelids from the northwestern Gulf of Mexico." M.S. Thesis, Texas A&M Univ. vi + 85 p.

Jones, M. L. 1963. "Four new species of *Magelona* (Annelida, Polychaeta) and a rediscription of *Magelona longicornis* Johnson." *Amer. Mus. Novit.* 2164:1–31.

Mackin, J. G. and F. Cauthron. 1952, "Effect of heavy infestations of *Polydora websteri* Hartman on *Crassostrea virginica* (Gmelin) in Louisiana," Conv. Natl. Shellfish. Assoc. for 1952:14–24.

Mangum, C. P. 1964. "Activity patterns in metabolism and ecology of polychaetes." *Comp. Biochem. Physiol.* 11:239–256.

Mangum, C. P. 1964. "Studies on speciation in maldanid polychaetes of the North American Atlantic coast. II. Distribution and competitive interaction of five sympatric species." *Limnol. Oceanogr.* 9:12–26.

Mangum, C. P., S. L. Santos, and W. R. Rhodes, Jr. 1968. "Distribution and feeding in the onuphid polychaete, *Diopatra cuprea* (Bosc)." *Mar. Biol.* 2:33–40.

McCarty, D. M. 1974. "Polychaetes of Seven and One–Half Fathom Reef." M.S. Thesis, Texas A&I Univ. 213 pp.

Myers, A. C. 1972. "Tube–worm sediment relationships of *Diopatra caprea*," *Mar. Biol.* 17:350–356.

Pettibone, M. H., 1965. "Two new species of *Aricidea* (Polychaeta, Paraonidae) from Virginia and Florida, and redescription of *Aricidea fragilis* Webster." *Proc. Biol. Soc. Wash.* 78:127–139.

Truman, E. R. 1966. "The mechanism of burrowing in the polychaete worm, *Arenicola marina* (L.)," *Biol. Bull.* 131:369–377.

Wilson, D. 1969. "Honeycomb worm," *J. Mar. Biol. Assoc.* U.K. 15:567–604.

## GASTROPODA

Apley, M. L. 1970. "Field studies on life history, gonadal cycle and reproductive periodicity in *Melampus bidentatus* (Pulmonata: Ellobiidae)," *Malacologica* 10:381–397.

Bandel, K., and D. Kadolsky. 1982. "Western Atlantic species of *Nodilittorina* (Gastropoda: Prosobranchia): Comparative morphology and its functional, ecological, phylogenetic and taxonomic implications." *Veliger* 25: 1–42.

Bayer, F. M. 1963. "Observations on pelagic mollusks associated with the siphonophores *Velella* and *Physalia*," *Bull. Mar. Sci.* 13:454–466.

Butler, P. A. 1953. "The southern oyster drill," Natn. Shellfish Assoc. 1953 Conv. Papers: 67–75.

Chapman, C. R. 1955. "Feeding habits of the southern oyster drill, *Thais haemastoma*," Proc. Natn. Shellfish. Assoc. for 1955:169–176.

Carriker, M. R. 1972. "Observations on removal of spines by muricid gastropods during shell growth," *Veliger* 15:69–74.

Craig, A. K. et al. 1969, "The gastropod, *Siphonaria pectinata*: a factor in destruction of beach rock," *Amer. Zool.* 9:895–901.

D'Asaro, C. N. 1966. "The egg capsules, embryogenesis, and early organogenesis of a common oyster predator, *Thais haemastoma floridana* (Gastropoda: Prosobranchia)," *Bull. Mar. Sci.* 16:884–914.

D'Asaro, C. N. 1970. "Egg capsules of prosobranch mollusks from South Florida and the Bahamas and notes on spawning in the laboratory," *Bull. Mar. Sci.* 20:414–440.

Dayan, N. S., and R. T. Dillon, Jr. 1995. "Florida as a biogeographic boundary: evidence from the population genetics of Littorina irrorata." *Nautilus.*

Demoran, W. J., and G. Gunter. 1956. "Ability of *Thais haemastoma* to regenerate its drilling mechanism," *Science* 123:1126.

Epstein, R. A. 1972. "Larval trematodes of marine gastropods of Galveston Island, Texas," M. Sc. Thesis. Texas A&M Univ.

Gore, R. H. 1966. "Observations on the escape response in *Nassarius vibex* (Say) (Mollusca: Gastropoda)," *Bull. Mar. Sci.* 16:423–434.

Gould, H. N. 1949. "The effects of temperature on growth and sexual changes in *Crepidula plana*," *Biol. Bull.* 97:239–240.

Hall, J. R. 1973. "Intraspecific trail–following in the marsh periwinkle *Littorina irrorata* Say," *Veliger* 16:72–75.

Hamilton, P. V. 1985. "Migratory molluscs, with emphasis on swimming and orientation in the sea hare, *Aplysia*," *Contr. Mar. Sci.* 27: 212–226.

Hausman, S. A. 1932. "A contribution to the ecology of the salt marsh snail, *Melampus bidentatus* Say," *Amer. Nat.* 6:541–545.

Hausman, S. A. 1936. "Food and feeding activities of the salt marsh snail (*Melampus bidentatus*)," *Anat. Rec.* 67:127.

Hopkins, S. H. 1956. "*Odostomia impressa* parasitizing southern oysters," *Science* 124:628–629.

Hurst, A. 1965. "The feeding habits of *Nassarius vibex* (Say)," Proc. Malac. Soc. Lond. 36:313–317.

Johnson, J. K. 1972. "Effect of turbidity on the rate of filtration and growth of the slipper limpet, *Crepidula fornicata* Lamarck, 1799," *Veliger* 14:315–320.

Kitchell, J. A., C. H. Boggs, J. A. Rice, J. F. Kitchell, A. Hoffman, and J. Martinell. 1986. "Anomalies in naticid predatory behavior: a critique and experimental observations," *Malacologia* 27:291–298.

Kornicker, L. S. 1961. "Observations on the behavior of the littoral gastropod *Terebra salleana*," *Ecology* 42:207.

Linsley, R. M., and M. Javidpour. 1980. "Episodic growth in gastropods," *Malacologia* 20:153–160.

Magalhaes, H. 1948. "An ecological study of snails of the genus *Busycon* at Beaufort, North Carolina," *Ecol. Monogr.* 18:377–409.

Marcus, E., and E. Marcus. 1960. "Some opisthobranchs from the northwestern Gulf of Mexico," *Publ. Inst. Mar. Sci. Texas* 6:251–264.

Mollick, R. S. 1973. "Some aspects of the biology of *Terebra dislocata* Say, 1822 (Gastropoda: Prosobranchia)," *Veliger* 16:82–84.

Olsson, A. A., and L. E. Crovo. 1968. "Observations on aquarium specimens of *Oliva sayana* Ravenal," *Veliger* 11:31–32.

Russell–Hunter, W. D., M. L. Apley, and R. D. Hunter. 1972. "Early life–history of *Melampus* and the significance of semilunar synchrony," *Biol. Bull.* 143:623–656.

Strenth, N. E., and J. E. Blankenship. 1978. "On the valid name of the common Texas and Florida species of *Aplysia* (Gastropoda, Ophistobranchia)." *Bull. Mar. Sci.* 28:249–254.

Tunnell, J. W., Jr. 1969. "The mollusks of Seven and One–Half Fathom Reef." M.S. Thesis, Texas A&I Univ, 83 pp.

Voss, N. A. 1959. "Studies on the pulmonte gastropod *Siphonaria pectinata* (Linnaeus) from the southeast coast of Florida," *Bull. Mar. Sci.* 9:84–99.

Wells, H. W. 1958a. "Predation of pelecypods and gastropods by *Fasciolaria hunteria* (Perry)," *Bull. Mar. Sci.* 8:152–166.

Wells, H. W. 1958b. "The feeding habits of *Murex fulvescens*," *Ecology* 39:556–558.

Wells, H. W. 1959. "Notes on *Odostomia impressa* (Say)," *Nautilus* 72:140–144.

Wilson, D. P., and M. A. Wilson, 1956. "A contribution to the biology of *Ianthina janthina* (L.)," *J. Mar. Biol. Assoc.* U.K. 35:291–305.

Zischke, J. A. 1974. "Spawning, development and growth in the pulmonate limpets *Siphonaria pectinata* Linnaeus, 1758, and *Siphonaria alternata* Say, 1822," *Veliger* 16:399–404.

## PELECYPODA

Ansell, A. D. 1968. "The rate of growth of the hard clam *Mercenaria mercenaria* (L.) throughout the geographical range," *J. Cons. Perm. Int. Explor. Mer.* 31:364–409.

Baugham, J. L., and B. B. Baker. 1951. "Oysters in Texas," *Texas Game, Fish and Oyster Comm. Bull.* 29:1–37.

Carriker, M. R. 1961. "Interrelation of functional morphology, behavior, and autecology in early stages of the bivalve *Mercenaria mercenaria*," *J. Elisha Mitchell Sci. Soc.* 77:168–241.

Cary, L. R. 1907. "The cultivation of oysters in Louisiana," *Bull. Gulf Biol. Sta.* 8:1–56.

Chanely, P. 1965. "Larval development of the brackish water mactrid clam, *Rangia cuneata*," *Chesapeake Sci.* 6:209–213.

D'Asaro, C. N. 1967. "The morphology of larval and postlarval *Chione cancellata* Linne (Eulamellibranchia: Veneridae) reared in the laboratory," *Bull. Mar. Sci.* 17:949–972.

Davis, H. C. 1953. "On food and feeding of larvae of the American oyster, *C. virginica*," *Biol. Bull.* 104:334–350.

Dillon, J., and J. J. Manzi. 1989. "Genetics and shell morphology of hard clams (Genus *Mercenaria*) from Laguna Madre, Texas." *The Nautilus* 103(2): 73–77.

Fairbanks, L. D. 1963. "Biodemographic studies of the clam *Rangia cuneata* Gray," *Tulane Stud. Zool.* 10:3–47.

Fraser, T. H. 1967. "Contributions to the biology of *Tagelus divisus* (Tellinacea: Pelecypoda) in Biscayne Bay, Florida," *Bull. Mar. Sci.* 17:111–132.

Gillard, R. M. 1969. "An ecological study of an oyster population, including selected associated organisms in West Bay, Galveston, Texas," M. Sc. Thesis. Texas A&M Univ.

Gunter, G. 1951. "The species of oysters of the Gulf, Caribbean and West Indian region," *Bull. Mar. Sci.* 1:40–45.

Gutsell, J. S. 1930. "Natural history of the bay scallop," *Bull. U.S. Bur. Fish.* 46:569–632.

Jones, C. C. 1979. "Anatomy of *Chione cancellata* and some other chiones (Bivalvia: Veneridae)," *Malacologia* 19:157–199.

Kane, H. E. 1961. "Occurrence of *Rangia cuneata* Gray and *Crassostrea virginica* (Gmelin) in Sabine Lake, Texas–Louisiana," *J. Sediment. Petrol.* 31:627.

Kuenzler, E. S. 1961. "Structure and energy flow of a mussel population in a Georgia salt marsh," *Limnol. Oceanogr.* 6:191–204.

Lent, C. M. 1969. "Adaptations of the ribbed mussel, *Modiolus demissus* (Dillwyn), to the intertidal habitat," *Amer. Zool.* 9:283–292.

Loesch, H. C. 1957. "Studies of the ecology of two species of *Donax* on Mustang Island, Texas," *Publ. Inst. Mar. Sci. Texas* 4:201–227.

Loesch, J. G., and D. S. Haven. 1973. "Estimated growth functions and size–age relationships of the hard clam, *Mercenaria mercenaria*, in the York River, Virginia," *Veliger* 16:76–81.

Loosanoff, V .L. 1966. "Time and intensity of settling of the oyster *Crassostrea virginica*, in Long Island Sound," *Biol. Bull.* 130:211–227.

Menzel, R. W., and F. E. Nichy. 1958. "Studies of the distribution and feeding habits of some oyster predators in Alligator Harbor, Florida," *Bull. Mar. Sci.* 8:125–145.

Moore, H. B., and N. N. Lopez. 1969. "The ecology of *Chione cancellata*," *Bull. Mar. Sci.* 19:131–148.

O'Heeron, M. K. 1966. "Some aspects of the ecology of *Rangia cuneata* (Gray)," M. Sc. Thesis. Texas A&M Univ.

Tiffany, W. J., III. 1971. "The tidal migration of *Donax variabilis* Say," *Veliger* 14:82–85.

Trussell, P. C. 1967. "Teredine borers," *Sea Frontiers* 13:234–243.

Tunnell, J. W., Jr., and A. H. Chaney. 1970. "A checklist of the mollusks of Seven and One–Half Fathom Reef, northwestern Gulf of Mexico." *Contrib. Mar. Sci.* 15:193–203.

Turner, H. J., Jr., and D. L. Belding. 1957. "The tidal migrations of *Donax variabilis* Say," *Limnol. Oceanogr.* 2:120–124.

Turner, R. D. 1954. "The family Pholadidae in the western Atlantic and eastern Pacific, Part I, Pholadinae," *Johnsonia* 3:1–63.

Turner, R. D., and J. Rosewater. 1958. "The family Pinnidae in the western Atlantic," *Johnsonia* 3:285–328.

Waller, T. R. 1984. "The ctenolium of scallop shells: functional morphology and evolution of a key family–level character in the Pectinacea (Mollusca: Bivalvia)," *Malacologia* 25:203–219.

Wardle, W. J. 1970. "Contributions to the biology of *Tagelus plebius* (Bivalvia: Tellinacea) in Galveston Bay, Texas," M. Sc. Thesis. Texas A&M Univ.

Wells, H. W., M. J. Wells, and I. E. Gray. 1964. "The calico scallop community in North Carolina," *Bull. Mar. Sci.* 14:561–593.

Wolfe, D. A., and E. N. Petteway. 1968. "Growth of *Rangia cuneata*," *Chesapeake Sci.* 9:99–102.

## SCAPHOPODA

Gainey, L. F., Jr. 1972. "The use of the foot and the captacula in the feeding of *Dentalium* (Mollusca: Scaphopoda)," *Veliger* 15:29–34.

## CEPHALOPODA

Arnold, J. M. 1962. "Mating behavior and social structure in *Loligo pealei*," *Biol. Bull.* 123:53–57.

Bruun, A. F. 1943. "The biology of *Spirula spirula*," Dana Rep. No. 24. Copenhagen. 44 pp. + 2 pl.

Bruun, A. F. 1955. "New light on the biology of *Spirula*, a mesopelagic cephalopod," *Essays in the Natural Sciences in Honor of Captain Allan Hancock*. Los Angeles: Univ. of So. Calif. Press. pp. 61–69.

Dillon, L. S., and R. O. Dial. 1962. "Notes on the morphology of the common Gulf squid *Lolliguncula brevis* (Blainville)," *Texas J. Sci.* 14:156–166.

Harry, H. W., and S. F. Snider. 1969. "Cuttlebones on the beach at Galveston," *Veliger* 12:89–94.

Kelly, J. A., Jr., and A. Dragovich. 1967. "Occurrence of the squid, *Lolliguncuia brevis*, in some coastal waters of western Florida," *Bull. Mar. Sci.* 17:840–883.

Lipka, D. A. 1975. "The systematics and zoogeography of cephalopods from the Gulf of Mexico." Ph.D. Diss., Texas A&M Univ. 347 pp.

Voss, G. L. 1954. "Cephalopoda of the Gulf of Mexico," *U.S. Fish Wildl. Serv. Fish. Bull.* 55:475–478.

Voss, G. L. 1956. "A review of the cephalopods of the Gulf of Mexico," *Bull. Mar. Sci.* 6:85–178.

## CIRRIPEDIA

Causey, D. 1961. "The barnacle genus *Octolasmis* in the Gulf of Mexico," *Turtox News* 39:51–55.

Causey, D. 1962. "The ivory barnacle," *Turtox News* 40:178–183.

Darwin, C. 1851. "A monograph on the subclass Cirripedia, with figures of all species. The Lepadidae; or, pedunculated cirripedes," Ray Soc., Lond.

Darwin, C. 1854. "A monograph on the subclass Cirripedia, with figures of all species. The Balanidae, (or sessile cirripedes); the Verrucidae, etc.," Ray Soc., Lond.

Dawson, C. E. 1957. "*Balanus* fouling of shrimp," *Science* 126:1068.

Doochin, H. D. 1951. "The morphology of *Balanus improvisus* Darwin and *Balanus amphitrite niveus* Darwin during initial attachment and metamorphosis," *Bull. Mar. Sci.* 1: 15–39.

Eldred, B. 1962. "The attachment of the barnacle, Balanus amphitrite niveus Darwin, and other fouling organisms to the rock shrimp, *Sicyonia dorsalis* Kingsley," *Crustaceana* 3:203–206.

Gordon, C. M. 1969. "The apparent influence of salinity on the distribution of barnacle species in Chesapeake Bay (Cirripedia)," *Crustaceana* 16:139–142.

Hulings, N. C. 1961. "The barnacles and decapod fauna from the nearshore area of Panama City, Florida," *Quart. J. Fla. Acad. Sci.* 24:215–222.

Jones, E. C. 1968. "*Lepas anserifera* Linne (Cirripedia: Lepodomorpha) feeding on fish and *Physalia*," *Crustaceana* 14:312–313.

Lang, W. H. 1976. "The larval development and metamorphosis of the pedunculate barnacle *Octolasmis mulleri* (Coker, 1902) reared in the laboratory." *Biol. Bull.* 150:255–267.

Minchin, D. 1996. "Tar pellets and plastics as attachment surfaces for lepadid cirripedes in the north Atlantic Ocean." *Mar. Poll. Bull.* 32: 855–859.

Moore, H. B., and A. C. Frue, 1959. "The settlement and growth of *Balanus improvisus*, *B. eburneus* and *B. amphitrite* in the Miami area," *Bull. Mar. Sci.* 9:421–440.

Pilsbry, H. A. 1916. "The sessile barnacles (Cirripedia) contained in the collections of the U.S. National Museum, including a monograph of the American species," *Bull. U.S. Natn. Mus.* 93:1–366.

Thomas, P. J. 1975. "The fouling community on selected oil platforms off Louisiana, with special emphasis on the Cirripedia fauna." M.S. Thesis, Fla. St. Univ. vi + 129 p.

## AMPHIPODA

Bousfield, E. L. 1973. *Shallow–water gammaridean amphipoda of New England.* Cornell Univ. Press.

Dougherty, E. C., and J. E. Steinberg. 1953. "Notes on the skeleton shrimps (Crustacea: Caprellidae) of California," *Proc. Biol. Soc. Wash.* 66:39–50.

Keith, D. E. 1969. "Aspects of feeding in *Caprella californica* Stimpson and *Caprella equilibra* Say (Amphi–poda)," *Crustaceana* 16:119–124.

McCain, J. C. 1965. "The Caprellidae (Crustacea: Amphipoda) of Virginia," *Chesapeake Sci.* 6:190–196.

McCain, J. C. 1968, "The Caprellidae (Crustacea: Amphipoda) of the western North Atlantic," *Bull. U.S. Natn. Mus.* 278:1–147.

McKinney, L. D. 1977. "The origin and distribution of shallow water gammaridean Amphipoda in the Gulf of Mexico and Caribbean Sea with notes on their ecology." Ph.D. Diss., Texas A&M Univ, xviii + 401 p.

Shoemaker, C. R. 1947. "Further notes on the amphipod genus *Corophium* from the east coast of America," *J. Wash. Acad. Sci.* 37:47–63.

Steinberg, J. E., and E. C. Dougherty. 1957. "The skeleton shrimps (Crustacea: Caprellidae) of the Gulf of Mexico," *Tulane Stud. Zool.* 5:265–288.

### ISOPODA

Markham, J. C. 1978. "Bopyrid isopods parasitizing hermit crabs in the northwestern Atlantic Ocean." *Bull. Mar. Sci.* 28:102–117.

Menzies, R. J. 1951 (1954). "A new subspecies of marine isopod from Texas," *Proc. U.S. Natn. Mus.* 101:575–579.

Menzies, R. J. 1957. "The marine borer family Limnoriidae (Crustacea; Isopoda)," *Bull. Mar. Sci.* 7:101–200.

Menzies, R. J., and D. Frankenberg. 1966. "Handbook of the common marine isopod Crustacea of Georgia," Univ. of Ga. Press.

Menzies, R. J., and M. A. Miller. 1955. "A redescription of the marine isopod crustacean 'Exosphaeroma' faxoni Richardson from Texas," *Bull. Mar. Sci.* 5:292–296.

Miller, M. A. 1968. "Isopoda and Tanaidacea from buoys in coastal waters of the continental United States, Hawaii, and the Bahamas (Crustacea)," *Proc. U.S. Natn. Mus.* 125:1–53.

Rehm, A., and H. J. Humm. 1973. "*Sphaeroma terebrans*: A threat to the mangroves of southwestern Florida," *Science* 182:173–174.

Reish, D. J., and W. M. Hetherington. 1969. "The effects of hyper– and hypochlorinities on members of the wood–boring genus *Limnoria*," *Mar. Biol.* 2:137–139.

Richardson, H. 1905. "A monograph on the isopods of North America," *Bull. U.S. Natn. Mus.* 54:1–727.

Schafer, R. D., and C. E. Lane. 1957. "Some preliminary observations bearing on the nutrition of *Limnoria*," *Bull. Mar. Sci.* 7:289–296.

### DECAPODA

Anderson, W. W., and M. J. Lindner. 1945. "A provisional key to the shrimps of the family Penaeidae with especial reference to American forms," *Trans. Amer. Fish. Soc.* 73:284–319.

Anderson, W. W., J. E. King, and M. J. Lindner. 1949. "Early stages in the life history of the common marine shrimp, *Penaeus setiferus* (Linnaeus)," *Biol. Bull.* 97:168–172.

Ayers, J. C. 1938. "Relationship of habitat to oxygen consumption by certain estuarine crabs," *Ecology* 19:523–527.

Baxter, K. N., and W. C. Renfro. 1967. "Seasonal occurrence and size distribution of postlarval brown and white shrimp near Galveston, Texas, with notes on species identification," *U.S. Fish Wildl. Serv. Fish. Bull.* 66:149–158.

Behre, E. H. 1954. "Decapoda of the Gulf of Mexico," *U.S. Fish Wildl. Serv. Fish. Bull.* 55:451–455.

Bert, T. M. 1986. "Speciation in western Atlantic stone crabs (genus *Menippe*): the role of geological processes and climatic events in the formation and distribution of species." *Marine Biology* 98: 157–170.

Bishop, J. M., and W. F. Herrnkind. 1976. "Burying and molting of pink shrimp, *Penaeus duorarum* (Crustacea: Penaeidae), under selected photoperiods of white light and UV–light," *Biol. Bull.* 150:163–182.

Bliss, D. E. 1968. "Transition from water to land in decapod crustaceans," *Amer. Zool.* 8:355–392.

Borradaile, L. A. 1915. "On the species of *Lucifer* and their distribution," *Ann. Mag. Nat. Hist.*, Set. 8, 16:226–231.

Brown, F. A., Jr., and G. C. Stephens. 1951. "Studies of the daily rhythmicity of the fiddler crab, *Uca*," Modifications by photoperiod, *Biol. Bull.* 101:71–83.

Burkenroad, M. D. 1934. "The Penaeidea of Louisiana with a discussion of their world relationships," *Bull. Amer. Mus. Nat. Hist.* 68:61–143.

Christensen, A. M., and J. J. McDermott. 1958. "Life–history and biology of the oyster crab, *Pinnotheres ostreum* Say," *Biol. Bull.* 114:146–179.

Christoffersen, M. L. 1984. "The western Atlantic snapping shrimps related to *Alpheus heterochaelis* (Crustacea: Caridea) with the description of a new species." *Pap. Avulsos Zool.* 35: 189–208.

Compton, H. 1965. "A study of Texas shrimp populations; biological survey of the commercial shrimp and associated organisms in the inshore Gulf of Mexico," Texas Parks Wildl. Dept., Coastal Fish Proj. Rept. 1964, Proj. No. MS–R–6:145–147.

Conte, F. S. 1971. "Ecological aspects of selected crustacea of two marsh embayments on the Texas coast," Ph.D. Diss., Texas A&M Univ.

Cook, H. L. 1965. "A generic key to the protozoean, mysis, and postlarval stages of the littoral Penaeidae of the northwestern Gulf of Mexico," *U.S. Fish Wildl. Serv. Fish. Bull.* 65:437–447.

Cook, H. L., and M. A. Murphy. 1965. "Early developmental stages of the rock shrimp, *Sicyonia brevirostris* Stimpson, reared in the laboratory," *Tulane Stud. Zool.* 12:109–127.

Costlow, J. D., Jr., and C. G. Bookhout. 1960. "The complete larval development of *Sesarma cinereum* (Bosc) reared in the laboratory," *Biol. Bull.* 118:203–214.

Costlow, J. D., Jr., and C. G. Bookhout. 1962. "The larval development of *Sesarma reticulatum* Say reared in the laboratory," *Crustaceana* 4:281–294.

Crane, J. 1957. "Basic patterns of display in fiddler crabs (Ocypodidae: Genus *Uca*), " *Zoologica* 42:69–82.

Cummings, W. C. 1961. "Maturation and spawning of the pink shrimp, *Penaeus duorarum* Burkenroad," *Trans. Amer. Fish. Soc.* 90:462–468.

Darnell, R. M. 1959. "Studies of the life history of the blue crab (*Callinectes sapidus* Rathbun) in Louisiana waters," *Trans. Amer. Fish. Soc.* 88:294–304.

Dobkin, S. 1961. "Early development stages of the pink shrimp, *Penaeus duorarum*, from Florida waters," *U.S. Fish Wildl. Serv. Fish. Bull.* 61:321–349.

Efford, I. E. 1967. "The antermule cleaning setae in the sand crab, *Emerita* (Decapoda, Hippidae)," *Crustaceana* 21:316–318.

Eisler, R. 1969. "Acute toxicities of insecticides to marine decapod crustaceans," *Crustaceana* 16:302–310.

Felder, D. L. 1971. "The decapod crustaceans of Seven and One–Half Fathom Reef," M.S. Thesis, Texas A&I Univ. 103 pp.

Felder, D. L. 1973. "An annotated key to crabs and lobsters (Decapoda, Reptantia) from coastal waters of the northwestern Gulf of Mexico," Louisiana St. Univ., Sea Grant Publ. No. LSU–SG–73–02.

Fingerman, M. R. 1957. "Relation between position of burrows and tidal rhythm of *Uca*," *Biol. Bull.* 112:7–20.

Fingerman, M. R., R. Nagabhushanam, and L. Philpott. 1961. "Physiology of the melanophores of the crab *Sesarma reticulatum*," *Biol. Bull.* 120:337–347.

Gifford, C. A. 1963. "Some observations on the general biology of the land crab, *Cardisoma guanhumi* (Latreille) in South Florida," *Biol. Bull.* 123:207–223.

Goodbody, I. 1965. "Continuous breeding in populations of two tropical crustaceans *Mysidium columbiae* (Zimmer) and *Emerita portoricensis* (Schmitt)," *Ecology* 46:195–197.

Gordon, J. 1956. "A bibliography of pagurid crabs, exclusive of Alcock, 1905," *Bull. Amer. Mus. Nat. Hist.* 108:255–352.

Gray, I. E. 1957. "A comparative study of the gill area of crabs," *Biol. Bull.* 112:34–42.

Haig, J. 1956. "The Galatheidae (Crustacea: Anomura) of the Allan Hancock Expedition with a review of the Porcellanidae of the western Atlantic," *Allan Hancock Atlantic Exp., Rept.* 8:1–44.

Haley, S. R. 1969. "Relative growth and sexual maturity of the Texas ghost crab, *Ocypode quadrata*," *Crustaceana* 17:285–297.

Haley, S. R. 1972. "Reproductive cycling in the ghost crab, *Ocypode quadrata*," *Crustaceana* 23: 1–11.

Harper, D. E., Jr. 1968. "Distribution of *Lucifer faxoni* (Crustacea: Decapoda: Sergestidae) in neritic waters off the Texas coast, with a note on the occurrence of *Lucifer typus*," *Contri. Mar. Sci., Univ. Texas Mar. Sci. Inst.* 13:1–16.

Hazlett, B. 1962. "Aspects of the biology of the snapping shrimp (*Alpheus* and *Synalpheus*)," *Crustaceana* 4:82–83.

Herreid, C. F. 1969. "Integument permeability of crabs and adaptation to land," *Comp. Biochem. Physiol.* 29:423–429.

Herreid, C. F., and C. A. Gifford. 1963. "The burrow habitat of the land crab *Cardisoma guanhumi* (Latreille)," *Ecology* 44:773–775.

Hinsch, G. W. 1972. "Some factors controlling reproduction in the spider crab, *Libinia emarginata*," *Biol. Bull.* 143:358–366.

Holland, C. A., and D. M. Skinner. 1976. "Interactions between molting and regeneration of the land crab," *Biol. Bull.* 150:222–240.

Hughes, D. A. 1969. "Responses to salinity change as a tidal transport mechanism of pink shrimp, *Penaeus duorarum*," *Biol. Bull.* 136:43–53.

Jensen, J. P. 1958. "The relation between body size and number of eggs in marine Malacostraca," *Meddr. Danm. Fisk. –og Havunders* 2:1–28.

Johnson, L. C. 1940. "The correlation of water movements and dispersal of pelagic littoral animals, especially the sand crab, *Emerita*," *J. Mar. Res.* 2:236–245.

Johnson, M. W., F. A. Everest, and R. W. Young. 1947. "The role of snapping shrimp (*Crangon* and *Synalpheus*) in the production of underwater noise in the sea," *Biol. Bull.* 93:122–138.

Kinne, O., E. K. Shirley, and H. E. Meen. 1963. "Osmotic responses of hermit crabs (*Pagurus longicarpus* Say) exposed to various constant temperatures and salinities," *Crustaceana* 5:317.

Landers, W. S., 1954. "Notes on the predation of the hard clam, *Venus mercenaria*, by the mud crab, *Neopanope texana*," *Ecology* 35:422.

Laughlin, R. B., Jr., L. G. L. Young, and J. M. Neff. 1978. "A long–term study of the effects of water–soluble fractions of No. 2 fuel oil on the survival, development rate, and growth of the mud crab, *Rhithro–panopeus harrisii*," *Mar. Biol.* 47:87–95.

Limbaugh, C., H. Pederson, and F.A. Chace, Jr. 1961. "Shrimps that clean fishes," *Bull. Mar. Sci.* 11:237–257.

Lunz, G. R. 1947. "*Callinectes* versus *Ostrea*," *J. Elisha Mitchell Sci. Soc.* 63:81.

MacGinitie, G. E. 1937. "Notes on the natural history of several marine Crustacea," *Amer. Midl. Nat.* 18:1031–1036.

Manning, R. 1987. "Notes on western Atlantic Callianassidae (Crustacea: Decapoda: Thallassinidae)." *Proc. Biol. Soc. Washington* 100: 386–401.

Menzel, R. W. 1955. "Crabs as predators of oysters in Louisiana," *Proc. Natn. Shellfish Assoc.* 46:177–184.

Miller, D. C. 1961. "The feeding mechanism of fiddler crabs, with ecological considerations of feeding adaptations," *Zoologica* 46:89–100.

Moffett, A. W. 1967. "The shrimp fishery in Texas," *Texas Parks Wildl. Dept. Bull.* 50:1–36.

Overstreet, R. M. 1973. "Parasites of some penaeid shrimps with emphasis on reared hosts," *Aquaculture* 2:105–140.

Parker, J. C. 1966. "A study of the distribution and condition of brown shrimp in the primary nursery areas of the Galveston Bay System, Texas," M. Sc. Thesis. Texas A&M Univ.

Pautsch, F., L. Lawinski, and K. Turboboyski. 1969. "Zur ökologie der Krabbe *Rithropanopeus harrisii* (Gould) (Xanthidae)," *Linmologica*, Berlin 7:63–68.

Pearse, A. S. 1945. "Ecology of *Upogebia affinis* (Say)," *Ecology* 26:303–305.

Porter, H. J. 1960. "Zoeal stages of the stone crab, *Menippe mercanaria* Say," *Chesapeake Sci.* 1: 168–177.

Powell, E. H., Jr., and G. Gunter. 1968. "Observations on the stone crab, *Menippe mercanaria* Say, in the vicinity of Port Aransas, Texas," *Gulf Res. Rept.* 2:285–299.

Powers, L. W. 1977. "A catalogue and bibliography to the crabs (Brachyura) of the Gulf of Mexico," *Contri. Mar. Sci.* 20 (Supp.): 1–190.

Provenzano, A. J. 1959. "The shallow–water hermit crabs of Florida," *Bull. Mar. Sci.* 9:349–420.

Pullen, E. J., and W. L. Trent. 1969. "White shrimp emigration in relation to size, sex, temperature and salinity," *F.A.0. Fish. Rept.* No. 57:1001–1014.

Rathbun, M. J. 1918. "The grapsoid crabs of America," *U.S. Natn. Mus. Bull.* 97:1–461.

Rathbun, M. J. 1925. "The spider crabs of America," *U.S. Natn. Mus. Bull.* 129:1–612.

Rathbun, M. J. 1930. "The cancroid crabs of America of the families Euryhalidae, Portunidae, Atelecyclidae, Cancridae and Xanthidae," *U.S. Natn. Mus. Bull.* 152:1–609.

Ray, C. 1967. "*Gecarcinus lateralis* Freminville in Texas," *Texas J. Sci.* 19:109.

Ray, J. P. 1974. "A study of the coral reef crustaceans (Decapoda and Stomatopoda) of two Gulf of Mexico reef systems: West Flower Garden, Texas, and Isla de Lobos, Veracruz, Mexico," Ph.D. Diss., Texas A&M Univ., xxxi + 323 p.

Reams, R. C., and A. B. Williams. 1983. "Mud crabs of the *Panopeus herbstii* H.M. Edw., s.l., complex in Alabama, U.S.A.," *Fish. Bull.* 81:885–890.

Rebach, S. 1969. "Seasonal migrations of the hermit crab, *Pagurus longicarpus*," *Amer. Zool.* 9:1075.

Rebach, S. 1974. "Burying behavior in relation to substrate and temperature in the hermit crab, *Pagurus longicarpus*," *Ecology* 55:195–198.

Roberts, M. H., Jr. 1968. "Functional morphology of mouthparts of the hermit crabs, *Pagurus longicarpus* and *Pagurus pollicaris*," *Chesapeake Sci.* 9:9–20.

Robertson, J. R., K. Bancroft, G. Vermeer, and K. Plaisier. 1980. "Experimental studies on the foraging behavior of the sand fiddler crab, *Uca pugilator* (Bosc)," *J. Exp. Mar. Biol. Ecol.* 44:67–83.

Robertson, J. R., and W. J. Pfeiffer. 1982. "Deposit feeding by the ghost crab *Ocypode quadrata* (Fabricius)," *J. Exp. Mar. Biol. Ecol.* 56:165177.

Ryan, E. P. 1956. "Observations on the life histories and the distribution of the Xanthidae (mud crabs) of Chesapeake Bay," *Amer. Midl. Nat.* 56:138–162.

Sandoz, M., and S. H. Hopkins. 1947. "Early life history of the oyster crab, *Pinnotheres ostreum* (Say)," *Biol. Bull.* 93:250–258.

Savage, T. 1971. "Mating of the stone crab, *Menippe mercenaria* (Say) (Decapoda, Brachyura)," *Crustaceana* 20:315–316.

Schmitt, W. L. 1935. "Mud shrimps of the Atlantic coast of north America." *Smithsonian Misc. Coll.* 93(2): 1–21.

Shoup, J. B. 1968. "Shell opening by crabs of the genus *Calappa*," *Science* 160:887–888.

Stauber, L. A. 1945. "*Pinnotheres ostreum*, parasitic on the American oyster, *Ostrea* (Gryphaea) *virginica*," *Biol. Bull.* 88:269–291.

Tashian, R. E., and F. J. Vernberg. 1958. "The specific distinctness of the fiddler crabs *Uca pugnax* (Smith) and *Uca rapax* (Smith) at their zone of overlap in northeastern Florida," *Zoologica* 43:89–91.

Teal, J. M. 1958. "Distribution of fidder crabs in Georgia salt marshes," *Ecology* 39:185–193.

Teal, J. M., and F. G. Carey, 1959. "The metabolism of marsh crabs under conditions of reduced pressure," *Physiol. Zool.* 40:83–91.

Voss, G. L. 1956. "Protective coloration and habitat of the shrimp *Tozeuma carolinesis* Kingsley (Caridae: Hippolytidae)," *Bull. Mar. Sci.* 6:359–363.

Wass, M. L. 1955. "The decapod crustaceans of Alligator Harbor and adjacent inshore areas of northwestern Florida," *Quart. J. Fla. Acad. Sci.* 18:129–176.

Wear, R. G. 1970. "Notes and bibliography on the larvae of xanthid crabs," *Pac. Sci.* 24:84–89.

Wickham, D. A., and F. C. Minkler, III. 1975. "Laboratory observations on daily patterns of burrowing and locomotor activity of pink shrimp, *Penaeus duorarum*, brown shrimp, *Penaeus aztecus*, and white shrimp, *Penaeus setiferus*," *Contrib. Mar. Sci.* 19:21–35.

Wilkins, J. G. 1975. "Contributions to the biology and ecology of *Petrolisthes armatus* (Anomura, Porcellanidae)," M.S. Thesis, Texas A&M Univ. 58 pp.

Williams, A. B. 1958. "Substrates as a factor in shrimp distribution," *Limnol. Oceanogr.* 3:283–290.

Williams, A. B. 1965. "Marine decapod crustaceans of the Carolinas," *U.S. Fish Wildl. Serv. Fish. Bull.* 65:1–298.

Williams, A. B. "Mud crabs of the genus *Panopeus* (Decapoda: Xanthidae): morphology, ecology, genetics, and rediagnoses," *Fish. Bull.* 81:863–890.

Williams, A. B., and D. L. Felder. 1986. "Analysis of stone crab: *Menippe mercenaria* (Say), restricted, and a previously unrecognized species described (Deca–poda: Xanthiidae)." *Proc. Biol. Soc. Washington* 99:517–543.

Wilson, E. B. 1903. "Notes on the reversal of asymmetry in the regeneration of the chelae in *Alpheus heterochaelis*," *Biol. Bull.* 4:197–210.

Wolcott, T. G. 1978. "Ecological role of ghost crabs, *Ocypode quadrata* (Fabricius) on an ocean beach: scavengers or predators?," *J. Exp. Mar. Biol. Ecol.* 31:67–82.

Wolcott, T. G. 1976. "Uptake of soil capillary water by ghost crabs," *Nature* 264:756–757.

Wood, C. E. 1967. "Physioecology of the grass shrimp, *Palaemonetes pugio*, in the Galveston Bay Estuarine System," *Contr. Mar. Sci.*, Inst. Mar. Sci. Texas 12:54–79.

## OTHER CRUSTACEA

Bowman, T. E. 1964. "*Mysidopsis almyra*, a new estuarine mysid crustacean from Louisiana and Florida," *Tulane Stud. Zool.* 12:15–18.

Hedgpeth, J. W. 1948 (1950). "The Pycnogonida of the western North Atlantic and Caribbean," *Proc. U.S. Natn. Mus.* 97:157–342.

Ives, J. E. 1891. "Crustacea from the northern coast of Yucatán, the harbor of Vera Cruz, the west coast of Florida and the Bermuda Islands," *Proc. Acad. Nat. Sci. Phila.* 43:176–207.

Molenock, J. 1969. "*Mysidopsis bahia*, a new species of mysid (Crustacea: Mysidacea) from Galveston Bay, Texas," *Tulane Stud. Zool. Bot.* 15:113–116.

Parks, H. B. 1940. "Descriptive catalogue of the crustacea of the Gulf coast of Texas," *Tech. Bull. Stephen F. Austin St. Teachers Coll.* 2: 1–5.

Pearse, A. S. 1952. "Parasitic crustacea from the Texas coast," *Publ. Inst. Mar. Sci. Texas* 2:5–42.

Price, W. W. 1976. "The abundance and distribution of Mysidacea in the shallow waters of Galveston Island, Texas," Ph.D. Diss., Texas A&M Univ. xvi + 207 p.

Reinhard, E. G. 1950. "The morphology of *Loxothylacus texanus* Boschma, a sacculinid parasite of the blue crab," *Texas J. Sci.* 2:360–365.

Say, T. 1818. "An account of the Crustacea of the United States," *J. Acad. Nat. Sci. Phila.* 1:37–401.

Tattersall, W. M. 1951. "The Mysidacea of the United States National Museum," *Bull. U.S. Natn. Mus.* 201:1–292.

## BRYOZOA

Cann, F., and R. S. Bassler. 1928. "Fossil and recent Bryozoa of the Gulf of Mexico region," *Proc. U.S. Natn. Mus.* 72:1–199.

Lagaaij, R. 1963. "New additions to the bryozoan fauna of the Gulf of Mexico," *Publ. Inst. Mar. Sci. Texas* 9:162–236.

Maturo, F. 1957. "Bryozoa of Beaufort, North Carolina," *J. Elisha Mitchell Sci. Soc.* 73:11–68.

Osborn, R. C. 1954. "The Bryozoa of the Gulf of Mexico," *U.S. Fish Wildl. Serv. Fish. Bull.* 89:361–362.

Ryland, J. S. 1976. "Physiology and ecology of marine bryozoans," *Adv. Mar. Biol.* 14:285–443.

## ECHINODERMATA

Bell, B. M., and R. W. Frey. 1969. "Observations on ecology and the feeding and burrowing mechanisms of *Mellita quanquiesperforata* (Leske)," *J. Paleont.* 43:553–560.

Burke, T. E. 1974. "Echinodermata of the West Flower Garden Reef Bank," M.S. Thesis, Texas A&M Univ. 165 pp.

Downey, M. E. 1973. "Starfishes from the Caribbean and the Gulf of Mexico," *Smithsonian Contrib. Zool.* 126:1–158.

Fell, H. B. 1966. "The ecology of ophiuroids," In *Physiology of Echinodermata*, R. A. Boolootian (Ed.). New York: Interscience.

Hyman, L. H. 1958. "Notes on the biology of the five–lunuled sand dollar," *Biol. Bull.* 114:54–56.

Moore, D. R. 1956. "Observations of predation on echinoderms by three species of Cassidae," *Nautilus* 69:73–76.

Gray, I. E., M. E. Downey, and M. J. Cerame–Vivas. 1968. "Sea–stars of North Carolina," *U.S. Fish Wildl. Serv. Fish. Bull.* 67:127–163.

Shirley, T. C. 1973. "The echinoderms of Seven and One–Half Fathom Reef," M.S. Thesis, Texas A&I Univ. 82 pp.

Thomas, L. P. 1965. "A new species of *Ophiophragmus* (Ophiuroidea, Echinodermata) from the Gulf of Mexico," *Bull. Mar. Sci.* 15:850–854.

Weihe, S. C., and I. E. Gray. 1968. "Observations on the biology of the sand dollar *Mellita quinquiesperforata* (Leske)," *J. Elisha Mitchell Sci. Soc.* 84:315–327.

Wells, H. W., M. J. Wells, and I. E. Gray. 1961. "Food of the sea–star *Astropecten articulatus*," *Biol. Bull.* 120:265–271.

## CHAETOGNATHA

Adelmann, H. C. 1967. "The taxonomy and summer and fall vertical distribution of the chaetognatha off Galveston, Texas," Ph.D. Diss., Texas A&M Univ.

Pierce, E. L. 1951. "The chaetognatha of the west coast of Florida," *Biol. Bull.* 100:206–228.

Pierce, E. L. 1962. "Chaetognatha from the Texas coast," *Publ. Inst. Mar. Sci. Texas* 8:147–152.

Reeve, M. R. 1964. "Feeding of zooplankton, with special reference to some experiments with *Sagitta*," *Nature*, Lond. 201:211–213.

Tokioka, T. 1955. "Notes on some chaetognaths from the Gulf of Mexico," *Bull. Mar. Sci.* 5:52–65.

## CHORDATA

Cory, R. L., and E. L. Pierce. 1967. "Distribution and ecology of lancelots (order Amphioxi) over the continental shelf of the southeastern United States," *Limnol. Oceanogr.* 12:650–656.

Fenaux, R. 1966. "Synonymie et distribution géographique des Appendiculaires," *Bull. Inst. Oceanogr. Monaco* 66:1–23.

Van Name, W. G. 1945. "The North and South American ascidians," *Bull. Amer. Mus. Nat. Hist.* 84:1–476.

**SUBPHYLUM VERTEBRATA**

Ackerman, R. A. 1980. "Physiological and ecological aspects of gas exchange by sea turtle eggs," *Amer. Zool.* 20:575–583.

Amos, A. F. 1989. "The occurrence of hawksbills *(Eretmochelys imbricata)* along the Texas coast." Proc. 9th Annual Workshop on Sea Turtle Conservation and Biology. NOAA Technical Memorandum NMFS–SEFC–232. pp. 9–11.

Bjorndal, K. 1996. "Foraging ecology and nutrition of sea turtles." In *The Biology of Sea Turtles.* (eds. P. L. Lutz and J. A. Musick). Boca Raton, Fl.: CRC Press, pp. 199–231.

Bjorndal, K. A., A. B. Bolten, D. A. Johnson, and P. J. Eliazar, compilers. 1994. Proceedings of the Fourteenth Annual Symposium on Sea Turtle Biology and Conservation. U.S. Dept. Commer. NOAA Tech. Memo. NMFS–SEFSC–351. 323 pp.

Bjorndall, K. A. 1980. "Nutrition and grazing behavior of the green turtle *Chelonia mydas,*" *Mar. Biol.* 56:147–155.

Bjorndal, K. A. 1985. "Nutritional ecology of sea turtles," *Copeia* 1985:736–751.

Bourne, W. R. P. 1985. "Turtles and pollution," *Mar. Pollut. Bull.* 16:177–178.

Byles, R., and Y. Fernnandes, compilers. 1998. Proceedings of the Sixteenth Annual Sea Turtle Symposium on Sea Turtle Biology and Conservation. U.S. Dept. Commer. NOAA Tech. Memo. NMFS–SEFSC–412. 158 pp.

Caillouet, C. W., Jr., D. L. Shaver, W. G. Teas, J. M. Nance, D. B. Revera, and A. C. Cannon. 1995. "Relationship between sea turtle stranding rates and shrimp fishing intensities in the northwestern Gulf of Mexico: 1986–1989 versus 1990–1993." *Fish. Bull.* 94(2): 237–249.

Caine, E. A. 1986. "Carapace epibionts of nesting loggerhead sea turtles: .Atlantic coast of U.S.A.," *J. Exp. Mar. Biol. Ecol.* 95:15–26.

Caldwell, D. 1968. "Baby loggerhead turtle associated with *Sargassum* weed," *Quart. J. Fla. Acad. Sci.* 31:271–272.

Caldwell, D. K., A. Carr, and T .H. Hellier, Jr. 1955. "A nest of the Atlantic leatherback turtle *Dermochelys coriacea coriacea* (L.), on the Atlantic coast of Florida, with a summary of American nesting records," *Quart. J. Fla. Acad. Sci.* 18:279–284.

Carr, A. 1980. "Some problems of sea turtle ecology," *Amer. Zool.* 20:489–498.

Carr, A. 1980. "Impact of non–degradable marine debris on the ecology and survival outlook of sea turtles," *Mar. Pollut. Bull.* 18:352–356.

Committee on Sea Turtle Conservation, Board on Environmental Studies and Technology, Board on Biology, Commission on Life Sciences, National Research Council. 1990. Washington D.C.: National Academy Press. 259 pp.

Conley, W. J., and B. A. Hoffman. 1987. "Nesting activity of sea turtles in Florida 1979–1985," *Florida Sci.* 50:201–210.

Crouse, D. T., L. B. Crowder, and H. Caswell. 1987. "A stage–based population model for loggerhead sea turtles and implications for conservation," *Ecology* 68:1412–1423.

Davenport, J. 1987. "Locomotion in hatchling leather–back turtles *Dermochelys coriacea,*" *J. Zool.* 212:85–101.

Davenport, J., and W. Clough. 1985. "The use of limb–scales or 'pseudoclaws' in food handling by young loggerhead turtles," *Copeia* 1985:786–788.

Eckert, K. L., and S. A. Eckert. 1988. "Pre–productive movements of leatherback sea turtles *(Dermochelys coriacea)* nesting in the Caribbean," *Copeia* 1982:400–405.

Ehrenfeld, D. W. 1968. "The role of vision in the sea–finding orientation of the green sea turtle *(Chelonia mydas)*. 2. Orientation mechanism and range of spectral sensitivity," *Anim. Behav.* 16:281–287.

Encalada, S. E. , K. A. Bjorndal, A. B. Bolten, J. C. Jurita, B. Schroeder, E. Possardt, C. J. Sears, and B. W. Bowen. 1998. "Population structure of loggerhead turtle *(Caretta caretta)* nesting colonies in the Atlantic and Mediterranean as inferred from mitochondrial DNA control sequences." *Marine Biology* 130(4): 567–575.

Epperly, S. P., and J. Braun, compilers. 1998. Proceedings of the Seventeenth Annual Sea Turtle Symposium. U.S. Dept. Commer. NOAA Tech. Memo. NMFS–SEFSC–415. 294 pp.

Fletemeyer, J. R. 1978. "Underwater tracking evidence of neonate loggerhead sea turtles seeking shelter in drifting *Sargassum,*" *Copeia* 1978: 148–149.

Frair, W., R. G. Ackman, and N. Mrosovsky. 1972. "Body temperature of *Dermochelys coriacea*: warm turtle from cold water," *Science* 177:791–793.

Frazer, N. B., and L. M. Ehrhart. 1985. "Preliminary growth models for green, *Chelonia mydas,* and loggerhead, *Caretta caretta,* turtles in the wild," *Copeia* 1985:73–79.

Frazer, N. B., and J. I. Richardson. 1985. "Seasonal variation in clutch size for loggerhead sea turtles, *Caretta caretta,* nesting on Little Cumberland Island, Georgia, U.S.A.," *Copeia* 1985:1083–1085.

Frick, J. A. 1976. "Orientation and behavior of hatchling green turtles *(Chelonia mydas)* in the sea," *Anim. Behav.* 24:849–857.

Garnett, S. J., I. R. Price, and F. J. Scott. 1985. "The diet of the green sea turtle *Chelonia mydas* (L.) in the Torres Strait," *Aust. Wildl. Res.* 12:103–112.

Grassman, M., and D. Owens. 1987. "Chemosensory imprinting in juvenile green sea turtles," *Anim. Behav.* 35:929–931.

Greer, A. E., J. D. Laxell, and R. M. Wright. 1973. "Anatomical evidence for a counter–current heat exchanger in the leatherback turtle (*Dermochelys coriacea*)," *Nature* 244:181.

Gudger, E. 1949. "Natural history notes on tiger sharks, *Galeocerdo triqrinus*, caught at Key West, Florida, with emphasis on food and feeding habits," *Copeia* 1949:39–47.

Hendrickson, J. R. 1980. "The ecological strategies of sea turtles," *Amer. Zool.* 20:597–608.

Henwood, T., W. Stuntz, and N. Thompson. 1992. "Evaluation of U.S. turtle protective measures under existing TED regulations, including estimates of shrimp trawler related mortality in the wider Caribbean." U.S. Dept. Commer., NOAA Tech. Memo. NMFS–SEFSC–303, 15 pp.

Henwood, T. A., and W. E. Stuntz. 1987. "Analysis of sea turtle captures and mortalities during commercial shrimp trawling," *Fish. Bull.* 85:813–817.

Hirth, H. F. 1997. Synopsis of the biological data on the green turtle, *Chelonia mydas* (Linnaeus 1758). *U.S. Dept. of the Interior, Fish and Wildlife Service, Biological Report* 97(1). 120 pp.

Hirth, H. F. 1980. "Some aspects of the nesting behavior and reproductive biology of sea turtles," *Amer. Zool.* 20:507–523.

Keinath, J. A., D. E. Barnard, J. A. Musick, and B. A. Bell, compilers. 1996. Proceedings of the Fifteenth Annual Workshop on Turtle Biology and Conservation. U.S. Dept. Commer. NOAA Tech. Memo. NMFS–SEFSC–387. 355 pp.

Killingley, J. S., and M. Lutcavage. 1983. "Loggerhead turtle movements reconstructed from $^{18}O$ and $^{13}C$ profiles from commensal barnacle shells," *Estuarine, Coastal and Shelf Sci.* 16:345–349.

King, F. W. 1995. "Historical review of the decline of the green turtle and the hawksbill." In *Biology and Conservation of Sea Turtles*, revised edition. (Ed. Bjorndal, K.). Washington and London: Smithsonian Institution Press. pp. 183–188.

Leary, T. R. 1957. "A schooling of leatherback turtles *Dermochelys coriacea coricea* on the Texas coast," *Copeia* 1957:232.

Lazell, J. D. 1980. "New England waters: Critical habitat for marine turtles," *Copeia* 1980:290–295.

Limpus, C. J. 1984. "A benthic feeding record from neritic waters for the leathery turtle (*Dermochelys coriacea*)," *Copeia* 1984:552–553.

Lutcavage, M., and J. A. Musick. 1985. "Aspects of the biology of sea turtles in Virginia," *Copeia* 1985:449–456.

Mack, D., N. Duplaix, and S. Wells. 1995. "Sea turtles, animals of divisible parts: international trade in sea turtle products. In *Biology and Conservation of Sea Turtles*, revised edition. (Ed. Bjorndal, K.). Washington and London: Smithsonian Institution Press. pp. 545–562.

Mendonca, M. T., and L. M. Ehrhart. 1982. "Activity, population size and structure of immature *Chelonia mydas* and *Caretta caretta* in Mosquito Lagoon, Fla.," *Copeia* 1982:161–167.

Meylan, A. 1995. "Sea turtle migration—evidence from tag returns." In *Biology and Conservation of Sea Turtles*, revised edition. (Ed. Bjorndal, K.). Washington and London: Smithsonian Institution Press. pp. 91–100.

Mortimer, J. A. 1995. "Feeding ecology of sea turtles." In *Biology and Conservation of Sea Turtles*, revised edition. (Ed. Bjorndal, K.). Washington and London: Smithsonian Institution Press. pp. 103–109.

Mrosovsky, N. 1980. "Thermal biology of sea turtles," *Amer. Zool.* 20:531–547.

Mrosovsky, N., S. R. Hopkins–Murphy, and J. F. Richardson. 1984. "Sex ratios of sea turtles: seasonal changes," *Science* 225:739–741.

National Marine Fisheries Service and U.S. Fish and Wildlife Service. 1998. "Recovery plan for U.S. Pacific populations of the leatherback turtle *(Dermochelys coriacea)*." National Marine Fisheries Service, Silver Spring, Md. 65 pp.

National Marine Fisheries Service and U.S. Fish and Wildlife Service. 1998. "Recovery plan for U.S. Pacific populations of the hawksbill turtle *(Eretmochelys imbricata)*." National Marine Fisheries Service, Silver Spring, Md. 82 pp.

National Marine Fisheries Service and U.S. Fish and Wildlife Service. 1998. "Recovery plan for U.S. Pacific populations of the green turtle *(Chelonia mydas)*." National Marine Fisheries Service, Silver Spring, Md. 84 pp.

National Marine Fisheries Service and U.S. Fish and Wildlife Service. 1998. "Recovery plan for U.S. Pacific populations of the loggerhead turtle *(Caretta caretta)*." National Marine Fisheries Service, Silver Spring, Md. 59 pp.

Ogden, J. C., S. Tighe, and S. Miller. 1981. "Foraging behavior of juvenile green turtles *Chelonia mydas* on St. Croix," *Proc. Assoc. Isl. Mar. Lab. Caribb.* 16:7.

Ogren, L. H., J. W. Watson, Jr., and D. A. Wickham. 1977. "Loggerhead sea turtles, *Carretta carretta*, encountering shrimp trawls," *Mar. Fish. Rev.* (NOAA) 39(11):15–17.

Pritchard, P. C. H. 1973. "International migrations of South American sea turtles (Cheloniidae and Dermochelidae)," *Anim. Behav.* 21:18–27.

Pritchard, P. C. H. 1971. "Post–nesting movements of marine turtles (Cheloniidae and Dermochelidae) tagged in the Guianas," *Copeia* 1976:749–754.

Pritchard, P. C. H. 1982. "Nesting of the leatherback turtle, *Dermochelys coriacea* in Pacific Mexico, with a new estimate of the world population status," *Copeia* 1982:741–747.

Pruter, A. T. 1987. "Sources, quantities and distribution of persistent plastics in the maritime environment," *Mar. Pollut. Bull.* 18:305–310.

Rabalais, S. C., and N. N. Rabalais. 1980. "The occurrence of sea turtles on the south Texas coast," *Contrib. Mar. Sci.* 23:123–129.

Rebel, T. P. 1974. *Sea Turtles and Turtle Industry of the West Indies, Florida, and the Gulf of Mexico.* Coral Gables, Florida: University of Miami Press.

Rester, J., and R. Condrey. 1996. "The occurrence of the hawksbill turtle, *Eretmochelys imbricata,* along the Louisiana coast." *Gulf of Mexico Science* 14 (2): 112–114.

Richardson, J. I., and T. H. Richardson, compilers. 1995. Proceedings of the Twelfth Annual Workshop on Sea Turtle Biology and Conservation. U.S. Dept. Commer. NOAA Tech. Memo. NMFS–SEFSC–361. 274 pp.

Rimblot, F., J. Fretey, J. Lescure, and C. Pieae. 1985. "Influence de la temperature sur la differentiation sexuelle des gonades chez la tortue luth (*Dermochelys coriacae*)." In M. Amanieu, L. Laubier, and A. Guille (eds.) *Bases Biologiques de l'Aquaculture,* Montpellier 12–16 Decembre. IFREMER (Paris) Actes Colloq. No. 1:355–362.

Rhodin, A. G. J. 1985. "Comparative chondro–osseous development and growth of marine turtles," *Copeia* 1985:752–771.

Ross, J. P. 1995. "Historical decline of loggerhead, ridley and leatherback turtles." In *Biology and Conservation of Sea Turtles,* revised edition. (Ed. Bjorndal, K.). Washington and London: Smithsonian Institution Press. pp. 189–195.

Salmon, M., and J. Wyneken, compilers. 1992. Proceedings of the Eleventh Annual Workshop on Sea Turtle Biology and Conservation. U.S. Dept. Commer. NOAA Tech. Memo. NMFS–SEFSC–302. 195 pp.

Shaver, D. J. 1991. "Feeding ecology of wild and head–started Kemp's ridley sea turtles in south Texas waters." *J. Herpetology* 25(3): 327–334.

Shaver, D. J. 1994. "Relative abundance, temporal patterns and growth of sea turtles at the Mansfield Channel, Texas." *J. Herpetology* 28(4): 491–497.

Shaver, D. J. 1998. "Sea turtle strandings along the Texas coast, 1980–94." In Roger Zimmerman (ed.), *Characteristics and Causes of Texas Marine Strandings.* U.S. Dept. Commer., NOAA Tech. Rep. NMFS 143: 57–72.

Shaver, D. J., and C. W. Caillouet, Jr. 1998. "More Kemp's ridley turtles return to south Texas to nest." *Marine Turtle Newsletter* 82: 1–5 plus errata, *Marine Turtle Newsletter* 83: 28.

Shaver, D. J., D. W. Owens, A. H. Chaney, C. W. Caillouet, Jr., P. Burchfield, and R. Marquez M. 1988. "Sty-

ofoam box and beach temperatures in relation to incubation and sex ratios of Kemp's ridley sea turtles." In Proceedings of the Eighth Annual Workshop on Sea Turtle Conservation and Biology. NOAA Tech. Memo. NMFS–SEFC–214: 103–108.

Spotila, J. R., M. P. O'Connor, and F. V. Paladino. 1996. "Thermal biology." In *The Biology of Sea Turtles.* (Eds. P. L. Lutz and J. A. Musick). Boca Raton, Fl.: CRC Press. pp. 297–314.

Spotila, J. R., and E. A. Standora. 1985. "Environmental constraints on the thermal energetics of sea turtles," *Copeia* 1985:694–702.

Standora, E. A., and J. R. Spotila. 1985. "Temperature dependent sex determination in sea turtles," *Copeia* 1985:711–722.

Thayer, G. W., D. W. Engel, and K. A. Bjorndal. 1982. "Evidence for short–circuiting of the detritus cycle of seagrass beds by the green turtle, *Chelonia mydas* L.," *J. Exp. Mar. Biol. Ecol.* 62:173–183.

Timko, R. E., and D. BeBlanc. 1981. "Radio tracking juvenile marine turtles," *Mar. Fish. Rev.* (NOAA) 43(3):20–24.

Timko, R. E., and A. L. Kolz. 1982. "Satellite sea turtle tracking," *Mar. Fish. Rev.* (NOAA) 44(4):19–24.

Turtle Expert Working Group. 1998. "An assessment of the Kemp's ridley *(Lepidochelys kempii)* and loggerhead *(Caretta caretta)* sea turtle populations in the western North Atlantic." NOAA Technical Memorandum NMFS–SEFSC–409. 96 pp.

Witham, R. 1974. "Neonate sea turtles from the stomach of pelagic fish," *Copeia* 1974:548.

Witham, R. 1980. "The 'lost year' question in young sea turtles," *Amer. Zool.* 20:525–530.

Witzell, W. N., and W. G. Teas. 1994. "The impacts of anthropogenic debris on marine turtles in the western north Atlantic Ocean." NOAA Technical Memorandum NMFS–SEFSC–355. 21 pp.

Witzell, W. N. 1982. "Observations on the green sea turtle (*Chelonia mydas*) in Western Samoa," *Copeia* 1982:183–185.

Witzell, W. N. 1983. "Synopsis of biological data on the hawksbill turtle, *Eretmochelys imbricata* (Linnaeus, 1766)," *FAO Fish. Synop.* 137:78 pp.

Witzell, W. N. 1984. "The incidental capture of sea turtles in the Atlantic U.S. Fishery Conservation Zone by the Japanese tuna longline fleet, 1978–81," *Mar. Fish. Rev.* (NOAA) 46(3):56–58.

Wood, J. R., and F. E. Wood. 1980. "Reproductive biology of captive green sea turtles *Chelonia mydas*," *Amer. Zool.* 20:499–505.

Yerger, R. W. 1965. "The leatherback turtle on the Gulf coast of Florida," *Copeia* 1965:365–366.

## MISCELLANEOUS TAXA

Chitwood, B. G. 1951 a. "A marine tardigrade from the Gulf of Mexico," *Texas J. Sci.* 3:111–112.

Chitwood, B. G. 1951 b. "North American marine nematodes," *Texas J. Sci.* 3:617–672.

Coe, W. R. 1951. "The nemertean faunas of the Gulf of Mexico and of southern Florida," *Bull. Mar. Sci.* 1:149–186.

Fisher, W. K. 1947 (1950). "New genera and species of echiuroid and sipunculoid worms," *Proc. U.S. Natn. Mus.* 97:351–372.

Gerauld, J. H. 1913. "The sipunculids of the eastern coast of North America," *Proc. U.S. Natn. Mus.* 44:373–437.

Henry, C. A. 1976. "The commensal clam, *Paramya subovata* (Bivalvia: Myidae) and *Thalassema hartmani* (Echiuroidae) off Galveston, Texas," *Nautilus* 90:73–74.

Hopper, B. E. 1961. "Marine nematodes from the coast line of the Gulf of Mexico," *Canad. J. Zool.* 39:183–199.

Long, C. D. 1960. "A phoronid from the Gulf of Mexico," *Bull. Mar. Sci.* 10:204–207.

Paine, R. T. 1961. "Observations on *Phoronis architecta* in Florida waters," *Bull. Mar. Sci.* 11:457–462.

Paine, R. T. 1963. "Ecology of the brachiopod *Glottidia pyramidata*," *Ecol. Monogr.* 33:187–213.

Short, R. B. 1962. "Two new dicyemid mesozoans from the Gulf of Mexico," *Tulane Stud. Zool.* 9: 101–111.

Willis, H. L. 1968. "Artificial key to the species of *Cicindela* of North America, north of Mexico (Coleoptera: Cicindelidae)," *J. Kans. Ent. Soc.* 41:303–317.

## GENERAL REFERENCES

Abbott, R. E. 1975. "The faunal composition of the algal–sponge zone of the Flower Garden Banks, northwest Gulf of Mexico," M.S. Thesis, Texas A&M Univ., 205 pp.

Adams, J. A. 1960. "A contribution to the biology and postlarval development of the *Sargassum* fish, *Histrio histrio* (Linnaeus), with a discussion of the *Sargassum* complex," *Bull. Mar. Sci.* 10:55–82.

Behre, E. H. 1950. "Annotated list of the fauna of the Grand Isle Region, 1928–1946," Occ. Pap. Mar. Lab. La. St. Univ. 6:1–66.

Bird, S. O. 1970. "Shallow–marine and estuarine benthic molluscan communities from the area of Beaufort, North Carolina," *Bull. Amer. Assoc. Petrol. Geol.* 54:1651–1676.

Breuer, J. P. 1957. "Ecological survey of Baffin and Alazan Bays, Texas," *Publ. Inst. Mar. Sci. Texas* 4:134–155.

Breuer, J. P. 1962. "An ecological survey of the lower Laguna Madre of Texas, 1953–1959," *Publ. Inst. Mar. Sci. Texas* 8:153–183.

Bright, T. J., and R. Rezak. 1976. "A biological and geological reconnaissance of selected topographic features on the Texas continental shelf. A final report to the U.S. Dept. of the Interior, Bureau of Land Management Outer Continental Shelf Office, New Orleans, Louisiana," Contract No. AA550–CT5–4. Texas A&M University Research Foundation and Texas A&M University Dept. of Oceanography.

Cary, L. R. 1906. "A contribution to the fauna of the coast of Louisiana," *Gulf Biol. Sta. Bull.* 6:50–59.

Chambers, G. V., and A. K. Sparks. 1959. "An ecological survey of the Houston Ship Channel and adjacent bays," *Publ. Inst. Mar. Sci.* 6:213–250.

Chandler, A. C. 1935. "Parasites of fishes in Galveston Bay," *Proc. U.S. Natn. Mus.* 83:123–155.

Connell, C. H., and J. B. Cross. 1950. "Mass mortality of fish associated with the protozoan *Gonyaulax* in the Gulf of Mexico," *Science* 112:359–363.

Copeland, B. J., and T. J. Bechtel. 1974. "Some environmental limits of six Gulf coast estuarine organisms," *Contrib. Mar. Sci.* 18:169–204.

Cross, J. C., and H. B. Parks, 1937. "Marine fauna and sea–side flora of the Nueces River basin and the adjacent islands," *Bull. Texas Coll. Arts & Indust.* 8:1–36.

Cuzon du Rest, R. P. 1962. "Distribution of the zooplankton in the salt marshes of southeastern Louisiana," M. Sc. Thesis, Texas A&M Univ.

Darnell, R. M. 1958. "Food habits of fishes and larger invertebrates of Lake Pontchartrain, Louisiana, an estuarine community," *Publ. Inst. Mar. Sci. Texas* 5:353–416.

Darnell, R. M. 1961. "Trophic spectrum of an estuarine community, based on studies of Lake Pontchartrain, Louisiana," *Ecology* 42:553–568.

David, P. M. 1965. "The surface fauna of the ocean," *Endeavour* 24:95–100.

Dawson, C. E. 1966. "Additions to the known marine fauna of Grand Isle, Louisiana," *Proc. La. Acad. Sci.* 29:175–180.

Defenbaugh, R. E. 1976. "A study of the benthic macroinvertebrates of the continental shelf of the northern Gulf of Mexico," Ph.D. Diss., Texas A&M Univ., 476 pp.

Dooley, J. K. 1972. "Fishes associated with the pelagic *Sargassum* complex, with a discussion of the *Sargassum* community," *Contrib. Mar. Sci.* 16:1–32.

Frazer, R. D. 1921. "Early records of tropical hurricanes on the Texas coast in the vicinity of Galveston, Texas," *Monthly Weather Rev.* 49:454–457.

Gettleson, D. A. 1976. "An ecological study of the benthic microfauna and macrofauna of a soft bottom area on the Texas outer continental shelf," Ph.D. Diss., Texas A&M Univ., xiv + 257 p.

Geyer, R. A. 1950. "A bibliography on the Gulf of Mexico," *Texas J. Sci.* 2:44–93.

Goodbody, I. 1961. "Mass mortality of a marine fauna following tropical rains," *Ecology* 42:150–155.

Gordon, M. 1938. "Animals of the Sargasso Sea merry–go–round," *Nat. Hist.* 42:12–20.

Gudger, E. W. 1937. "*Sargassum* week fish 'nests' made by flying fishes and not by *Sargasso* fish (Antennariidae): a historical review," *Amer. Nat.* 71:363–381.

Gunter, G. 1941. "Death of fishes due to cold on the Texas coast, January, 1940," *Ecology* 22:203–208.

Gunter, G. 1945. "Studies on marine fishes of Texas," *Publ. Inst. Mar. Sci. Texas* 1:1–190.

Gunter, G. 1950. "Seasonal population changes and distributions as related to salinity, of certain invertebrates of the Texas coast, including the commercial shrimp," *Publ. Inst. Mar. Sci. Texas* 1:7–51.

Gunter, G. 1952. "The import of catastrophic mortalities for marine fisheries along the Texas coast," *J. Wildl. Manag.* 16:63–69.

Gunter, G. 1956. "Some relations of faunal distributions to salinity in estuarine waters," *Ecology* 37:616–619.

Gunter, G. 1961. "Some relations of estuarine organisms to salinity," *Limnol. Oceanogr.* 6:182–190.

Gunter, G., and G. E. Hall. 1965. "A biological investigation of the Caloosahatchee Estuary of Florida," *Gulf Res. Rept.* 2:1–71.

Gunter, G., and H. H. Hildebrand. 1951. "Destruction of fishes and other organisms on the south Texas coast by the cold wave of January 28–February 3, 1951," *Ecology* 32:731–736.

Gunter, G., and R. A. Geyer. 1955. "Studies of fouling organisms of the northwest Gulf of Mexico," *Publ. Inst. Mar. Sci. Texas* 4:37–67.

Gunter, G., and W. E. Shell. 1958. "A study of an estuarine area with water–level control in the Louisiana marsh," *Proc. La. Acad. Sci.* 21:5–34.

Harper, D. E. 1970. "Ecological studies of selected level bottom macroinvertebrates off Galveston, Texas," Ph.D. Diss., Texas A&M Univ.

Heck, K. L. 1976. "Community structure and the effects of pollution in seagrass meadows and adjacent habitats," *Mar. Biol.* 35:345–357.

Hedgpeth, J. W. 1950. "Notes on the marine invertebrate fauna of salt flat areas in the Aransas National Wildlife Refuge, Texas," *Publ. Inst. Mar. Sci. Texas* 1:103–119.

Hedgpeth, J. W. 1953. "An introduction to zoogeography of the northwestern Gulf of Mexico with reference to the invertebrate fauna," *Publ. Inst. Mar. Sci. Texas* 3:107–224.

Hedgpeth, J. W. 1958. "Estuaries and lagoons. II. Biological aspects," *Geol. Soc. Amer. Mem.* 67; Vol. 1:693–749.

Henry, C. A. 1976. "A study of offshore benthic communities in natural areas and in areas affected by dredging and dredged material disposal," M.S. Thesis, Texas A&M Univ. x + 190 p.

Hildebrand, H. H. 1954. "A study of the fauna of the brown shrimp grounds in the western Gulf of Mexico," *Publ. Inst. Mar. Sci. Texas* 3:225–366.

Hildebrand, H. H. 1955. "A study of the fauna of the pink shrimp grounds in the western Gulf of Mexico," *Publ. Inst. Mar. Sci. Texas* 4:171–232.

Hill, G. 1975. "Animal–sediment relationships," In "Environmental assessment of the south Texas outer conti-

nental shelf–geologic investigations," U.S.G.S. report to the Bureau of Land Management, Contract No. 08550–MU5–20, pp. 133–187.

Hoese, H. D. 1960. "Biotic changes in a bay associated with the end of a drought," *Limnol. Oceanogr.* 5:326–336.

Hoese, H. D., and R. S. Jones. 1963. "Seasonality of larger animals in a Texas turtle grass community," *Publ. Inst. Mar. Sci. Texas* 9:37–47.

Hoese, H. D., B. J. Copeland, et al. 1968. "Fauna of the Aransas Pass Inlet, Texas. 3. Diel and seasonal variations in trawlable organisms of the adjacent area," *Texas J. Sci.* 20:33–60.

Holland, J. S. 1977. "Invertebrate epifauna and macroinfauna," In "Environmental studies, South Texas Outer Continental Shelf, Biology and Chemistry," Univ. of Texas final report to the Bureau of Land Management, Contract No. AA550–CT6–17, pp. 9–1 to 9–79.

Holland, J. S. 1977. "Invertebrate epifauna and macroinfauna," In "Environmental studies, South Texas Outer Continental Shelf, Biology and Chemistry," Univ. of Texas fourth quarterly report for 1976 to the Bureau of Land Management, Contract No. 08550–CT6–17, pp. 415–459.

Humm, H. J. 1956. "Sea grasses of the northern Gulf Coast," *Bull. Mar. Sci.* 6:305–308.

Johnson, C. W. 1934. "List of marine mollusca of the Atlantic coast from Labrador to Texas," *Proc. Boston Soc. Nat. Hist.* 40:1–104.

Kalke, R. D. 1972. "Species composition, distribution, and seasonal abundance of macro–zooplankton in intake and discharge areas before and during early operation of the Cedar Bayou generating station," M. Sc. Thesis, Texas A&M Univ.

Karlson, R. H. 1978. "Predation and space utilization patterns in a marine epifaunal community," *J. Exp. Mar. Biol. Ecol.* 31:225–239.

Keith, D. E., and N. C. Huling. 1965. "A quantitative study of selected nearshore infauna between Sabine Pass and Bolivar Point, Texas," *Publ. Inst. Mar. Sci. Texas* 10:33–40.

Ladd, H. S. 1951. "Brackish–water and marine assemblages of the Texas coast, with special reference to mollusks," *Publ. Inst. Mar. Sci. Texas* 2:125–163.

Ladd, H. S., J. W. Hedgpeth, and R. Post. 1957. "Environments and facies of existing bays on the central Texas coast," *Geol. Soc. Amer. Mem.* 56, Vol. 2:599–640.

La Fleur, N. C. 1940. "The beach fauna of Grand Isle, La.," *Bios* 11:112–119.

Lebour, M. V. 1922. "The food of plankton organisms," *J. Mar. Biol. Assoc. U.K.* 12:644–677.

Lebour, M. V. 1923. "The food of plankton organisms (Part II)," *J. Mar. Biol. Assoc. U.K.* 13:70–92.

Loesch, H. 1960. "Sporadic mass shoreward migrations of demersal fish and crustaceans in Mobile Bay, Alabama," *Ecology* 41:292–298.

McDougall, K. D. 1943. "Sessile marine invertebrates of Beaufort, N.C.," *Ecol. Monogr.* 13:321–374.

McNulty, J. K. 1961. "Ecological effects of sewage pollution in Biscayne Bay, Florida: sediments and the distribution of benthic and fouling micro–organisms," *Bull. Mar. Sci.* 11:394–447.

Moore, D. R. 1963. "Distribution of the sea grass, *Thalassia*, in the United States," *Bull. Mar. Sci.* 13:329–342.

Nowlin, W. D., and H. J. McClellan. 1967. "A characterization of the Gulf of Mexico waters in winter," *J. Mar. Res.* 25:29–59.

Odum, H. T. 1963. "Productivity measurements in Texas turtle grass and the effects of dredging in intracoastal channel," *Publ. Inst. Mar. Sci. Texas* 9:48–58.

O'Gower, A. K., and J. W. Wacasey. 1967. "Animal communities associated with *Thalassia*, *Diplanthera*, and sand beds in Biscayne Bay. I. Analysis of communities in relation to water movements," *Bull. Mar. Sci.* 17:175–210.

Oppenheimer, C. H. 1963. "Effects of Hurricane Carla on the ecology of Redfish Bay, Texas," *Bull. Mar. Sci.* 13:59–72.

Osman, R. W. 1977. "The establishment and development of a marine epifaunal community," *Ecol. Monogr.* 47:37–63.

Parker, R. H. 1955. "Changes in the invertebrate fauna, apparently attributable to salinity changes, in the bays of central Texas," *J. Paleont.* 29:193–211.

Parker, R. H. 1959. "Macro–invertebrate assemblages of central Texas coastal bays and Laguna Madre," *Bull. Amer. Assoc. Petrol. Geol.* 43:2100–2166.

Parker, R. H., and J. R. Curray. 1956. "Fauna and bathymetry of banks on the continental shelf, Gulf of Mexico," *Bull. Amer. Assoc. Petrol. Geol.* 40:2428–2439.

Partner, D. L. 1970. "Some mechanisms of organism limitations in the Inland Houston Ship Channel," M. Sc. Thesis, Texas A&M Univ.

Partner, D. L., S. H. Hopkins, and R. W. Hann, Jr. 1971. "Biological studies of the Houston Ship Channel," Texas A&M Univ., Estuarine Systems Projects, Tech. Rept. No. 20.

Parr, A. E. 1939. "Quantitative observations on the pelagic *Sargassum* vegetation of the western North Atlantic," *Bull. Bing. Oceanogr. Coll.* 6:1–94.

Pearse, A. S. 1936. "Estuarine animals at Beaufort, North Carolina," *J. Elisha Mitchell Sci. Soc.* 52:174–222.

Perry, L. M., and J. S. Schwengel. 1955. "Marine shells of the western coast of Florida," *Paleont. Res. Inst.*, Ithaca, N.Y.

Puffer, E. L., and W. K. Emerson. 1953. "The molluscan community of the oyster–reef biotope on the central Texas coast," *J. Paleont.* 27:537–544.

Reid, G. K., Jr. 1955. "A summer study of the biology and ecology of East Bay, Texas. Part I. Introduction, description of the area, methods, some aspects of the fish community, the invertebrate fauna," *Texas J. Sci.* 7:316–343.

Reid, G. K., Jr. 1956. "Ecological investigations in a disturbed Texas coastal estuary," *Texas J. Sci.* 8:296–327.

Richmond, E. A. 1962. "The fauna and flora of Horn Island, Mississippi," *Gulf Res. Repts.* 1:59–106.

Saloman, C. H. 1975. "A selected bibliography of the nearshore environment: Florida West Coast," Misc. Paper No. 5–75, U.S. Army Corps of Engineers.

Sievers, A. M. 1969. "Comparative toxicity of *Gonyaulax monilata* and *Gymnodinium breve* to annelids, crustaceans, mollusks and a fish," *J. Protozool.* 16:401–404.

Simmons, E. G. 1957. "An ecological survey of the upper Laguna Madre of Texas," *Publ. Inst. Mar. Sci. Texas* 4:156–200.

Tabb, D. C., and R. B. Manning. 1961. "A checklist of the flora and fauna of northern Florida Bay and adjacent brackish waters of the Florida mainland collected during the period July, 1957–September, 1960," *Bull. Mar. Sci.* 11:553–648.

Tabb, D. C., and A. C. Jones. 1962. "Effect of Hurricane Donna on the aquatic fauna of north Florida Bay," *Trans. Amer. Fish. Soc.* 91:375–378.

Teal, J. M. 1962. "Energy flow in the salt marsh ecosystem of Georgia," *Ecology* 43:614–624.

Thomas, L. P., D. R. Moore, and R. C. Work. 1961. "Effects of Hurricane Donna on the turtle grass beds of Biscayne Bay, Florida," *Bull. Mar. Sci.* 11:191–197.

Torres, J. J., and C. P. Mangum. 1974. "Effects of hyperoxia on survival of benthic marine invertebrates," *Comp. Biochem. Physiol.* (A). 47:17–22.

Trueman, E. K., and A. D. Ansell. 1969. "The mechanisms of burrowing into soft substrata by marine aminals," *Oceanogr. Mar. Biol. Ann. Rev.* 7:315–366.

Weiss, C. M. 1947. "The comparative tolerances of some fouling organisms to copper and mercury," *Biol. Bull.* 93:56–63.

Weiss, J. S. 1968. "Fauna associated with pelagic *Sargassum* in the Gulf Stream," *Amer. Midl. Nat.* 80:554–558.

Wells, H. W. 1961. "The fauna of oyster beds with special reference to the salinity factor," *Ecol. Monogr.* 31:239–266.

Whitten, H. L., H. F. Rosene, and J. W. Hedgpeth. 1950. "The invertebrate fauna of Texas coast jetties; a preliminary survey," *Publ. Inst. Mar. Sci. Texas* 1:53–87.

Williams, H. F. 1951. "The Gulf of Mexico adjacent to Texas," *Tex. J. Sci.* 3:237–250.

Wurtz, C. B., and S. S. Roback. 1955. "The invertebrate fauna of some Gulf Coast rivers," *Proc. Acad. Nat. Sci. Phila.* 107:167–206.

# Index

Boldface page numbers indicate illustrations.